THE WORLD BOOK INDUSTRY

THE WORLD BOOK INDUSTRY

Peter Curwen

Facts On File Publications
New York, New York ● Oxford, England

THE WORLD BOOK INDUSTRY
First edition 1986

4/3/86 *app publ*

Copyright © Euromonitor Publications Ltd, 1986

Library of Congress Cataloging-in-Publication Data

Curwen, Peter J.
  The world book industry.

    1. Book industries and trade. 2 Publishers and publishing. 3. Book industries and trade—Technological innovations. 4. Publishers and publishing—Technological innovations. I. Title.
Z278.C87 1986   338.4'70705   85-27591
ISBN 0-8160-1405-1

Phototypeset by The Fosse Bureau, Yeovil, Somerset.
Printed by Woolnough Bookbinding, Irthlingborough, Northamptonshire.

FOREWORD

In THE WORLD BOOK INDUSTRY Peter Curwen examines the book publishing industry throughout the world, a subject which has been relatively neglected in the past. Drawing on information collected from a variety of sources he explores many key aspects of the world publishing industry which will be of interest to anyone involved in the world of books.

Peter Curwen is Principal Lecturer in Economics at Sheffield City Polytechnic and a leading authority on book industry trends.

CONTENTS

Chapter One

INTRODUCTION

This book attempts to assemble together as much as possible of the accessible information about the book industry around the world. Not altogether surprisingly this task has never before been attempted, and it has certainly not been without its difficulties. Like all first attempts, however, it will hopefully prove to be merely an opening gambit in the struggle to acquire knowledge about this diverse industry. A similar struggle has already taken place in a small number of individual countries, and in the case of, for example, the UK, the battle is now well on its way to being won, thanks in part to Euromonitor's own efforts over the years.

Much, however, remains to be done elsewhere in the world. Looked at in relation to the aggregate size of manufacturing and retail sectors the book industry is inevitably something less than big business, even in the developed world, and undoubtedly this has held back the development of a proper statistical framework for its analysis. Nevertheless, this must not be treated as an excuse for neglecting research and information gathering activities, for quite apart from any other consideration the industry can scarcely expect those outside the industry in positions of influence to appreciate the important role which it plays, both economically and culturally, when hard facts about its operation are at a premium. In a curious way it may be argued that it is better for the industry to feel besieged, since this pressure forces its adherents to marshall their arguments and the data in defence of their position, which might otherwise never occur.

Many members of the book industry prefer to give the impression that books are not mere commodities, but items which possess special qualities which entitle them to rise above the hurly-burly of the economic and political environment. Generally speaking it has been possible to persuade the outside world that these qualities merit special treatment, but it is dangerous to assume that the matter is self-evident. Where politicians remain unmoved they are inclined to see the industry's restrictive practices as no less restrictive than anyone else's, and books as no less taxable commodities than any other. Far too often the industry responds negatively to such matters by issuing ritual cries of horror and outrage, and by refusing to acknowledge that there is any case to answer. What is needed is for the industry to treat such intrusions as a stimulus which forces it to rationalise its position, and to accept that it conducts its affairs in the market place rather than in some culturally pure environment.

What this book may help to show, as in the section on pricing agreements, is that such intrusions are rarely unique to an individual country. Their absence today is no long-term guarantee. Experiences clearly need to be shared on a supra-national level, with at least one important aim in view, namely the need to construct a clearer picture of how the pieces of the worldwide book industry jigsaw fit together. This book does not pretend to have filled in all the missing pieces, but it does at least show what is still missing, and it is for those who have something to add to come forward.

One particular innovation of this book is the attempt to trace trade flows in books around the world. Obviously, many such flows involve relatively small sums of money, and cannot be examined in any detail in a text of this kind. Nevertheless, the curious way in which one country's exports are mysteriously transformed into another country's imports worth twice as much may give one cause to reflect. Books are, after all, rather easy to recognise and to count, or at least members of the book industry may think so. The statistics do not, unfortunately, bear out this simple proposition, and there is still much to do to sort out what really is going on.

Let us for the moment turn from exhortation, to some of the matters revealed by this study. For the most part the book is likely to reinforce existing conceptions of the industry. It shows, unsurprisingly, the dominant role of the English-speaking countries, especially the USA and the UK, although the rest of the pecking order may be more revealing. Colonial links between developed and developing countries are still strong, but these are going through a period of reappraisal which is likely to transfer control of their own destinies gradually to the latter. This causes trading patterns to alter, and it may well prove generally instructive to the reader to see who is trading with whom, on what scale, and how the trading patterns have changed historically. Obviously, trade grows with increases in the size of national markets, and most trade therefore flows between developed countries. The biggest problem here is, unfortunately, nationalism itself, for national governments do have a way of changing the rules to suit themselves, and market agreements and consent decrees are never going to meet with worldwide acclaim.

Trade is also bedevilled by exchange rates, and indeed by shortages of hard currency. One can well sympathise with any publisher who finds that a rapid rise or fall in the exchange rate completely upturns his careful calculations about profitability, but again it is a simple fact that, if one takes a worldwide view, then for every gain there is an exactly equal loss and vice versa.

Home markets are, on the face of it, considerably more secure. Analytically, however, they present great difficulties because the industrial structure in any individual market is typically both heterogeneous and complex. This will become apparent enough later in the book. Suffice it to say that there is no such thing as a typical publisher nor a typical bookseller or printer, although virtually every national book industry shares some structural features in common. For example, there is always easy entry into the market. Publishers, printers and booksellers can start up on a small scale with little capital. This is both a virtue, in so far as it constantly introduces new blood, and a vice in so far as it tends to lead to over-production and poor profitability. The latter wouldn't be true, of course, if the markets themselves were large and growing rapidly. Here again, however, the text shows that book markets are really rather small even in developed countries, although it is simultaneously true that book buying, albeit on a modest scale, has proved a fairly resilient sector when other competing uses for disposable income are examined.

The small size of markets is linked with library provision. Institutional buying can be both complementary to, and a substitute for, individual purchase. The text shows that few countries have a well developed library system, but in one or two cases, as in the UK, there clearly are conflicts between borrowing and buying. Equally, small markets raise thorny issues about the nature of the product. In a simple economic sense the smaller the range of products on offer the bigger the print runs and the higher the level of profitability. This, however, conflicts with a desire to meet the demands of individual groups, however small, and raises issues about the culturally insignificant driving out the culturally significant. Many countries, as the text indicates, deliberately allow policies to be pursued to protect the culturally significant texts, even though this may conflict with common practice in other industries. But like everything else, a price does have to be paid in this respect in so far as this sustains an industrial structure containing huge numbers of very small publishers producing very short print runs.

Such a structure is neither good nor bad *per se,* but it does make the industry very vulnerable. An excellent example was the problem created by the alleged intention to introduce Value Added Tax on books in the UK for the first time. The severity of such a change would clearly have affected some parts of the industry far more than others. Some books would continue to be bought as before but at higher prices. Others would not, and the balance between the commercial and the cultural would be altered. In a rapidly changing world such destabilising factors are ever-present, and there may well be a need for both national and international book industries to engage in more strategic planning in order to head off some of these potential problems, and to determine the grounds on which particular industrial structures can be defined as optional.

On the marketing side there are also many things to be done. It is very difficult to find any national book industry which can be said to employ marketing skills comparable to those used in other consumer product industries. This may, of course, simply reflect a preference for regarding books as non-comparable with, for example, electronic equipment, especially insofar as the production side, and the quality of the product, are regarded as an end in themselves, with the decision to purchase left entirely in the unpersuaded hands of the public. No doubt many members of the book industry are genuinely not very commercially minded, but one is inclined to the view that without commercial survival other worthy aims become somewhat academic.

The fact is that marketing books is rather tricky. There is no single market for books, therefore each type of book must have its own marketing channels devised with care. Some books are best sold through bookstores, others through direct selling methods. So long as little is done to expand the overall market it is inevitable that one marketing channel is seen as taking custom away from another, but it would seem more sensible to devise marketing strategies whereby different channels become complementary, because they all serve to persuade the public that books are there to be bought. In this respect it is interesting to examine the tables in the text which set out the different channels used in different national markets. Although differences are clearly related to the variations in the historical development of each industry, it surely makes one realise that underutilised channels are foregone opportunities, rather than either unacceptable to the public or necessarily destructive to those already heavily utilised.

4

In general, therefore, there is much to be said, if only from a purely financial view point, for treating books as mere commodities. It must be accepted, however, that aggressive marketing is generally unpopular because of the tendency to see the overall market as static, and hence the success of one book as implying the failure of another. In the UK, the recent altercation over the repackaging of Pan Books especially for Marks and Spencer was illustrative of this point. The industry's reaction was to cry foul play on the grounds that far fewer books would be sold through other outlets as a result. But if such an approach were universal in commerce then innovation would be stifled, and nothing would be learnt by experience. No doubt if the rest of the industry had suffered because of Pan's policy, then Pan itself may well have come to appreciate that the policy was not even in its own interest to pursue, but it seems very undesirable to assume specific outcomes before any experimentation takes place.

So far as government is concerned, there appears to be little of a positive nature that it can do to assist the book industry, and it does therefore tend to be perceived as a threatening force in the market for books. However, given our preference for separating the commercial from the cultural aspects of the book industry, perhaps more pressure should be placed upon government to treat the cultural aspect as one that can be dealt with separately, say, through a system of subsidies. So long as the industry is obliged to cross-subsidise in order that the cultural responsibilities are met, these considerations will divert attention away from the need to market the product in the most effective way.

At the end of the day the market place for books must be seen as presenting opportunities for those in the industry who are prepared to take a view on where the world industry is going, and who are prepared to plan strategically on the basis of that view. It is to be hoped that this book will provide at least a starting point of reference for that task.

Are Books Consumer Products?

In the course of this introduction we have noted that one of the key questions which has yet to be faced head on in the great majority of countries is whether to sell books as a unique kind of product, or whether to sell them as an alternative to buying any other kind of consumer product. Because publishing was for so long considered a far more gentlemanly pursuit than, say, producing dustbins, it was not considered seemly to

5

market books aggressively. Rather, anyone with any claims to culture would seek out a bookseller in the hope of finding something suitable. This is why, for example, the advent of book clubs, with the seemingly vulgar approach to the consumer, caused such consternation in many publishing circles. Despite such intrusions, however, books are still not marketed aggressively, and it is not unreasonable to suppose that one consequence is that book buying constitutes only a small proportion of total consumer expenditure in most markets.

Generic advertising and marketing is fairly commonplace in developed consumer markets, but generic promotion of books is not. Attempts have been made to engender progress in this respect, but these have mostly floundered. The National Book Committee, for example, set up in America in 1954, died the death in 1974 ultimately because publishers would not put up enough money to make it work.

Many publishers would of course argue that what they want is to promote their own books, not other publishers'. The fact that other publishers would be chipping in on the same basis is not regarded as particularly helpful. It may also be argued, with some conviction, that there are a number of book markets, and not just one, so efforts should only be directed towards those markets where publishers have no existing lines of communication to potential customers. However, such markets do exist. For example, books for the home, or books as gifts, would suggest themselves as suitable themes.

Publishers place a great deal of faith in existing methods of reaching readers, for example book reviews in newspapers and magazines. But these are preaching to the converted who already read and buy books. What such reviews don't do is stimulate those who don't read or buy to do so. In the Netherlands a book promotion house was set up in order to expand the market to the non-buyer or infrequent buyer, funded by an obligatory levy on publishers of ½% of their turnover, but other countries have been disinclined to follow suit.

Partly as a consequence of the lack of attention paid to marketing it is fair to say (on the whole) that the odds of making a fortune in the book publishing industry are rather poor. In the first place there are too many products, and in the second place there are too many producers. It is difficult to become sufficiently large to take advantage of potential economies of scale, and even more difficult to remain operating at an optimum scale. There are few guaranteed bestsellers, but a vast number of products on which you can lose your shirt. The system of distributing the product leaves much to be desired. Your retail outlets do not always seem to be on your side, and too few buy in bulk. Hence you have too many customers and know too little about them. You have to sell too many of your products on a sale or return basis. Technological advances have been slow in making real savings on your relatively short-run, bread and butter business. Finally, too many producers still think publishing is an activity for gentlemen to engage in, rather than as a tough, competitive business.

This is not to imply, however, that the book industry is entirely hidebound by convention. For example, the past few years have seen a considerable switch from hardback to paperback format in book publishing. This has resulted primarily from consumer price resistance to books in hardback format combined with reductions in library budgets. The process has taken place primarily in the area of fiction, with the growth of mass-market paperbacks, but has now spread fairly extensively into the educational areas as well.

Originally a paperback was merely the cheap, non-durable, version of a hardback original which had completed its main sales cycle. Today, however, the picture is far more diverse. Some paperbacks are original format titles, and some are published simultaneously in hard and soft editions. No longer are all paperbacks the same size, aimed at the same segments of the reading public, and priced within a fairly narrow price band.

The institutional market traditionally preferred books in hardback format because of their durability, but paperbacks are being bought in increasing numbers for a variety of reasons, of which the most important are:

1.   budgetary constraints mean that cheaper books are having to be acquired if the range of choice is to be maintained;

2.   an increasing number of titles appear only in paperback format;

3.   with suitable reinforcing, a paperback can survive an economically attractive number of issues when the cost savings in relation to hardback editions are taken into account;

7

4. savings can be made in handling and processing costs by simply arranging paperbacks randomly on shelves rather than on a catalogue basis;

5. many users have perhaps never owned a hardback book, and therefore actually show a preference for books in paperback format.

The main growth area for paperbacks has been in mass-market fiction, appealing to the consumer's desire for something which can be purchased cheaply, absorbed with a minimum of intellectual effort, and allowed to fall apart rather than collected as part of a personal library. Nevertheless, in recent years, commencing in America, the most interesting trend has been towards the development of the so-called trade paperback, which amongst other things would not be subject to the bestseller/high returns syndrome described above.

Originally such paperbacks were a halfway house between normal hardback and paperback editions, but treated as more similar to the former than to the latter in terms of book trade practice, only being sold at a cheaper price. The format was typically larger than for normal paperbacks, and the subject matter more serious, either non-fiction or up-market fiction. Increasingly this latter distinction is becoming blurred, and the trade paperback is replacing the hardback edition of a title, being issued as a mass-market paperback a year or so after publication. The selling point is quality at a relatively low price, and publishing houses often set up separate imprints for trade paperbacks to distinguish them in the eyes of the consumer. Institutions often find this type of book fulfils their requirements, and the regular output of books in identical format with an identical imprint obviously helps to build up institutional purchases, although the general public is not very conscious of imprints.

Few publishers can afford to ignore these developments, so the growth of the trade paperback market seems assured. Nevertheless, the process of jumping on the bandwagon brings its own dangers. Although hardback sales are in decline, an inevitable consequence has been an increase in sales at less than full retail price. Clearly many trade paperbacks, the prices of which have tended recently to escalate, do not look attractive in comparison with, say, remaindered hardbacks, and churning them out regardless may run into precisely the same difficulties as are faced in the mass market for paperbacks, namely too much competition between too many different titles. The success of the trade paperback operation must be linked to a clear specification of the target market. For many hardback houses this involves selective culling of backlists, and for newer imprints it means commissioning only those titles which fit in with a clearly established marketing philosophy.

It is difficult to assess market trends when one has just been through a period of extended recession, but one thing is reasonably clear, and that is the eventual disappearance of the exclusively hardback publisher. Furthermore, if book prices continue to escalate, the margin between mass-market and trade paperbacks will become increasingly blurred as price differentials between the formats reduce in real terms. In America the concept of the mass-market trade paperback is already with us, and presumably it is only a matter of time before it becomes established elsewhere.

Demographic Trends

A final matter which merits attention in this introductory section is demography. One of the obvious determinants of book buying behaviour in future years are demographic changes. It is obviously the case that some parts of the world have rapidly rising populations, yet, partly as a consequence, very little disposable income left for the purchase of books, whereas other parts have static, or even falling populations, but high disposable incomes accessible to publishers.

The average pattern can be seen in table 1.1

TABLE 1.1   WORLD POPULATION TRENDS

Unit: millions

	1969-70	1975-76	1979-80	1985-86	1989-90	1995-96
North America	226.2	238.2	246.7	257.5	268.1	278.1
Latin America	278.7	327.3	365.9	421.9	479.0	538.9
EEC	260.4	267.9	270.7	272.1	274.6	277.3
Other Western Europe	73.6	77.1	79.1	81.5	84.1	85.8
Eastern Europe/USSR	368.4	387.7	400.0	417.5	432.7	449.8
Africa/Middle East	456.6	538.0	604.2	692.1	791.4	897.9
Asia	1,990.1	2,240.9	2,407.0	2,634.7	2,893.8	3,156.2
Oceania	19.3	21.6	22.7	24.1	25.5	27.1
TOTAL	3,670.3	4,098.6	4,396.4	4,801.4	5,249.3	5,711.2

Source: UNESCO Yearbook 1981/Predicasts

From a publisher's viewpoint this is not particularly helpful because he needs to know something further both about the distribution of the population into age cohorts, and about the level of disposable income in each region. We will be looking at the latter issue later in the book, and with respect to the former it will come as no real news to learn that although large families are still commonplace in underdeveloped and developing countries, they have gone right out of fashion in developed countries. There is inevitably a wave effect as the post-war bulge in developed countries recurs in a diminished way with each successive generation, and the wise publisher will plot this into the future. But so far as the immediate future is concerned the child/school market is unquestionably going to be depressed. Equally, it is obvious that literacy is the key to opening up the market for books in developing countries, yet the acute financial difficulties faced not merely by the newly developing, but by many of the fairly well developed South American and African countries — Nigeria is an obvious case in point — is going to postpone the expenditure of the very large sums required to conquer illiteracy.

An ageing population with lots of money to spend is good news for the publisher who can gear his product to his market. If one looks, for example, at Japan one discovers a country with the longest life span in the world, with 32% of the population currently over 40, set to rise to 38% in 1995, equivalent to a total market of 50 million. Equivalent markets have never existed before, but the opportunity is clearly now there to be taken.

The American market is the largest of all, and we also know a great deal about demographic trends there. We know, for example, the number of those under 18 and over 65 in every large American city, courtesy of the US Bureau of the Census[1], who also provide projections of the total population by race, sex and age from 1985 to 2000. The basic lessons to be learned are as follows:

1. the total population is edging up very slowly, adding roughly 10 million every five years (total in 1982 — 232 million);

2. females outnumber males (119 million to 113 million in 1982);

3. the biggest age cohort is 25-34 years, currently 17% of the total and rising steadily;

4. 12% of the population are currently over 65, and this is set to rise;

5. the number of under 5s hit rock bottom in 1980 and is now on the way up again;

6. all other age cohorts up to age 21 are still on the way down, but will bottom out as the current under 5 group grows up;

7. the number of middle-aged Americans is fairly constant.

The UK provides something of a contrast because, partly as a result of much tighter immigration controls, the population barely changed during the second part of the 1970s, and at one point actually fell, an almost unheard of occurrence. Population projections are notoriously unreliable, but population growth will probably pick up to a rate of 100,000 per annum during the 1980s, and perhaps half as much again during the 1990s. Among developed countries as a whole the 0-21 years age cohort is on the decline, and is not expected to bottom out until the 1990s, hence the dire results for sales of children's books discussed elsewhere in the text. It is much the same in the UK and, although the 0-5

---

[1] Would-be exporters will find this information in the library of the American Embassy in London, and doubtless the equivalent libraries elsewhere.

age group has now bottomed out, it will obviously be a further decade before there is a significant boost in the number of teenagers in the UK. These factors do not, of course, necessarily offer an accurate guide to the prospects for sales of educational books. More children may stay on at school, and there will always be enough children qualified to go on to higher education, irrespective of the size of the 0-21 age cohort, so the key question is whether the number of places will be maintained. The age cohort which is set to grow most rapidly during the second half of the 1980s is aged 21-35 years. The number of pensioners is set to grow slowly. The best prospects therefore appear to be in books for young children, although disposable income and unemployment are going to make a big difference here, and in pandering to the tastes of those setting up homes, starting families, and looking for recreation, probably in the company of children.

Outside of Western Europe, of which the UK is fairly typical, developed countries show rather more buoyant population growth. One distinction may be room or lack of it to expand. Western Europe suffers from a population density which discourages further growth, but if one looks at, for example, Australia, this is much less of a consideration, and immigration policy may be more benign. Certainly Australian population growth runs at a consistent $1\frac{1}{2}\%$ per annum, which, although insufficient to ensure continuous growth in every age cohort because the inter-generational swing is larger in magnitude, prevents the kind of sudden drop in school age children experienced in other developed countries. The latter part of the 1980s offers few opportunities in the school-age cohorts, but all age cohorts beyond the age of 20 are expected to expand in a roughly equivalent way, so there are excellent prospects across a wide range of publishing activities. Inevitably, European publishers will be eyeing up these markets because prospects at home are indifferent, and no doubt those publishing in the indigenous language will have a major advantage, although competition from US publishers is also likely to intensify.

Chapter Two

THE STRUCTURE OF THE BOOK INDUSTRY

Worldwide Book Production

Allowing for the inevitable imprecision of the aggregate magnitudes, the rate of growth of worldwide production of books in terms of number of titles has been as follows:

1950-1955	17%
1955-1960	23%
1960-1965	28%
1965-1970	22%
1970-1975	10%
1975-1980	27%
TOTAL	317%

Guesswork is required for the comparable change in the number of copies printed, but it is generally considered to lie between 350% and 400%. By contrast the world's population only grew by 180%, and the numbr of literate adults and children by 210%. As a consequence, book availability throughout the world advanced significantly although, as table 2.1 below shows, it is only during the past decade that this has shown any tendency to favour developing as well as developed countries, partially because of wide differences in birth rates.

Escarpit[1] has identified what he refers to as a 'quantum jump' in 1962. The twelve-year period 1950 to 1962 saw total output of titles rise by 120,000, or 10,000 per year. But by 1965 the total had risen by a further 76,000, roughly 25,000 per year. From 1965 to 1970 the average fell back to roughly 20,000 per year, and from 1970 to 1975 it returned to an average of 10,000, although from 1975 to 1980 it shot up to 30,000 per annum. 1981, the latest year available saw only a negligible change. It is interesting that there is no tendency for book production to rise geometrically. Indeed the pattern is very irregular.

---

[1] Escarpit (1982) p.3

TABLE 2.1   NUMBER OF TITLES PER MILLION INHABITANTS

	1955	1960	1965	1970	1975	1980	1981
Africa	13	19	23	23	27	28	29
Asia	64	84	57	62	65	56	56
Europe (inc. USSR)	307	374	385	464	471	542	534
North America	77	91	271	367	389	468	461
Latin America	60	79	77	78	89	93	103
Oceania	68	121	286	361	428	548	478
WORLD TOTAL	131	144	168	187	184	164	162
Developed countries	249	296	357	420	431	500	489
Developing countries	38	35	40	41	45	44	46

Source: UNESCO

As table 2.2 shows, a major cause of the quantum jump was a redefinition of the statistics for the United States which resulted in the North American share of the much increased total rising from 5.4% in 1960 to 13.6% in 1965[1]. Escarpit goes on to claim that a more valid explanation was the achievement of independence by former colonies. Their starting up their own book industries did have some impact, although the table shows that the African share of the total altered very little. Escarpit sees the real significance of the changes as stimulating 'book production less in the new nations than in the old colonising countries which had now to meet the new demands from their former colonies for literacy campaigns or educational development'.[2]

The other large absolute increase in output up to 1965 came in Europe, but as table 2.2 shows, not in the USSR (nor Eastern Europe generally). The previously mentioned factor was a consideration in this, but the main explanation was the spread of the paperback, that is the entry of the book into the mass distribution and consumption systems of market economies. The approximate sequence over time was the USA, the UK,

[1] Federal government publications and university theses were added, raising the US total for 1965 from 28,000 to 54,400.
[2] Escarpit (1982) p.4

14

TABLE 2.2 NUMBER OF BOOK TITLES PUBLISHED WORLDWIDE[1]

	1955 No	1955 %	1960 No	1960 %	1965 No	1965 %	1970 No	1970 %	1975 No	1975 %	1980 No	1980 %	1981 No	1981 %
Africa	3,000	1.1	5,000	1.5	7,000	1.6	8,000	1.5	11,000	1.9	13,000	1.8	14,000	1.9
Asia	54,000	20.1	51,000	15.4	61,000	14.3	75,000	14.4	88,000	15.4	145,000	20.0	147,000	20.2
Europe	131,000	48.7	163,000	49.1	200,000	46.9	247,000	47.4	264,000	46.1	313,000	43.1	308,000	42.3
USSR	55,000	20.4	76,000	22.9	76,000	17.8	79,000	15.2	79,000	13.8	93,000	12.7	94,000	12.9
North America	14,000	5.2	18,000	5.4	58,000	13.6	83,000	15.9	92,000	16.1	116,000	16.0	117,000	16.0
Latin America	11,000	4.1	17,000	5.1	19,000	4.5	22,000	4.2	29,000	5.1	34,000	4.7	38,000	5.2
Oceania[2]	1,000	0.4	2,000	0.6	5,000	1.2	7,000	1.4	9,000	1.6	12,500	1.7	11,000	1.5
WORLD TOTAL	269,000	100.0	332,000	100.0	426,000	100.0	521,000	100.0	572,000	100.0	726,500	100.0	729,000	100.0
Africa (excluding Arab States)[3]	1,600	0.6	2,400	0.7	4,300	1.0	4,600	0.9	8,300	1.4	9,700	1.4	10,500	1.5
Asia (excluding Arab States)[3]	53,200	19.7	49,900	15.0	59,700	14.0	73,700	14.1	85,800	15.0	141,300	19.4	143,000	19.6
Arab States[3]	2,200	0.9	3,700	1.2	4,000	0.9	4,700	0.9	4,900	0.9	7,000	1.0	7,500	1.0
Developed countries[4]	225,000	83.6	285,000	85.8	366,000	85.9	451,000	86.6	484,000	84.6	582,000	80.1	576,000	79.0
Developing countries[4]	44,000	16.4	47,000	14.2	60,000	14.1	70,000	13.4	88,000	15.4	144,500	19.9	153,000	21.0

[1] data prior to 1980 for World Total, Asia, Developing Countries and Asia (excluding Arab States) do not include China; [2] mainly Australia, New Zealand, Fiji, Guam, Samoa, Papua New Guinea, French Polynesia; [3] reformulations of the total for Africa and Asia; [4] these two new headings also add up to the World Total

Source: UNESCO

15

West Germany, Japan, France and Spain, and the simultaneity of the paperback expansion in these countries between 1962 and 1965 largely accounted for the 'Jump' effect. In Escarpit's opinion, the effect was to change substantially the landscape of book publishing, bookselling and reading in Western Europe.

The huge increase in title production between 1965 and 1970 showed a proportionate movement away from the developing nations towards both Europe and especially North America. In absolute terms, Europe accounted for 47,000 of the 95,000 increase, and North America 25,000, 77% of the total increase between them.

The effect was to raise dramatically the number of titles per million inhabitants in these areas whilst it stood still in the developing nations.

Fortunately, on the whole, the 1970s saw a reversal of this trend. Between 1970 and 1975 the total grew by 57,000 titles, and 23,000 of these were published in Africa, Asia and Latin America. Between 1975 and 1980 the total grew by 154,000, of which 64,000 were published in those regions, but the Asian increase, much the largest of the three, was centred in Japan, its main developed nation, so the picture for the developing countries as a whole was a little less auspicious. As table 2.2 shows, the latter group accounts for only 56,000 of the increase between 1975 and 1980. Taking the developed nations as the 34 countries of Western Europe, USSR, USA, Canada, Australia, New Zealand and Japan, the continuing slowdown in the rate of population growth resulted in yet another sharp increase in the number of titles per million inhabitants, especially between 1975 and 1980, a period when the developing nations could only achieve a stand-still position. 1981 data suggest a reversal of these trends, but it would be inadvisable to place too much emphasis upon the results of a single year.

Table 2.3 shows the relative position over the period since 1965 of the major developed nations.

TABLE 2.3   POSITION OF DEVELOPED NATIONS IN WORLDWIDE BOOK PRODUCTION, 1965-1980

Titles '000s	1965	1970	1978	1980	Subsequent
80-90			1. USSR 2. USA·	1. USSR	
70-80	1. USSR	1. USA 2. USSR		2. USA	
60-70				3. W.Germany	
50-60	2. USA		3. W.Germany		UK (1983)
40-50		3. W.Germany	4. Japan	4. UK 5. Japan	
30-40		4. UK 5. Japan	5. UK	6. France	Spain (1982)
20-30	3. UK 4. W.Germany 5. Japan 6. France	6. France	6. France	7. Spain	
10-20	7. Spain	7. Spain	7. Spain		

Source: UNESCO

Throughout the 1970s the USA and the USSR kept abreast of one another. The US statistics, as previously noted, were raised in the 1960s, but as Escarpit points out, quite a number of Soviet titles are counted several times as a result of the multiplicity of languages in use, and this may be 'engineered' in relation to US output. By 1980, the USA seems to have yielded second best, but it is in reality very hard to say which would produce more books if a uniform, conventional measure was to be applied. Third place has been held by West Germany for over a decade, and the UK has now positioned itself significantly above Japan, whose output growth has ground to a halt.

Just how dominant the top six countries are among the developed nations can be better understood when one realises that although Canada just makes the 20,000 mark, Australia and New Zealand can only just rustle up 10,000 between them. Indeed, the real challenge comes from the Republic of Korea and, insofar as the statistics can be relied upon, from China, both now in the 20-30,000 range.

The dominant role played by a limited number of languages is most obviously the end result of colonisation, but one can also appreciate just how unassailable English is as the foremost world language for written communication. Perhaps one quarter of all books are published in English, with Russian and German accounting for roughly another quarter. Russian is virtually unused outside Russia itself whereas German is the main alternative to English throughout Western Europe.

Further light can be shed upon the role of different languages if one looks at data on translations. Table 2.4, below, lists the main countries publishing translations in 1978. As can be seen, the UK and USA play little part in this process which is dominated by France, West Germany and the USSR.

TABLE 2.4   MAIN COUNTRIES PUBLISHING TRANSLATIONS, 1978

Country	No	Country	No	Country	No
WORLD TOTAL	57,147				
Albania	137	East Germany	812	Netherlands	3,847
Argentina	344	West Germany	7,168	Norway	1,013
Austria	351	Greece	589	Poland	942
Belgium	621	Hungary	840	Portugal	640
Brazil	522	Iceland	165	Romania	650
Bulgaria	632	India	890	Spain	5,543
Canada	336	Indonesia	382	Sweden	1,275
Colombia	101	Israel	211	Switzerland	838
Czechoslovakia	984	Italy	1,738	Turkey	792
Denmark	2,014	Japan	2,307	USSR	7,023
Egypt	173	South Korea	237	UK	1,494
Finland	701	Malaysia	100	USA	1,479
France	8,350	Mexico	205	Yugoslavia	1,352

Source: UNESCO Statistical Yearbook

Table 2.5 looks at languages rather than countries, and illustrates the huge number of books translated from English, followed predictably by Russian, German and French although interestingly the latter three languages are not translated as extensively as one might have expected into English.

Table 2.6 gives a good idea of the topic areas which are popularly translated. Not surprisingly, what people most want to read are other countries' best-selling literature. This is especially true for literature published originally in English, though it is proportionately even more significant for Scandinavian languages. Social science translations run literature a not very close second, although work of this nature published in English is not much sought after for translation purposes.

French and German books on the arts and philosophy are much translated, as are German books on applied sciences, whereas Russian books most sought after for translation are in the social and pure sciences.

A final point worth making at this juncture is that very few previously colonised countries publish in any language other than that of the nation which colonised them. This is especially noticeable in Africa where English and French predominate, and in South America where Spanish is predominant. Only in India is a real exception to be found, where roughly one half of all publications are in a language other than English.

TABLE 2.5 TRANSLATION OF TITLES BY ORIGINAL LANGUAGE AND BY SELECTED LANGUAGES INTO WHICH TRANSLATED IN 1978

Translated into

Translated from	English	French	Spanish	Russian	Arabic	German	Italian	Japanese	Dutch	Danish	Norwegian	Swedish	Polish	Turkish
English		4,922	2,760	453	59	4,878	808	1,568	2,129	1,022	619	759	199	299
French	886		1,467	125	15	1,231	476	280	434	177	32	83	94	95
German	810	999	854	154	9		250	236	751	227	53	103	105	56
Hebrew	95	50	10	6	7	29	10	1	12	3	1	0	0	2
Hungarian	95	45	13	79	1	127	7	1	7	2	2	5	19	10
Italian	178	534	435	13	0	275		22	33	25	5	10	17	9
Japanese	97	44	1	10	2	27	4		9	2	1	1	2	1
Latin	82	112	51	3	0	69	37	5	15	5	2	21	4	0
Polish	108	69	11	83	0	124	5	9	3	3	1	6		3
Russian	668	552	361		110	680	71	108	71	34	20	52	191	79
Spanish	111	237		28	3	129	60	18	38	16	10	15	26	10
Swedish	102	81	21	5	0	181	5	8	54	349	184		9	7

Note: A more detailed breakdown of this table can be found in the Statistical Appendix

Source: UNESCO Statistical Yearbook

TABLE 2.6 TRANSLATIONS BY ORIGINAL LANGUAGE BY UDC CLASSES

Translated from	Total	General Titles	Philosophy	Religion	Social sciences	Pure sciences	Applied sciences	Art	Literature	Geog/history
English	23,715	135	1,287	1,086	1,994	1,819	2,221	1,154	12,712	1,384
Russian	6,745	22	299	25	2,112	1,040	470	265	2,013	481
French	6,220	42	414	424	646	252	509	678	2,711	346
German	5,663	49	468	408	808	326	758	574	1,902	370
Italian	1,731	15	57	131	170	160	188	329	593	88
Swedish	1,177	6	29	29	87	51	128	62	739	45
Spanish	879	1	14	81	85	39	31	90	477	63
Danish	625	1	20	11	29	63	53	42	384	22
Czech	584	6	4	2	87	115	54	46	225	45
Polish	578	4	17	13	100	36	62	57	251	38
Hungarian	565	17	8	1	68	38	73	76	245	39
Dutch	528	1	9	52	50	32	93	112	147	32
Latin	508	1	55	203	17	12	13	25	134	48
Serbo-Croatian	477	2	2	1	281	8	20	17	109	37
Romanian	454	5	5	1	136	46	32	37	131	61
Classical Greek	437	0	64	178	7	7	6	9	143	23
Chinese	352	0	15	10	163	5	8	21	116	14
Arabic	318	2	10	83	113	2	2	7	83	16
Japanese	308	0	9	14	24	20	47	54	126	12
Norwegian	264	1	2	26	17	2	8	13	176	19
Bulgarian	256	4	2	1	51	12	18	10	130	28
Hebrew	246	2	3	131	34	3	6	12	34	21
Sanskrit	221	0	25	101	6	3	4	1	80	1
Portuguese	215	3	7	21	45	2	3	12	112	10
TOTAL (inc. others)	57,147	347	2,908	3,357	7,709	4,197	4,935	3,890	26,199	3,585

Source: UNESCO Statistical Yearbook

World Survey

Table 2.7 presents details of title production for different regions of the world. A few brief comments follow on the major regions, before individual studies of selected national industries.

a)   *Africa:* In Africa, an extremely small number of titles per head combines with the extensive use of European languages for written communication. Between them these two factors offer few opportunities for African book development. There are too few languages in widespread use throughout Africa in any event, so a major difficulty exists in getting agreement between the main African trading nations that an indigenous language should be substituted for an imported one. Failing this, the well-established subsidiaries of European and American publishers are likely to continue their stranglehold on the region.

b)   *Asia:* The Asian situation is much more varied because of the vast populations involved. To begin with, Japan can now be treated as a developed nation with its own large-scale publishing industry; and Korea is fast catching up. China remains something of an enigma with a low output of titles for its size and a very low per capita consumption. Nevertheless, the high population results in print runs on a scale which would make a western publisher green with envy. According to Escarpit[1], large printings are the order of the day with priority being given to children's and school books, the availability of which is relatively satisfactory.

 The Indian experience is quite different. Rather surprisingly, the period 1977 to 1981 saw title production fluctuate erratically between 11,000 and 13,000, a level no better than for the early 1960s despite a modest upsurge in between. British colonisation had bequeathed to India a comparatively well developed book industry, but this appears to have been insufficient to cope with widespread illiteracy and linguistic disparities.

[1] Escarpit (1982) p.18

TABLE 2.7 BOOK PRODUCTION : NUMBER OF TITLES BY UDC CLASSES

Region	Total	Gener-alities	Philos-ophy	Religion	Social sciences	Pure sciences	Applied sciences	Arts	Litera-ture	Geog/history
Africa	5,357	271	69	506	1,734	450	810	211	884	402
North America	103,534	2,422	2,237	2,668	15,939	4,943	11,179	4,486	6,505	3,984
South America	17,142	1,176	245	924	4,864	1,142	2,406	1,495	3,359	1,359
Asia	134,327	4,072	5,873	6,142	30,012	12,691	13,234	9,341	39,034	7,084
Europe	318,548	14,644	9,140	13,424	72,690	21,167	54,779	26,174	80,632	23,565
USSR	94,646	2,899	1,702	278	24,354	9,436	37,089	2,836	14,007	2,045
Oceania	10,802	396	124	235	3,521	851	1,973	1,043	1,603	976

Note: a more detailed country breakdown is presented in the Statistical Appendix
Source: UNESCO Statistical Yearbook

c) *South America:* The major producer in this area is Brazil, which unfortunately does not appear in the table. Brazilian output is comparable to that of Spain, rising inexorably from 5,000 in 1965 to 20,000 in 1976. Paper consumption is on a par with Europe, essentially because pulp is an indigenous industry. Print runs are large, but the size of the population results in a rather low level of volumes per capita. In 1976 textbooks accounted for 4,900 titles and 100 million copies, and children's books for 2,420 titles and 37 million copies.

The Brazilian experience is especially noteworthy because none of the other long-standing publishing nations in this region have achieved their potential. Argentina, for example, is currently producing at the same level as in 1970, with virtually no change in between, and Chile cannot even muster the modest total achieved in 1965. Uruguay looked to be making headway by the end of the 1970s, but ran into a period of stagnation. Only Colombia's respectable total has resulted from significant growth in recent years.

d) *The Arab States:* Data with respect to the Arab States are at best sketchy and unreliable. One or two oil rich nations such as Iraq have increased their output considerably, although over the longer term Egypt has always been at the centre of the Arabic publishing world. Colonial languages still exert a hold, for example French in Algeria and Tunisia. It is now hard to believe that Arabic was one of the world's great international languages. Of what is produced, an unusually high proportion is directed towards children.

United States

The UNESCO statistics cover what they define as commercial book production. However, this definition includes publications of the Federal Government (10,566) and university theses (31,358), so it is sensible to examine the data to be found in Bowker's *Weekly Record,* which is based upon a narrower definition closer to that used by other countries. This appears as Table 2.8 opposite.

**TABLE 2.8   US : NEW BOOKS AND NEW EDITIONS PUBLISHED BY
SUBJECT**

	1965	**1970**	**1975**	**1980**	**1982**	**1983[1]**
TOTAL	28,595	36,071	39,372	42,377	46,935	41,888[2]
Agriculture	270	265	456	461	439	440
Art	974	1,169	1,561	1,691	1,722	1,472
Biography	685	1,536	1,968	1,891	1,752	2,059
Business	537	797	820	1,185	1,327	1,666
Education	954	1,178	1,038	1,011	1,046	806
Fiction	3,241	3,137	3,805	2,835	5,419	4,946
General reference	634	846	1,113	1,643	2,398	2,216
History	1,682	1,995	1,823	2,220	2,177	1,961
Home economics	300	321	728	879	1,099	1,006
Juvenile	2,895	2,640	2,292	2,859	3,049	2,651
Language	527	472	438	529	576	631
Law	436	604	915	1,102	1,451	1,245
Literature	1,686	3,085	1,904	1,686	1,742	1,597
Medicine	1,218	1,476	2,282	3,292	3,229	2,869
Music	300	404	305	357	346	323
Philosophy, psychology	979	1,280	1,374	1,429	1,465	1,277
Poetry, drama	994	1,474	1,501	1,179	1,049	967
Religion	1,855	1,788	1,773	2,055	2,075	1,781
Science	2,562	2,358	2,942	3,109	3,124	2,605
Sociology, economics	3,242	5,912	6,590	7,152	7,449	6,759
Sports, recreation	591	799	1,225	971	1,191	1,056
Technology	1,153	1,141	1,720	2,337	2,328	2,223
Travel	883	1,394	794	504	482	442

[1] provisional, the eventual total is likely to be at least as high as 1982; [2] prior to 1979,
book entries comprise all titles submitted for listing in Bowker's Weekly Record during
calendar year. Beginning 1979, covers listings in year shown, plus titles issued in that year
which were listed in following six months. Comprises new books (published for first time)
and new editions (with changes in text or format). Excludes government publications,
books sold only by subscription, dissertations, periodicals and quarterlies, and pamphlets
under 39 pages.
Source: R.R.Bowker Co., *Publishers Weekly*

It will be apparent that the scale of publishing is not dissimilar to that
of the UK despite an enormous difference in the size of the home market.
Whether that is any kind of indictment of either country, neither or both,
is a matter of opinion. It may be observed that whereas 1981 was a peak

year for the USA, and 1980 a trough, it was the other way around for the UK (studied next). As in the UK, the proportion of new titles runs at around 75% of the total output.

The breakdown by category is individual to the USA, although one can also obtain the UNESCO division for the equivalent number of publications. From 1975 on, biography went into decline, but was evidently going to hit a record high in 1983. Fiction declined until 1980 then rose by an extraordinary 100% in 1981 to a level which is currently being maintained. Reference books have increased steadily, but poetry and drama have taken a tumble. Rather curiously, travel books are nothing like as popular as they were prior to 1975 even though travel itself is so much more popular. The other categories show no obvious trends.

Information is also available on mass-market paperback titles covering the past three years. These totalled 4,175 in 1981 and 3,985 in 1982, and look to have totalled 3,835 in 1983. Fiction titles have paralleled this decline exactly, retaining 75% of the total, and only juveniles at 6%, and sport and recreation at 5%, otherwise take a significant share of the market. The only growth area is in books on technology.

If one turns to paperbacks other than mass-market, one finds the total building up to a peak of 12,658 in 1982 before declining to 10,962 in 1983 (which may not represent the year's full total). Of these, fiction represented 4% in 1980, but only 2½% in 1982.

United Kingdom

UK data on titles published appears as table 2.9 below, and is especially noteworthy because it has been produced by the same organisation over a very long period of time. Between 1949 and 1959 the total increased by 21.5%; between 1959 and 1969 by 56.6%; between 1969 and 1979 by 29.5%; and it is already up 22% since 1979, so the current decade should easily set a new record. The 1960s were a decade of continuous, but fairly slow, growth. Subsequently, the pattern became more variable, with reductions at times of recession, but the inexorable upwards movement does suggest that even significant recessions fail to cause publishers to reconsider the wisdom of churning out more and more titles other than in the very short term.

TABLE 2.9   UK: NUMBER OF TITLES PUBLISHED

Year	Total	New books	%	Reprints/ new editions	%
1950	17,072	11,738	68.8	5,334	31.2
1955	19,962	14,192	71.1	5,770	28.9
1960	23,783	18,794	79.0	4,989	21.0
1965	26,358	21,045	79.9	5,313	20.1
1970	33,489	23,512	70.2	9,977	29.8
1975	35,608	27,247	76.5	8,361	23.5
1976	34,434	26,207	76.1	8,227	23.9
1977	36,322	27,684	76.2	8,638	23.8
1978	38,766	29,530	76.2	9,236	23.8
1979	41,940	32,854	78.3	9,086	21.7
1980	48,158	37,382	77.6	10,776	22.4
1981	43,083	33,696	78.2	9,387	21.8
1982	48,307	37,947	78.6	10,360	21.4
1983	51,071	38,980	76.3	12,091	23.7

Source: *The Bookseller*

The proportion of titles which are new has for many years varied in the 76-79% range, which is much higher than, for example, in France. It is obviously debatable whether the market can handle so many books whilst remaining profitable, and this issue is examined elsewhere in the text. Certainly a buoyant export market can make all the difference, although this is subject to potentially fierce competition from the USA. Indeed, many of the titles technically published in the UK are originated abroad, especially in America, so the upward trend in output is not solely the responsibility of UK publishers. In recent years, between 40 and 50 of the 100 imprints publishing the largest number of new titles in the UK have been foreign-owned, and some of these, especially US university presses, have flooded the market with their full lists as a result of signing up an agent within the UK to distribute on their behalf. This does not operate in reverse on anything like the same scale, nor indeed between other pairs of countries, and it is a little ironic that the UK should contain a population with a clear preference for borrowing rather than buying books.

One can obtain an impression of changes in the popularity of subject areas by analysing the breakdown produced by The Publishers' Association. This appears below in table 2.10 where the two most recent three-year periods are compared, each consisting of a sequence of three increasing total magnitudes, the first off a base of 38,766 titles, and the second off a base of 43,083 titles.

TABLE 2.10   UK: TITLES PUBLISHED BY CATEGORY

	Average 1978-80	1981	1982	1983	Average 1981-83	% change 81/83 : 78/80
Aeronautics	183	237	238	206	227	+ 24
Agriculture & forestry	447	451	512	427	463	+ 4
Architecture	407	347	384	426	386	− 5
Art	1,313	1,383	1,279	1,312	1,325	+ 1
Astronomy	138	120	155	171	149	+ 8
Bibliography & library economy	742	788	776	675	746	0
Biography	1,266	1,243	1,491	1,961	1,568	+ 24
Chemistry & physics	736	682	754	697	711	− 3
Children's books	3,236	2,934	2,917	3,449	3,100	− 4
Commerce	1,122	1,213	1,493	1,377	1,361	+ 21
Customs, costumes & folklore	148	158	172	172	167	+ 13
Domestic science	695	695	776	781	751	+ 8
Education	1,083	1,040	1,175	1,421	1,212	+ 12
Engineering	1,397	1,488	1,662	1,714	1,621	+ 16
Entertainment	576	630	717	598	648	+ 13
Fiction	4,691	4,747	4,879	5,265	4,964	+ 6
General	387	557	777	856	730	+ 89
Geography & archaeology	379	476	683	437	532	+ 40
Geology & meteorology	293	340	418	348	369	+ 26
History	1,434	1,432	1,503	1,740	1,558	+ 9
Humour	123	171	215	242	209	+ 70
Industry	538	492	569	612	558	+ 4

Continued...

Table 2.10 continued...

	Average 1978-80	1981	1982	1983	Average 1981-83	% change 81/83 : 78/80
Language	554	657	664	708	676	+ 22
Law & public administration	1,366	1,399	1,464	1,787	1,550	+ 13
Literature	1,134	1,151	1,612	2,187	1,650	+ 46
Mathematics	667	726	924	1,011	887	+ 33
Medical science	2,713	2,838	3,274	3,165	3,092	+ 14
Military science	157	113	143	167	141	+ 11
Music	419	365	498	489	451	+ 8
Natural sciences	1,194	1,234	1,507	1,177	1,306	+ 9
Occultism	248	251	193	188	211	− 15
Philosophy	458	431	521	695	549	+ 20
Photography	204	237	268	294	266	+ 30
Plays	300	256	253	381	297	0
Poetry	762	620	794	925	780	+ 2
Political science & economics	3,529	3,764	4,263	4,177	4,068	+ 15
Psychology	726	725	834	705	755	+ 4
Religion & theology	1,509	1,363	1,856	2,257	1,825	+ 21
School textbooks	2,128	1,991	1,807	1,964	1,921	− 10
Science, general	87	55	58	76	63	− 28
Sociology	1,050	1,031	1,174	1,162	1,122	+ 7
Sports & outdoor games	629	511	541	610	554	− 12
Stock breeding	308	264	297	265	275	− 11
Trade	571	536	606	563	568	0
Travel & guide books	666	677	869	956	834	+ 25
Wireless & TV	240	264	342	267	291	+ 21
TOTAL	42,955	43,083	48,307	51,071	47,487	+ 11

Source: Publishers' Association

The subject breakdown is interesting because it reflects how the general inexorable rise in total output shows up in individual categories, and because it provides some guidance to publishers as to which categories to be involved in. Given an overall change of + 11%, the main interest obviously lies in these categories which deviate significantly from this figure. The biggest gains, in declining order of magnitude, are general (rather too ambiguous to analyse), humour, literature, geography and archaeology, mathematics, photography, geology and meteorology, travel, aeronautics and biography. The biggest losers, in declining order of magnitude, are general science (off a small base), occultism, sports, stockbreeding and school textbooks. Children's books, alas, did badly, though they look to have had a resurgence in 1984. The biggest gains perhaps suggest a touch of escapism during the recession. Taking a longer view back through the 1970s, the most resilient sectors have been history, literature and mathematics, and those continuously below par have been architecture, occultism, school textbooks, general science and sports.

West Germany

West Germany has long been the world's third largest publishing nation. Like the UK output peaked in 1980, but the recovery in 1982 was much smaller than the UK's, perhaps because there were far fewer foreign-originated titles. Despite this recovery, the proportion of new titles in the total fell slightly in 1982, as shown in table 2.11 below.

TABLE 2.11   WEST GERMANY: TITLES PUBLISHED BY TYPE OF EDITION

	Total	First edition	New edition	First/New
1977	48,736	39,044	9,692	80:20
1978	53,137	43,270	9,867	81:19
1979	62,082	50,306	11,776	81:19
1980	67,176	54,572	12,604	81:19
1981	59,168	47,260	11,908	80:20
1982	61,332	48,730	12,602	79:21

Source: BDB

30

West Germany's high level of education and the popularity of self-improvement have led to a demand for variety in the book market and a preference for new ideas. Nevertheless, the rapid growth in the number of titles published during the 1970s coupled with a decline in print runs, is giving cause for concern exactly as in the UK. Consumer interest in many of the titles being published is generally not very high, and many titles are being pushed on to the market with no real prospects of breaking even.

The division of output by categories appears in table 2.12 below:

TABLE 2.12   WEST GERMANY: TITLES PUBLISHED BY CATEGORY

	1977	1978	1979	1980	1981	1982
General	750	808	937	1,095	901	633
Religion, theology	2,438	2,464	3,085	3,845	3,082	3,547
Philosophy, psychology	1,289	1,283	1,616	1,769	1,838	1,944
Law, administration	2,739	3,021	3,329	3,517	2,847	2,864
Economics, statistics, social sciences	4,043	4,456	5,312	6,658	5,598	5,326
Politics, defence	1,224	1,204	1,406	1,737	1,256	1,238
Languages and literature	2,032	1,783	2,267	2,208	2,124	2,407
Belles lettres	9,465	12,164	12,453	12,404	11,963	10,875
Children's books	2,873	2,636	2,932	3,115	2,695	4,096
Education	2,230	2,706	3,376	3,572	2,600	2,540
Schoolbooks	2,652	1,803	2,529	2,148	1,913	3,679
Fine arts, art	2,313	2,669	3,348	3,861	3,219	3,480
Music, dance, theatre, cinema	814	796	1,317	1,198	1,196	1,272
History, culture, folklore	2,013	2,233	2,630	2,969	2,665	2,137
Geography, travel, ethnology	960	1,158	1,416	1,730	1,667	1,840
Maps, atlases	2,150	2,123	2,416	2,415	2,600	2,767
Medicine	1,923	2,263	2,301	2,757	2,699	2,758
Natural sciences	1,798	1,979	2,104	2,281	1,779	1,733
Mathematics	680	702	1,170	960	847	890
Technology industry	2,262	2,335	3,056	3,656	2,615	2,315
Communications	424	527	817	739	682	541
Agriculture, forestry, domestic science	1,113	1,301	1,449	1,743	1,660	1,630
Sport, games	429	626	693	718	637	618
Miscellaneous	45	48	29	50	51	81
Calendars, almanacs	77	49	94	31	70	121
TOTAL	48,736	53,137	62,082	67,176	59,168	61,332

Source: BDB

If one compares 1979 with 1982, these being years with a similar total output, one discovers a substantial reduction in the largest category of belles lettres. Law and administration, education, history and culture, natural sciences, technology, communications, general and sports books also showed significant decreases. On the other hand, school books increased enormously, and good gains were shown by philosophy, children's books and geography and travel.

The number of titles published as paperbacks rose to 8,600 in 1982, a 100% increase over a decade earlier. However, the rise was not continuous, hitting a low of 11.6% of the total in 1980, but rising to 14.0% in 1982. Paperbacks are concentrated in the belles lettres category which accounts for 49% of paperback titles, and in children's books (9.7%). In 1982, 41% of paperback titles were either reprints or new editions, so the switch from a hardback to a paperback edition in many categories is now a very common practice. The only significant exceptions to this practice are fine arts and music and dance books.

Between 10% and 12% of titles published in West Germany are translated from a foreign language, a proportion which has remained fairly stable over the past twenty years. This gives a clear indication of the importance of invisible imports in the form of licences and publishing rights. Translations are primarily from English, with French a long way behind. Translations are fairly commonplace in children's literature, followed by general literature and philosophy and psychology, these being the strongest paperback markets. English general literature is extensively translated.

France

The official figures produced by the Syndicat National des Éditeurs are considerably lower than those registered by UNESCO in 1981, although the UNESCO figure for 1979 was only 25,000, well below the SNE figure. There is a reasonable agreement in both years about such areas as literature, but UNESCO registers an increase in Social Science output from 3,000 in 1980 to 12,400 in 1981 although no definitional change is indicated. Sticking to the SNE figures we find in fact a remarkably consistent output over the past six years, with only practical books and atlases showing a definite tendency to grow, and general literature a definite tendency to diminish.

The proportion of new titles in the total is unusually low at 45%, which suggests a rather different approach to that in, say, the UK where the figure is 76-78%. The bulk of the rest are reprints rather than new editions, so one must assume that the French bookbuyer is content to select from what is ultimately a rather narrowly defined range of titles for a country of that size. Scientific and technical books tend, not surprisingly, to be two-thirds new titles whereas dictionaries and encyclopaedias are 75% reprints.

The proportion being published in paperback format is rising steadily, with a clear tendency for reprints to be reissued in this format (up 21% in 1982). Although average print runs are necessarily limited in the information they convey, because the average includes some very long and some very short runs, it is interesting to examine the table below since information on print runs is rather scarce on the ground. As one would expect, there is some tendency for the size of print runs to decline over time, although this is by no means true of individual categories.

TABLE 2.13   FRANCE: TITLES PUBLISHED BY SUBJECT

	1970	1978	1979	1980	1981	1982
School textbooks	3,171	3,325	3,207	3,438	3,139	3,270
Scientific, technical	2,134	1,831	1,823	1,847	1,791	1,987
Social sciences	2,943	3,440	3,550	3,601	3,380	3,572
General literature	8,882	9,066	9,367	8,860	8,472	8,518
Encyclopaedias/dictionaries	386	677	673	458	476	456
Fine arts	635	1,018	1,106	1,182	1,080	1,027
Children's	2,282	4,795	4,939	4,549	4,532	4,774
Practical, atlases	1,041	1,905	2,022	2,700	2,732	2,764
TOTAL	21,571	26,584	26,687	26,635	25,602	26,348
of which						
New books	10,924	11,966	12,215	11,891	11,639	11,887
New editions	1,406	1,133	1,239	1,230	1,582	1,748
Reprints	9,241	13,485	13,233	13,514	12,381	12,713

Source: Syndicat National des Editeurs

Spain

From 1973 to 1979 Spanish title output remained remarkably constant, varying between 23,500 and 24,900 titles. Subsequently, however, the number of titles rose steadily to a provisional total of 32,200 in 1982, and this trend, if continued would establish Spain as very much a big league publishing country. Table 2.14 below divides up the totals by category. As can be seen annual fluctuations can be extremely large, although there are no definitional changes to explain this. 1982 was particularly changeable, making it difficult to interpret trends until the 1983 figures are available. However, it is reasonable to conclude that religious, legal, medical, town planning and language books are on the increase, whereas books on philosophy, sociology and history and biography are in decline. Literature is, as usual, the most popular category, but the number of medical books is remarkably large, perhaps reflecting the needs of export markets in developing countries.

The titles published in 1979 accounted for 225 million copies, some 9,200 per title, which is a very satisfactory figure. Literature was average in this respect, but general books managed 14,000 copies per title. Business-related books sold in far fewer numbers, whereas language books sold in very large numbers.

Over 5,000 of the titles published in 1979 were translations, mainly from English, French, German and Italian. These fell predominantly into the literature category. Clearly Spain forms a clearing house in this respect, making available to Spanish-speaking export markets the cream of European literature.

TABLE 2.14   SPAIN: TITLES PUBLISHED BY CATEGORY

	1979	1980	1981	1982[1]
General	3,915	4,601	4,721	6,707
Philosophy, psychology	1,180	1,215	1,056	1,028
Religion, theology	1,497	1,569	1,628	1,765
Sociology, statistics	518	508	351	302
Politics and economics	867	951	793	953

Continued...

Table 2.14 continued...

	1979	1980	1981	1982[1]
Law, public administration	708	875	887	957
Military science	46	43	76	58
Teaching and education	1,069	1,297	1,334	903
Business, communication, transport	268	312	327	600
Ethnography, folklore	216	188	200	306
Mathematics	570	541	598	700
Natural science	1,056	1,321	1,164	1,253
Medicine, public hygiene	893	1,069	1,298	1,296
Engineering, technology	705	1,056	872	976
Agriculture, forestry	294	366	408	474
Home economics	242	203	285	374
Business management	123	177	81	373
Town planning and architecture	174	222	249	351
Fine art, photography	1,025	1,201	1,270	1,013
Music, theatre, cinema	169	329	300	255
Games, sport	502	349	277	414
Language, philology	1,179	1,547	1,605	1,853
Literature	5,673	7,323	8,098	7,558
Geography, travel	183	283	241	507
History, biography	1,497	1,366	1,324	1,237
TOTAL	24,569	28,912	29,443	32,213

[1] provisional

Source: Anuario Estadistico

Italy

UNESCO data appears to underestimate title production in Italy. According to ISTAT the figures were as follows:

TABLE 2.15   ITALY: NUMBER OF TITLES PUBLISHED

	New titles	New editions	Reprints	Total
1978	9,209	1,470	6,939	17,618
1979	9,716	1,446	6,676	17,838
1980	10,498	1,531	7,665	19,694

No individual category, according to Annuario Statistico Italiano, accounted for as much as 10% of the total. Curiously it was public administration which led the field at 8% of total output, followed more predictably by history and biography at 6½% and religion at 6%. Classical literary texts have risen significantly in numbers whilst modern literary texts have declined by the same amount. Business management is also rapidly declining in interest, whereas philosophy, religion, and art and photography are increasingly popular.

The titles printed in 1979 accounted for 5.7 million copies. 3,930 titles were translations into Italian, and textbooks numbered 3,607 titles.

Japan

UNESCO data shows Japan reaching the 40,000 titles mark rather earlier than is suggested by the Research Institution for Publications, whose figures appear in table 2.16 below:

TABLE 2.16   JAPAN: NUMBER OF TITLES PUBLISHED

	All titles	First editions	
		Number	%
1977	36,815	25,808	70
1978	37,710	27,150	72
1979	39,027	27,132	70
1980	39,462	27,709	70
1981	40,439	29,362	73

Source: Prime Minister's Office

The trend is one of steady, slow growth, with the proportion of first editions tending towards an equilibrium of 70%. The native population is much larger than the UK's, whose output is similar, but Japan lacks the UK's export potential. Of the first editions published in 1981 23% were in the social sciences, 20% literature and 12% art, although the latter's high value presumably reflects a wider definition than is customary in the West. Science and engineering are not as prominent as we might expect, nor industry at a mere 3% of the total.

Under 10% of the titles published in 1981 were translated works, although this included 17% of the total for philosophy and religion, natural science and literature.

South Korea

The existence of a single language in Korea, which is very uncommon in Asia, denies publishers export opportunities, but simultaneously keeps out imports. As a result the number of titles published has shot up in recent years from 13,000 in 1977 to 26,000 in 1981, and the number of copies from 50 million in 1979 to 80 million in 1981. Of the latter just under 50% were textbooks, although these accounted for only 3,000 titles (12%).

The UNESCO data are the best available, and these illustrate the popularity of literature. Children's books represented 3,859 titles and 5.2 million copies.

China

China has in recent years become a major force in the publishing arena, as shown by the table below.

TABLE 2.17   PEOPLES REPUBLIC OF CHINA: NUMBER OF TITLES AND COPIES PUBLISHED

	Titles	Copies (million)	% growth rate Titles	Copies
1977	12,886	33.1		
1978	14,487	37.7	12.4	14.1
1979	17,212	40.7	18.8	7.9
1980	21,621	45.9	25.6	12.8
1981	25,601	55.8	18.4	21.4

Source: Economic Research Centre/State Council/State Statistical Bureau

The breakdown according to publishing category is rather limited, but appears as follows:

TABLE 2.18   PEOPLES REPUBLIC OF CHINA: TITLES PUBLISHED BY SUBJECT

	Titles	Copies ('000)
Political and social science	2,559	25,864
Culture and education	3,901	129,240
Literature and art	3,934	31,230
Natural science and technology	5,862	18,078
Children's	2,520	78,674
TOTAL GENERAL	18,776	283,086
Textbooks	4,144	199,841
Picture books	2,681	74,903
TOTAL	25,601	557,830

Source: Economic Research Centre/State Council/State Statistical Bureau

Picture books comprise an unusually large proportion of the total, and literature for children is flourishing generally. Textbooks comprise a much bigger share of copies (36%) than of titles (16%). Books for middle and primary schools accounted for only 1,184 titles, but 183.5 million copies. Books are published in 14 minority languages, and these account for 7½% of all titles but only 5% of all copies.

India

India has been known to lay claim to the title of seventh-largest book publisher in the world as measured by titles issued, and the third-largest publisher of titles in English. The first of the claims is certainly no longer true, as title output has shown a tendency to decrease in recent years, as indicated in the table below.

TABLE 2.19   INDIA: NUMBER OF TITLES PUBLISHED

1976	1977	1978	1979	1980	1981
21,922	19,629	18,584	16,392	17,168	11,562

Source: The National Library, Calcutta

As in the USSR, there is probably quite a lot of duplication of titles issued in more than one of the thirteen languages in widespread use. The 1981 total looks unreasonably low, so a later adjustment may be called for, but a decline in 1980 is fairly certain.

English is the most common published language, and its position has been strengthened during the past decade from 34% of titles in 1970 to 45% in 1981, although over 50% was recorded in 1975. Hindi, the national language, is the only other language to account for over 10% of the total. 67% of all social science titles are published in English and 20% in Hindi, whereas only 5% of literature is in English and 22% in Hindi.

Australia

It is interesting to examine briefly title output in Australia, since this is a country where indigenous publishers are in direct competition with other nationalities of much longer standing. Analysis is clouded slightly by the existence of two sets of data: the first, published by the *Australian Book-seller and Publisher,* gives the following aggregate output of new titles, produced by publishers of different nationalities:

TABLE 2.20 AUSTRALIA: TITLES PUBLISHED BY NATIONALITY OF PUBLISHER

	1976	1977	1978	1979	1980	1981	1982
New Titles	1,781	2,243	2,183	2,412	2,656	2,171	2,443
% breakdown:							
Main UK imprints	17.6	16.5	21.8	21.0	21.7	26.9	23.7
Main US imprints	6.7	6.9	6.7	8.1	7.5	6.5	9.1
Main Australian imprints	24.3	29.4	29.0	20.5	24.3	19.6	21.9
Other imprints[1]	51.4	47.2	42.6	50.4	46.5	47.0	45.4

[1] mainly Australian

Source: *Australian Bookseller and Publisher*

Of the 19 main UK imprints, only one had produced over 100 new titles in any one year, and only four others more than 50 new titles. Interestingly, more imprints (5) produced their peak outputs in 1978 (total 475), than in 1979 and subsequent years, despite total output rising to 580. Hence, although large UK imprints are important in aggregate, the market is tending to be divided up more evenly over time rather than the reverse. Of the 10 main US imprints only one produces over 50 new titles each year, and five reached their peak output in 1978 or earlier, the 1982 figure being caused by a single publisher's abnormal output. Of the five main Australian imprints, one published around 200 new titles a year, and two others over 100, although here again no peak outputs occurred after 1980. Nevertheless, indigenous publishing appears currently to be holding its own pretty well in the face of overseas competition, and US imprints have so far failed to make any real inroads, preferring to rely on exporting from the USA.

The Australian Book Publishers Association present a somewhat different picture for 1982, as indicated in table 2.21, where reprints are also listed.

TABLE 2.21   AUSTRALIA: TITLES PUBLISHED BY NATIONALITY OF OWNERSHIP

		Australian	USA	UK	Other	Total
New Australian books						
a)	Educational	471	204	495	11	1,181
	% of total	39.9	17.3	41.9	0.9	100
b)	General	919	48	256	28	1,251
	% of total	73.5	3.8	20.5	2.2	100
TOTAL NEW BOOKS		1,390	252	751	39	2,432
	% of total	57.1	10.4	30.9	1.6	100
Australian titles reprinted						
a)	Educational	361	405	862	2	1,630
	% of total	22.2	24.8	52.9	0.1	100
b)	General	537	27	195	5	764
	% of total	70.3	3.5	25.5	0.7	100
TOTAL REPRINTS		898	432	1,057	7	2,394
	% of total	37.5	18.0	44.2	0.3	100

Source: Australian Book Publishers Association

The table gives the UK a higher market share than indicated above, at the expense of Australian imprints, and shows Australian imprints operating primarily in the general market whilst UK and US imprints are disproportionately significant in educational publishing, a predictable division. The reprint market is, however, largely in the control of US and UK imprints, so the picture painted by ABRA is rather less propitious for indigenous publishing than was suggested above.

Production in developing countries

Little attention has been paid so far to production in developing countries because the scale of production is too low. It may appear superficially that this scarcity of titles is itself a factor holding back the

41

development of such countries, and that an expansion of title output, especially in the educational field, should be a priority. There is unquestionably an element of truth in this assertion, but it is subject to a number of reservations which need to be pointed out at this juncture.

In the first place it may be observed that existing facilities in many developing countries are already capable of producing many more products. The problem is that there is insufficient money available to buy them. This is not due to a lack of potential consumers, for, as we pointed out earlier, the majority of the world's population virtually consumes no books at all. If these potential consumers individually lack enough disposable income to acquire books then they obviously need to be purchased and supplied centrally, either by government or through the auspices of an international agency. Educational books are the key item since they are needed to instil the reading habit in the first place, yet there are misconceptions about the scale of provision. Elsewhere in this book we will be looking at educational and library provision, and noting that far less than is popularly imagined of institutional budgets actually go on acquiring textual material in developed countries. Hence the cost to a developing country of acquiring a modest proportion of the per capita provision in developed countries would by no means be crippling, and would surely pay for itself in the longer term through an improvement in educational standards. It is ironical that certain developing countries actually raise the cost of such provision by imposing import duties upon materials needed for book production, when one might consider subsidies to be a more rational policy.

Multinational Publishing

Throughout the world today, certain publishing imprints are commonly to be found wherever books are distributed. In many cases these are straightforward imports from another country, but increasingly this is ceasing to be the pattern whereby, say, a book bearing the imprint of an American publishing house is to be found on sale in a foreign market.

As we have noted elsewhere, there were originally four countries which dominated worldwide publishing; namely the United Kingdom, West Germany, France and Spain. The entry of the USA into export markets subsequently stepped up the degree of competition in a big way, but it also led to co-operative ventures at the same time. The latter primarily took the form of books containing a large amount of illustrated material to which the text was subservient. The text could then be translated into a number of different languages at no great additional cost, and a variety of versions of the same book produced, thereby spreading the heavy initial cost of reproducing the illustrations. Fine art books obviously lent themselves to this process, as did books on travel and architecture. Dictionaries and encyclopaedias could also be produced in the same way, but the higher ratio of text to illustration reduced potential savings. Eventually, this genre became known as the coffee-table book because its extra-large format and weight required a substantial piece of furniture for it to repose on. The key international issue with such publications lies at the production stage, because each version must be marketed in whichever countries are appropriate to the language concerned (the UK and USA generally being considered not to share a common language for this purpose!) Hence totally independent publishing houses will generally be involved.

The above process is obviously rather different from true multinational publishing, where a single publishing house only is involved, although it may use a variety of imprints in different markets. Generally speaking the procedure by which a publishing house becomes established as a multinational goes as follows:

1. It becomes involved in the buying and selling of rights in foreign countries.

2. It makes an agreement with a distributor in a foreign country to handle all or part of its domestic list.

3. It sets up an office in a foreign country to assist with selling in that country, possibly involving the company's own representatives.

4. This office begins to expand into the production side with some translations, adaptations of home market texts, or the occasional novel by an indigenous author.

5. The indigenous list expands to the point at which the branch is incorporated either as a wholly owned subsidiary or as a partnership with an existing indigenous publisher. By this time, the imprint may have become one of the major indigenous imprints.

6.   The subsidiary itself begins to export, in come cases back to the country from which it originated.

7.   The subsidiary takes over other indigenous publishers.

   Typical multinationals are McGraw-Hill and Prentice-Hall; Longmans and Penguin; Bertelsmann and Von Holtzbrink, and Hachette. On the whole, publishing houses have not profited from rushing into the development of a multinational structure because foreign markets are never quite the same as those at home, and there are many pitfalls to avoid. Nevertheless, once the process is fully completed, a publishing house may well discover that it does considerably more business abroad than it does at home, thereby blurring the interpretation of that house's nationality.

   The classic illustration is McGraw-Hill, which currently operates in seventeen foreign countries and in three of which, Canada, the UK and Australia, has become a major indigenous publisher. Altogether it publishes in thirteen languages. Because it is spreading its risks it can shrug off poor results in individual foreign markets which might have proved far more damaging to another house operating on a more restricted scale. Sharp currency movements, and the sort of problems recently manifested in Nigeria are inevitably always a threat to profitability. How many other houses will consider following the same route is never easy to assess. Two consequences are, however, worth mentioning in passing. In the first place, the volume of exports flowing from, say, the USA or the UK will inevitably be much reduced by the operations of foreign subsidiaries as these develop indigenous publishing programmes, and one must be careful to make allowances for this when examining trading patterns. In the second place, the publishing operations of developing countries will benefit from the substitution of indigenous publishing for direct imports, although the extent of this benefit will inevitably depend upon the rate at which book consumption expenditure can be generated.

Industrial Structure

Information about the structure of the book industry around the world is extremely difficult to obtain, and the scale of the industry is rarely of sufficient size to warrant drawing any significant conclusions. Only in the United States has the issue of structure been examined in detail, and

44

this section therefore concentrates upon that country. It is not unreasonable to suggest, however, that as the industry develops elsewhere it will be subject to similar pressures.

United States

The US Department of Commerce produces concentration data on a much more extensive scale than in most countries. The basis data is presented in table 2.22 below.

TABLE 2.22   CONCENTRATION RATIOS FOR THE US BOOK PUBLISHING INDUSTRY, SELECTED YEARS

Category and year	Largest Companies				Value of shipments ($ million)
	4 largest	8 largest	20 largest	50 largest	
Total book publishing industry					
Estimated percent of titles accounted for					
1925-1930	20	30	49	73	n.a
Percent value of shipments accounted for					
1963	18	29	52	73	1,547.8
1972	16	27	52	75	2,915.4
1977	16	29	54	73	5,007.7
Textbooks, including teachers' editions					
1963	32	54	81	94	471.1
1972	33	54	80	95	809.6
1977	35	57	80	95	1,408.7
Technical, scientific and professional books					
1963	32	49	68	87	156.3
1972	39	57	76	92	403.0
1977	40	55	75	89	684.1
Religious books					
1963	22	37	65	89	81.1
1972	36	51	76	97	131.2
1977	26	42	68	91	236.3
General books (trade, etc.)					
1963	30	46	59	89	458.2
1972	29	47	74	92	1,006.7
1977	31	48	76	92	1,895.6

Continued...

45

Table 2.22 continued...

Category and year	4 largest	Largest Companies 8 largest	20 largest	50 largest	Value of shipments ($ million)
General reference books					
1963	87	96	100	NA	207.3
1972	71	82	94	99+	235.2
1977	62	74	92	99	305.4

n.a. = not available; NA = not applicable

Source: US Department of Commerce, Bureau of the Census, *1977 Census of Manufacture,* May 1, 1981

The table shows clearly that concentration ratios for the industry as a whole are much lower than, for example, the UK, but when one examines individual categories one finds, unsurprisingly, both considerably higher ratios and considerable variation between categories. The overall market ratios have remained remarkably stable since 1963, as have the two largest categories of textbooks and general books for 20-firm ratios and above, although both of the latter have shown a clear tendency for the largest firms to separate off in size from those in the next size grouping. Religious books have shown some longer term tendency to show a reduction in the ratios, whereas the rate of decline for general reference books has been quite marked, reflecting an equalising tendency amongst a relatively small number of firms.

United Kingdom

It is not all that easy to pin down the precise number of firms involved in the publishing of books. The structure of the publishing industry as a whole in 1981 is given in table 2.23.

The figures relate to a wider group than book publishers alone, and one can use the data published by Whitakers, which includes every firm which publishes a book in any specific year, to arrive at a total of between 2,200 and 2,400. A large proportion of these do not publish regularly, and have a total output of less than 10 titles per year. Around 150 can be said to be major publishers in the sense of producing over 50 new titles per annum. Very few of these have links either with printers or with booksellers, but an appreciable number are family concerns.

Table 2.23   UK: ANALYSIS OF ESTABLISHMENTS[1] BY SIZE 1981

Size Group[2]	Establishments	Enterprises[3]
1- 10	8,233	7,871
11- 19	1,861	1,783
20- 49	1,033	973
50- 99	380	329
100- 199	232	182
200- 299	81	62
300- 399	44	37
400- 499	40	32
500- 749	31	24
750- 999	17	14
1000-1499	13	11
1500-1999	5	5
2000-2499	5	5
2500-2999	3	3
3000-over	6	3
TOTAL	11,984	10,722

[1] all UK establishments classified to the industry including estimates for establishments not making satisfactory returns, non-response, and not selected for the Census;

[2] average number employed (full and part-time) during the year including working proprietors;

[3] some enterprises control establishments in more than one size group; the sum of the figures for the size groups therefore exceeds the total for the industry.
Source: Census of Production

Some rather out of date official estimates exist of the degree of concentration among book publishers, representing the proportion of the sales value of published books accounted for by the five largest publishers.

TABLE 2.24   UK: FIVE-FIRM CONCENTRATION RATIOS

Unit: %	All books	Hardback	Paperback
1963	33.9	n.a.	n.a.
1968	32.2	n.a.	n.a.
1975	32.8	30.9	45.3
1976	n.a.	31.2	45.0
1977	n.a.	28.9	43.0

Source: Census of Production 1968/Business Monitor

Hardback publishing is widely dispersed, with imprints tending to specialise in a limited number of segments of the overall market. This is also true of paperback imprints in, for example, educational fields, but popular fiction, generally called mass-market paperbacks, is highly concentrated.

Some idea of the degree of specialisation can be obtained from Business Monitor, which lists the largest number of enterprises contributing to each category in any one of the four quarters of each year.

TABLE 2.25   UK: NUMBER OF PUBLISHERS BY CATEGORY, 1983

	Hardback	Paperback
Bibles	11	—
Reference	44	31
Scientific, technical, medical	45	33
Academic and professional	27	27
Other adult non-fiction	50	40[1]
Fiction, literature, classics	35	21
School textbooks	27	26
Children's	32	23

[1] including bibles
Source: Business Monitor

Clearly some publishers are active in more than one category, and some in both hardback and paperback categories. The total number for hardbacks at 271 exceeds that for paperbacks other than in educational categories where price sensitivity has caused a major switch from hardback to paperback format.

A major study of concentration was conducted by the Cranfield School of Management on behalf of the EEC. This was based upon a sample of the 47 largest independent firms as identified from data in ICC Business Ratios, Jordan and Sons reports on book publishing, and filed company accounts. Analysis related to both sales turnover and exports and covered 1977-79 with a partial up-date to 1980. Some non-book publishing activities crept in because of the way company accounts are presented, and this may have biased the concentration ratios upwards because large book publishers have more related activities than small ones.

TABLE 2.26   UK: CONCENTRATION RATIOS BASED ON SALES TURNOVER

Unit: %	1977	1978	1979	1980[1]
1-Firm Ratio	11.7	11.7	11.2	12.6
4-Firm Ratio	37.4	36.9	35.1	35.4
8-Firm Ratio	55.7	54.5	53.5	53.8
12-Firm Ratio	68.7	67.7	67.2	67.2

[1] 41 firms sampled in 1980, the market shares of the remaining 6 assumed same as 1979
Source: The Cranfield School of Management

The Cranfield Report concluded that the concentration levels were 'well below those normally found'. Although financial links between publishers were ignored, the under-estimation which resulted was not considered to be statistically significant.

The Cranfield Report applied other statistical techniques to try to identify an 'oligopolistic nucleus' of companies, but came to the conclusion that "oligopoly is not a feature of book publishing". The Report also measured the concentration of export sales, but this resulted in similar ratios to those listed in table 2.26 above.

In my view, sales turnover is a somewhat inappropriate variable to use in measuring concentration in publishing, where the objective is to make a judgement about the extent of market power held by a core of firms. This is because of the extraordinary diversity of the product range, with nearly 40,000 unique new products coming onto the market each year. Clearly there is some association between market power and firm size as measured by turnover (for example a greater ability to 'hype'), but the association is necessarily rather weak given that the great majority of books are bought on account of their authors or their technical content rather than their imprints. It is interesting, therefore, to examine the extent to which firms can seek to control the market through the sheer volume of their output. I have calculated concentration ratios based upon the production of new titles, which appear as table 2.27 below.

TABLE 2.27   UK: PROPORTION OF NEW TITLES PRODUCED BY MOST PROLIFIC IMPRINTS

	1971	1977	1980	1981	1982
3-Firm Ratio	6.7	6.0	5.4	6.6	6.4
10-Firm Ratio	15.7	14.9	14.9	16.8	15.9
25-Firm Ratio	28.7	24.6	24.5	26.4	25.1
50-Firm Ratio	40.9	35.7	34.0	36.0	35.0
75-Firm Ratio	49.5	43.7	40.9	43.1	42.4
100-Firm Ratio	56.0	49.8	47.0	48.9	48.1

As can be seen, there was a steady decline in the degree of concentration between 1971 and 1980, with the position subsequently reversing somewhat as was to be expected in the course of the recession. On this basis concentration is extremely low in relation even to other measures, once again emphasising an individual imprint's lack of market power.

West Germany

While some publishers are very large, such as Bertelsmann, which is reputed to be one of the world's three largest communications operations, and the Axel Springer Verlag, and whilst only 2.9% of publishers accounted for over half of the titles appearing in 1979, there are many small publishing houses which publish less than five titles a year, a publishing structure which has changed little in recent years.

TABLE 2.28   STRUCTURE OF THE WEST GERMAN PUBLISHING INDUSTRY

No. of titles	1977		1981	
	% of 2,084 publishers	% of 39,026 titles	% of 2,493 publishers	% of 43,853 titles
1	31.7	1.7	32.6	1.9
2	12.4	1.3	14.4	1.6
3-5	16.8	3.4	17.1	3.7
6-10	11.3	4.6	12.2	5.4
11-20	11.8	9.2	9.0	7.6
21-30	4.7	6.2	4.4	6.3
31-40	2.7	5.1	2.4	4.5
41-50	1.6	3.8	1.3	3.1
51-100	3.9	14.2	3.7	14.9
100+	3.1	50.5	2.9	51.0

Note: excluding titles published by the author, authorities, institutes, societies and associations

Source: Borserverein des Deutschen Buchhandels EV (BDB)

France

There are over 600 publishers in France, but the results of the annual survey into the book publishing industry conducted by the Syndicat National de l'Edition is limited to 398 publishers which account for over 99% of total sales by the industry. The results of the survey may therefore be taken as being representative and indeed an accurate picture of the whole industry.

As in many other respects of the commercial life of France, the publishing industry is seen to be extremely concentrated both financially and geographically. Of the 398 major publishers, 298 are situated in Paris with 96 in the 6th *arrondissement* alone — in addition to which a further 23 of the remaining 100 are in the *Région Parisienne*. The degree of concentration is clear from the fact that while only 7% of all publishers produced in excess of 200 titles, these 28 publishers accounted for 56% of all titles appearing in 1982. It is, however, interesting to note that the larger publishers were responsible for 65% of reprinted titles as against only 48% of new titles.

In terms of turnover, 9% of publishers accounted for 68% of total sales, with the top 18 sharing 52% between them.

The French book market remains dominated by two established publishing groups:

1. Hachette

Founded originally in 1826, the Hachette group is by far the largest publisher in France, and the second largest in Europe, annually acounting for 20% of all books published on the French market with a turnover in books of around Fr.1.5 billion. In addition to its publishing activities (the publishers Grasset, Fayard and Stock also belong to the Hachette group), the group has a majority share in the French Newspaper distribution system and owns a number of newspapers and magazines such as *Elle, France-Dimanche, Le Point* and *Télé 7 Jour*. It is the largest publisher of encyclopaedias, publishes *Le Masque* collection of detective novels and other popular fiction which helped to develop supermarkets and hypermarkets as an increasingly important channel of distribution, and is perhaps best known at present for having launched into *Livre de Poche* back in 1953. Since then it has sold well over 500 million copies and with annual sales of some 20 million copies, one fifth of which are exported, gives the group 20% of the domestic pocket book market. Hachette Classics account for 20% of the schoolbook market and around 25% of the total market for childen's books, including its *Livre de Poche Jeunesse* series. Hachette dominates the distribution structure even more emphatically, accounting for 30% by value of all books sold in France with sales of 90 million books per year. The group is also a significant exporter, accounting for 17% of all French exports. At the end of 1980, Matra, the giant arms and electronics manufacturing group, bought a 35% share of Hachette and 83% of the stock, a development which may serve to alter the structure of the group's activities.

2.   *Presses de la Cité*

The second largest publishers after Hachette, the group Presses de la Cité currently holds 15% of the French market with annual sales of 36 million copies, excluding sales of some 15 million copies through its bookclub France Loisirs. The group's publishing departments include Librairie Plon, Editions Julliard, Fleuve Noir and Librairie Académique Perrin with its subsidiaries including Editions du Rocher, Editions Christian Bougois, Aredit and Presses Pocket. Particularly strong in less expensive editions, Presses de la Cité claims 85% of the market for detective stories (Simenon is one of the company' best known authors). This category gives it an important share of the rapidly developing supermarket trade, in addition to which it has 5% of the pocket book market, 15% of children's books and 20% of general literature. The company operates its own decentralised distribution network with outlets also in Brussels and Montreal. Its bookclub division, France Loisirs, has enjoyed considerable expansion since its foundation in 1969 with the German publisher Bertelsmann and, since then, membership has grown from 255,000 in 1973 to 2.6 million in June 1980 — a figure which is expected to increase to 3.5 millon over the next ten years. Some 25% of the club's sales are of books published by the parent company, and the club accounts for half of all mail order sales in France, its turnover in books of FF435 million in 1979 giving it 5.5% of the total book market. France Loisirs also sells books through 80 shops which it owns and a further 110 other bookshops. The club also established a subsidiary in Belgium in 1975 called Club Belgique Loisirs with five shops including two in Brussels; in Switzerland through France Loisirs Suisse with outlets in Lausanne and Geneva, and last year set up Quebec Loisirs in Canada.

TABLE 2.29 FRANCE: DISTRIBUTION OF PUBLISHERS BY TITLES ISSUED 1982

Titles published	Number of publishers 1979	1982	% of publishers 1979	1982	% of titles 1979	1982	Titles published 1979	1982
200 or more	28	29	6.9	7.3	53.9	56.2	14,387	14,808
150-199	14	10	3.5	2.5	8.9	6.6	2,388	1,740
100-149	17	22	4.2	5.5	7.7	10.5	2,044	2,783
50-99	50	39	12.4	9.8	13.0	10.0	3,484	2,627
20-49	87	90	21.5	22.6	10.4	10.6	2,780	2,798
10-19	77	69	19.6	17.3	4.0	3.7	1,066	975
5-9	55	67	13.6	16.8	1.5	1.8	387	467
1-4	60	58	14.8	14.5	0.6	0.6	151	150
No titles	16	14	4.0	3.5	—	—	—	—
TOTAL	404	398	100.0	100.0	100.0	100.0	26,687	26,348

Source: Syndicat National de l'Edition (SNE)

36 publishers recorded sales in excess of FF50 million in 1982 compared with 28 in the previous year. The majority of French publishers recorded sales of between FF2-5 million, accounting for 3.2% of total sales.

TABLE 2.30 FRANCE: DISTRIBUTION OF PUBLISHERS BY TURNOVER 1982

Turnover (million francs)	Number of publishers 1981	1982	% of total turnover 1981	1982
100 plus	15	18	49.10	52.29
50-100	13	18	12.94	15.30
20-50	41	35	19.55	15.00
10-20	36	41	7.11	7.39
5-10	51	54	5.45	5.09
2-5	72	72	3.63	3.14
1-2	57	57	1.25	1.03
0.5-1	65	55	0.71	0.56
0.2-0.5	55	48	0.26	0.20
TOTAL	405	398	100.00	100.00

Source: SNE

Lessons to be learned

If we assume, based upon UK and US experience, that in general concentration levels are neither unacceptably high, nor vary significantly betwen categories, does this imply either that all structural developments in publishing are fully compatible with the public interest, or that this is true for some categories but not for others? The Cranfield Report certainly did not appear to favour any form of intervention to control book industry structure, indeed its overall conclusion was that the UK industry is 'very competitive'.

It is possible, however, to take a rather less sanguine view, based upon certain trends in the USA[1]. The first point to note is that profitability is not determined by the degree of concentration in any direct way, as table 2.31, US publishers ranked by operating margins, indicates. One should, of course, bear in mind that the figures in this table are based upon returns from AAP membrs, and are not therefore absolutely indicative of the industry segments of which they are samples. The trendline estimates are the statistical expectation of the operating margin based on normalising operating margins over the industry segment for the 1971-1980 period, and are useful because a single year may be unrepresentative of general trends.

On the whole, the educational sectors offer secure returns over time, which is to be expected because the markets are reasonably easy to quantify, have specialised requirements which are known to publishers, and titles have a reasonably long shelf life. The large imprints have well-established back-lists, authors and distribution channels and, whereas a newcomer can enter the segment easily enough, it takes a long hard grind to build up a list comparable to the established majors.

[1] *The detailed argument is contained in D.A. Garvin, 'Mergers and Competition in Book Publishing',* The Antitrust Bulletin *(Summer 1980)*

TABLE 2.31   US: SAMPLES OF PUBLISHERS BY SECTOR, RANKED BY ESTIMATED OPERATING MARGINS, 1980[1]

Sector	Operating margin (%)	Rank	Trendline[2](%)	Rank
College textbooks	20.4	1	16.3	3
El-hi textbooks	19.0	2	17.4	2
Juvenile trade books	16.9	3	10.5	6
Business & other professional	14.2	4	0.9	8
Medical books	13.2	5	n.e.	—
Mail order publications	13.1	6	-2.2	10
Professional books (total)	12.4	7	10.6	5
Book clubs	11.0	8	12.4	4
Technical & scientific books	9.4	9	18.6	1
Trade books (total)	8.2	10	0.9	9
Adult hardbound trade	5.6	11	4.2	7
Adult paperbound trade books	3.8	12	n.e	—
Religious trade books	2.4	13	n.e.	—
Mass market paperbacks	1.4	14	-5.6	11

n.e. = not estimated

[1] operating margins are pretax

[2] see text for explanation

Sources: Paine Webber Mitchell Hutchins, Inc., calculations based on Association of American Publishers statistical reports

It is the trade sectors, including mass-market paperbacks, which are much more interesting because their levels of profitability are far inferior. From this one might well conclude that imprints would come and go on a regular basis, and that the concentration ratios would correspondingly fluctuate a good deal. However, this evidently doesn't happen, and it is interesting to speculate why not.

It is obviously not a question of entry barriers, nor of economies of scale, since neither is significant. Rather it is the result of the same few firms dominating the best-seller lists, earning most of the income from subsidiary rights, for example through dominating book club selections, and hence recording much higher profits than the rest. Best-sellers are important because they do not merely earn a disproportionate amount from the original printing, but are the main source of subsidiary rights, and it is particularly the case that successful bids for paperback rights to best-selling hardback titles are limited to a narrow range of imprints.

The overall effect is that profits are considerably more skewed than sales figures alone would suggest, and this protects the position of established firms against entry. The observable difficulty which minor imprints have in getting together the capital to make successful bids for reprint rights can be partially overcome by offering high royalty rates to successful authors, but authors appear to prefer large advances to high royalties, so most minor imprints get left out in the cold. It is also the case that whereas the customer pays little attention to the imprint, many authors like to be associated with imprints which have published other successful and important writers.

There are, therefore, two opposing forces at work in general book publishing. The first, an acceptably low level of concentration, is beneficial. The second, the ability of the largest imprints to hold on to their market shares in an industry superficially characterised by easy entry and few economies of scale, is less auspicious. One must remember that general books account for a major slice of turnover in the USA, so the failure of potential competition to become an actuality needs, perhaps, to be watched with more vigilance than has previously been the case.

Profitability of publishers

In order to give some idea of profitability trends, we can use the fairly extensive data available for the US and, to an even greater extent, the UK.

United States

Knowledge Industry Publications have produced figures for pre-tax profit as a percentage of sales for 1977-1980. The percentage for a sample of 25 publicly owned publishing companies primarily dependent upon books for their profits; for a sample of 19 publicly owned companies with a book publishing division; and for the entire sample of 44 companies was as follows:

TABLE 2.32   US PUBLISHERS' PROFIT MARGINS

Unit: %	25 companies	19 companies	44 companies
1977	13.2	12.2	12.7
1978	12.1	12.8	12.9
1979	12.8	11.8	12.3
1980	11.5	10.7	11.1

Source: Knowledge Industries Publications

If these figures are compared with the slightly bigger UK sample that follows, one can first of all detect a generally higher margin of profit in the USA and, secondly, a far more rapid rate of decline in the UK at the end of the 1970s. This is not altogether surprising because the UK industry is far more vulnerable to problems in overseas markets when a recession begins to bite. Nevertheless, some of the US publishing houses, like their UK counterparts, showed considerable difficulties in 1980, especially the book divisions of diversified companies, and of course some of the losses were on a truly American scale: in one case $8.5 million.

United Kingdom

Table 2.33 sets out three critical ratios for a sample of 60 UK publishers covering two adjacent three-year periods, the first a relatively prosperous period during the mid-1970s, and the second an increasingly depressed period at the turn of the 1980s.

TABLE 2.33   UK PUBLISHERS' FINANCIAL RATIOS

	Pre-tax profit ÷ sales					
	1975-1976	1976-1977	1977-1978	1978-1979	1979-1980	1980-1981
Mean average	7.2%	10.0%	10.4%	9.9%	4.7%	2.1%
Highest value	24.0%	29.1%	34.3%	29.0%	28.7%	26.8%
Lowest value	− 31.8%	− 32.1%	− 10.1%	− 5.8%	− 12.4%	− 20.4%

continued...

Table 2.33 continued...

	Pre-tax profit ÷ sales					
	1975-1976	1976-1977	1977-1978	1978-1979	1979-1980	1980-1981
Over 50%	0	0	0	0	0	0
40-50%	0	0	0	0	0	0
30-40%	0	0	1	0	0	0
20-30%	1	4	5	3	3	2
10-20%	18	25	23	20	10	6
0-10%	32	25	23	34	35	24
Negative	9	5	5	2	12	21
TOTAL	60	59	57	59	60	53

TABLE 2.34   UK PUBLISHERS' FINANCIAL RATIOS

	Pre-tax profit ÷ total assets					
	1975-1976	1976-1977	1977-1978	1978-1979	1979-1980	1980-1981
Mean average	8.6%	12.0%	12.0%	12.6%	7.0%	3.3%
Highest value	35.2%	38.5%	40.9%	40.3%	49.3%	52.2%
Lowest value	− 32.5%	− 26.8%	− 10.2%	− 4.5%	− 17.0%	− 32.6%
Over 50%	0	0	0	0	0	1
40-50%	0	0	1	1	1	0
30-40%	3	4	3	1	3	2
20-30%	4	7	6	6	0	1
10-20%	22	24	25	25	16	7
0-10%	22	19	17	24	28	21
Negative	9	5	5	2	12	20
TOTAL	60	59	57	59	60	52

TABLE 2.35 UK PUBLISHERS' FINANCIAL RATIOS

	Return on capital employed					
	1975-1976	1976-1977	1977-1978	1978-1979	1979-1980	1980-1981
Mean average	15.8%	23.0%	23.8%	31.7%	18.2%	9.6%
Highest value	78.2%	175.2%	245.0%	211.1%	303.9%	288.5%
Lowest value	− 105.3%	− 51.9%	− 18.2%	− 4.5%	− 219.1%	− 127.2%
Over 50%	6	12	11	8	5	3
40-50%	7	4	8	5	0	0
30-40%	9	11	7	8	5	4
20-30%	12	13	11	14	10	5
10-20%	13	12	13	17	16	9
0-10%	4	2	2	5	12	11
Negative	9	5	5	1	11	20
TOTAL	60	59	57	58	59	50

Note: Large publishers
Source: ICC Business Ratios

During the first three years surveyed sales, assets and profits were all reasonably buoyant, with profits running ahead of the other two variables during the first two years and hence causing the first two ratios to rise sharply. In the third year all moved together, but rather slowly, so the ratios were largely unaffected. Of the 57 companies reporting in every year, 15 recorded an above average profit margin (profits divided by sales) in all three years, and 20 consistently achieved above average profitability (profits divided by assets) in all three years. Among these were to be found a number of very large companies such as Heinemann, A.B.P. and Macmillan, whereas some smaller companies were consistently unprofitable. Rather curiously the largest companies were noticeably absent from the list of twenty companies earning the highest rates of return on capital employed, many of whom were on the distinctly small side.

If one examines the second three-year period the picture is initially very satisfactory for 1978/79, but the subsequent two years make gloomy reading indeed, with all three ratios plunging into single figures by 1980/81. It was not a question of the best companies collapsing, since they continued to do well, nor even of the worst results becoming much worse, but rather of a widespread across-the-board reduction in performance. 15 companies again managed to achieve an above-average profitability (of whom 13 were common to both groups). A significant difference compared to the earlier period was, however, that 10 of these also achieved an above-average rate of return on capital employed in all three years.

Not surprisingly there were differences in the make-up of the two roughly equal groups of companies which led the field during the two periods. For example, one of the largest companies, Macmillan, was not included in the leading group during the latter period. Obviously, therefore, the most interesting question concerns the characteristics of the companies which came through the full six-year period in a relatively prosperous condition. The first characteristic, and there is no reason to believe that UK experience is unrepresentative of developed markets generally, is that there is no great virtue in being very big. Companies such as Collins, Macmillan and A.B.P. suffered quite badly as the recession bit hard. Clearly size allows risk diversification over different publishing sectors, and this can be something of a virtue, but specialisation would seem to be the real key to success. Mills and Boon continued to do outstandingly well with its range of romantic novels, and specialists in the medical, legal, academic and business fields, such as Butterworth, Wolfe Medical and Holt Saunders, proved extremely resilient. The other, and by and large associated, key, is tight financial control. The most successful companies generally showed an unusually rapid turnover of stock for the type of books being traded, and mostly managed to cut down their credit periods. The largest companies, by way of contrast, proved unable to use capital efficiently in order to generate sales, and were slow to recognise the need to become more agressive in attracting customers. Another, less reliable pointer, is that high rates of return on capital were often associated with very low liquidity, although there are obvious dangers in pressing that virtue too far. Certainly high liquidity was an inhibitory factor. Another looming danger was the noticeable increase in the indebtedness of the majority of companies; although this was perhaps inevitable in a recessionary world.

61

Chapter Three

INTERNATIONAL TRADE IN BOOKS

The section attempts to pull together what is known about trade flows in books between various countries throughout the world. Some countries are vastly more important than others in this respect, and the major trading nations are the only ones to provide useful, up to date, statistics. This whole area is ringed around with difficulties, and for this reason table 3.1, which presents trade flows in 1982 between 20 important trading countries, all expressed uniformly in £ sterling, gives two figures wherever possible, the top figure representing what the exporting nation claims to have exported, and the bottom one what the importing nation claims to have imported. Sometimes these are close to agreement, sometimes, bluntly, they differ to a degree which is almost staggering. How can, for example, two neighbouring nations such as France and Italy disagree by over 100% about the value of Italian exports of books to France, when Belgium exports to France are close to agreement. Why does America, whose statistics are comprehensive, reckon to export so much less to the UK, Australia, Japan and Canada than those countries reckon to purchase, when the latter's statistics are, on the face of it, equally sound.

Unfortunately, there are no easy answers to these questions. It will be observed that the majority of entries are developed countries, but elsewhere in the section an attempt is made to comment upon what is known about the other parts of the world. Eastern Europe is reticent, South America and Africa unreliable and out of date, but this is at least a first step to pull the information together and express as much of it as possible in a uniform currency and in a uniform year. Nothing is ultimately more confusing than to see every country's data expressed solely in its own currency. For those interested, the conversions were all done using the exchange rates posted in the Financial Times for June 28th 1982, but some more detailed exchange rate information is contained in the Appendices for the major trading nations.

TABLE 3.1 MAJOR INTERNATIONAL TRADE FLOWS IN BOOKS

£ m[1] 1982

Top figure in each cell represents amount of exports by column country to row country; bottom figure represents amount of imports by row country from column country.

Exporters \ Importers	Australia	Austria	Belgium	Canada	France	Hong Kong	Italy	Japan	Mexico	Netherlands	New Zealand	South Africa	Spain	Sweden	Switzerland	UK	USA	West Germany
Australia											11.1					0.9 / 0.1	0.7	
Austria			1.1							0.2			0.1	0.1	1.6	3.5 / 3.9	0.3	24.4
Belgium				2.1 / 1.8	24.9 / 26.9					23.6 / 17.3				2.8 / 2.0	2.1 / 2.0	2.1 / 2.2	3.5 / 3.4	2.1 / 2.9
Canada	0.6				5.3 / 1.4											3.0	43.9 / 27.1	
France			30.2 / 20.5	13.7 / 12.8			3.5 / 2.6	1.3		2.1 / 2.1			2.5 / 1.3	0.3	21.2 / 18.4	14.6 / 21.5	4.1 / 3.7	5.9 / 5.4
Hong Kong	11.0 / 10.0			1.1	3.1											9.7 / 13.6	8.1 / 11.0	
Italy		0.7	1.6	0.9 / 0.6	14.7 / 32.4			1.0		0.6	1.7		2.0		7.5	2.6 / 4.2	4.6 / 8.9	5.4 / 7.2
Japan	1.8 / 3.4		1.9 / 2.4		0.8	0.8					0.7		0.1	4.1		8.5 / 10.5	16.7 / 26.8	2.0
Netherlands			24.4 / 33.7	0.9 / 1.1	6.2 / 6.2		0.6	2.2 / 0.4					0.2	2.4 / 2.0	2.0	2.6 / 3.1	6.9 / 5.4	10.9 / 7.2
Singapore	6.3 / 5.6					1.0				1.3	0.7 / 0.7					3.0	1.0 / 3.0	
Spain		0.4	1.8		14.9 / 13.0		1.6	1.3	25.7 / 24.5	3.7 / 5.2				0.5		6.8 / 6.1	8.9 / 9.5	1.7 / 1.2
Switzerland		2.4 / 1.8	1.6 / 2.3	0.6 / 0.9	20.6 / 15.8		1.4 / 1.1	5.4		0.9 / 0.8	0.6		0.5	0.9		2.6 / 3.2	3.8 / 4.0	19.2 / 18.2
UK	37.6 / 45.2	0.8	1.6 / 2.5	10.8 / 10.6	7.8 / 6.2	7.6	3.9 / 3.5	9.3		13.9 / 12.6	8.2 / 11.7	20.6 / 19.5	3.4 / 2.1	6.2 / 5.9	3.0 / 2.2		50.4 / 48.6	8.3 / 8.4
USA	32.6 / 41.0	1.0	1.1 / 1.6	135.8 / 188.8	2.9 / 4.9	3.2	3.1 / 2.0	14.2 / 21.8	8.9 / 6.4	9.9 / 10.9	4.7 / 9.1	7.0 / 8.5	1.3 / 1.6	1.6 / 2.2	3.8 / 3.5	47.2 / 68.5		6.8 / 12.6
West Germany		49.5 / 47.8	6.2 / 4.9		11.1 / 10.4	5.7	6.9 / 2.8	5.5 / 6.9		14.8 / 11.6			2.6 / 0.9	2.4 / 2.5	47.1 / 45.3	4.0 / 4.1	14.4 / 9.4	

Notes: [1] Top figure represents amount of exports by column country to row country. Bottom figures represent amount of imports by row country from column country. An expanded version of this table appears in the Statististical Appendix

Issues in exporting

Exporting is necessarily constrained by organisational issues, so it is worth pausing to examine briefly the historical development of exporting from the USA (the world's key source for trade in books) and the relationship between US and UK publishers. Before World War II, the scale of the home market left US publishers disinclined to go to the effort of exporting. The inability of UK publishers to supply during the war allowed US publishers an entry into export markets, and they gradually opened up branch offices abroad on a regionalised pattern. Prosperity and experience combined to transform many of these branches into subsidiary corporations during the 1960s, and foreign imprints began to be taken over. By 1982, 32 US publishers owned 82 foreign subsidiaries, mostly located in Canada, the UK and Australia. These produced titles primarily in English, and subsidiaries elsewhere also published in foreign languages. The inevitable end-result of this process is that some of these subsidiaries have become major publishers in their own right in overseas markets, in direct competition with titles produced by the parent company in the USA. Obviously, this factor has constrained the export potential of US publishers, and it helps account for what may appear to be a surprisingly poor export performance.

An associated factor tends to confuse the geographical distribution of exports. Once an American publisher has an overseas subsidiary it may choose to export to that subsidiary, leaving it to the subsidiary to dispense the books around the region. This obviously causes the exports to be recorded as having been sent to the subsidiary's country rather than to the ultimate markets.

A further significant factor was the British Market Agreement. This was a system whereby British publishers agreed together that they would not publish in the UK any book first published outside the bounds of their Traditional Market unless they were granted the exclusive rights to publish that book throughout the market. In effect UK publishers promised to keep their editions of an American book out of the USA if US publishers promised to keep their editions of a UK book out of the UK's Traditional Market. This protected UK publishers' export market, but it also suited US publishers because the competitive nature of UK publishing allowed them to get good prices for the sale of rights for the Traditional Market as a whole. Also UK publishers had much better distribution networks than their US counterparts. Unfortunately, it didn't suit the Australian book trade who were for the most part prevented from

65

obtaining American books direct from the USA. This didn't matter so long as US editions were typically more expensive than UK ones, but by the early 1970s this no longer held true, and in November 1974 the Anti-Trust Division of the American Department of Justice began proceedings to dismantle the Agreement. Faced by the potentially high costs of defending the Agreement, UK publishers agreed to revoke the Agreement in July 1976.

It is now possible for US books to enter, for example, Australia (i) directly or through a subsidiary or agent of the US publisher, (ii) through the sale of rights to the Australian market to any interested publisher. The initial effects of relocation were, interestingly, rather perverse. In the first place, UK publishers initially supplied a bigger proportion of the Australian market, and US publishers rather less. This reflected a disinclination on the part of US publishers of non-professional books to take advantage of the opportunities presented. Secondly, it stimulated a number of UK publishers to try their luck in the USA. At the end of the day, it may well be that exchange rate movements are a more significant determinant of who supplies the markets such as Australia than the existence or otherwise of market agreements.

Principal trading nations

The following paragraphs briefly outline trends in international trade for the more significant national industries.

United States

The most important country in terms of world trade in books is, not surprisingly, the USA and it is therefore worthwhile examining its trade pattern in some detail. Table 3.2 shows the aggregate trade picture, in both money and real terms, from 1970 to 1983. However, adjusting for inflation reveals a rather different picture, one in which the five year period of stagnation from 1976 to 1980 is followed by a sharp upsurge in 1981, which collapses back to the previous level in 1983. With respect to exports alone the picture is one of very modest real growth right through to 1982, and a decline back to the 1979 level in 1983. On the import side, which starts from a much lower level in money terms, there is sharp growth in 1973, 1977 and 1983, but declines in-between, so the 1983 figure is also comparable to that of 1979.

66

TABLE 3.2   US OVERSEAS TRADE STATISTICS, BOOKS

Unit: $ million

	Exports[1]			Imports[1]			Trade balance	
	Units[2] million	Money value	Real value	Units[3] million	Money value	Real value	Money value	Real value
1970	125.7	174.9	174.9	143.4	92.0	92.0	82.9	82.9
1971	134.6	176.7	169.4	183.4	101.0	96.8	75.7	72.5
1972	138.0	172.1	159.9	222.4	136.9	92.9	35.2	32.7
1973	160.2	194.5	170.2	227.2	133.9	117.1	60.6	53.0
1974	199.1	242.7	191.2	215.2	150.7	118.7	92.0	72.5
1975	205.0	269.3	194.4	178.5	147.6	106.6	121.7	87.9
1976	210.0	298.8	204.0	169.4	157.9	107.8	140.9	96.2
1977	217.0	314.2	201.4	142.6	168.5	108.0	145.7	93.4
1978	226.9	370.6	220.7	180.3	232.3	138.4	138.3	82.4
1979	242.5	439.2	235.1	205.1	268.7	143.8	170.5	91.3
1980	267.0	511.6	241.3	216.8	306.5	144.6	205.1	96.7
1981	285.6	603.2	257.6	238.0	294.9	125.9	308.3	131.7
1982	294.9	641.4	258.3	284.0	314.9	126.8	326.5	131.5
1983	243.1	609.0	237.5	352.2	367.8	143.4	241.2	94.1

[1] Prior to August 1979 export data exclude shipments valued at less than $250; subsequently data exclude shipments valued at less than $500.   Import data exclude shipments valued at less than $250; [2] Units of textbooks not collected; [3] Units of toy books not collected

Source: US Department of Commerce, Bureau of the Census

A number of considerations need to be taken account of at this stage. Firstly, export shipments since late 1979 have only been counted if they were worth over $500. Since books are rather low value items, an unknown but appreciable understatement of exports is implied. Estimates of its magnitude vary from 10% to 30%. Also, some underestimation was occurring prior to 1979, but this applied to both imports and exports, whereas the exemption limits differed after 1979. Therefore, taking a conservative view, the real trade balance after 1979 should be aised by between 5% and 10%.

Secondly, US book publishers are heavily involved in the sale of translation, foreign manufacture and syndication rights to foreign publishers, co-publication and co-distribution of books with foreign firms, and overseas production and sale of books in foreign markets. This again probably amounts to at least another 10% of export earnings. This factor is likely to have a fairly consistent effect throughout the period. Overall, the picture is not as bad as it first appears, but this does not disguise the fact that 1983 was no better than 1979.

If we turn now to look at exports, we can break down the aggregate firstly according to the category of books, as in table 3.3 below. The real data are expressed here at constant 1976 prices. In proportionate terms certain categories, such as bibles, have moved very little over the years. Dictionaries sold well in 1977 and badly in 1982. Encyclopaedias are down substantially from their mid-1970s peak and textbooks also show a general tendency to decline. On the other hand, technical and scientific books are currently doing well after a very bad patch in the late 1970s. The big gains have been made by the category often referred to as 'Other Books', which, despite a patchy performance recently, are still holding on to a half share of the market.

TABLE 3.3   US EXPORTS OF BOOKS

Unit: $ million at current and (1976) prices								
	1976	1977	1978	1979	1980	1981	1982	1983[3]
Bibles, testaments,	15.3	18.4	20.7	24.0	31.9	33.9	31.9	32.0
other religious books	(15.3)	(17.3)	(18.1)	(18.8)	(22.0)	(21.2)	(18.8)	(18.3)
Dictionaries and	4.4	6.1	4.0	5.7	6.0	7.0	5.8	7.2
thesauri	(4.4)	(5.7)	(3.5)	(4.5)	(4.1)	(4.4)	(3.4)	(4.1)
Encyclopaedias	28.6	24.6	32.3	29.9	27.9	25.8	25.3	26.9
	(28.6)	(23.1)	(28.2)	(23.5)	(19.3)	(16.1)	(14.9)	(15.4)
Textbooks	70.4	72.1	70.3	83.6	99.7	118.7	130.8	108.6
	(70.4)	(67.8)	(61.3)	(65.6)	(68.9)	(74.3)	(77.2)	(62.1)
Technical, scientific &	47.1	45.3	49.5	51.6	53.9	79.7	118.5	120.1
professional books	(47.1)	(42.6)	(43.2)	(40.5)	(37.2)	(49.9)	(69.9)	(68.6)
Books, nepf[2]	126.1	142.4	187.5	237.9	284.2	327.2	319.7	305.4[4]
	(126.1)	(133.8)	(163.6)	(186.6)	(196.4)	(204.8)	(188.7)	(174.5)
Toy books,	6.9	5.3	6.4	6.7	8.0	10.9	9.4	8.8
colouring books	(6.9)	(5.0)	(5.6)	(5.3)	(5.5)	(6.8)	(5.5)	(5.0)
TOTAL	298.8	314.1	370.6	439.2	511.6	603.2	641.4	609.0
	(298.8)	(295.2)	(323.5)	(344.6)	(352.5)	(377.5)	(378.4)	(348.0)

[1] Prior to August 1979 data included shipments valued at $250 or more; post August 1979 data includes shipments valued at $500 or more; [2] not especially provided for; [3] not fully compatible with previous years due to reclassification; [4] includes paperbound books worth $61.1 million
Source: US Department of Commerce/Bureau of the Census

Table 3.4 examines the issue of how dependent the USA has been recently on its five main markets in each category. The only big customer for bibles is Canada, the rest of the pecking order being rather volatile. The small dictionary market is increasingly dominated by the UK, with Canada a consistent runner-up. Encyclopaedias remain the English-speaking preserve of Australia, Canada and the UK, with Italy getting an unexpected look-in, and Canada and Australia also dominate the small export market for toy and colouring books. Canada predictably dominates the three big categories of textbooks, technical and scientific, and especially other, with the UK runner-up in each category followed by Australia. Overall, the degree of dependence upon a limited number of export markets rose in every category bar the largest between 1980 and 1983, the loss of sales to the UK accounting for the exception.

TABLE 3.4   US EXPORT DEPENDENCE BY CATEGORY[1] 1980 AND 1983

Unit: %

Bibles	1980 Canada 21.5 + Brazil, Mexico, Australia, UK = 52.8
	1983 Canada 29.6 + Australia, Brazil, UK, Nigeria = 64.2
Dictionaries	1980 UK 30.3 + Canada 21.8 + Mexico, Nigeria, Australia = 69.7
	1983 UK 42.4 + Canada 15.9 + Brazil, Australia, S.Africa = 85.1
Encyclo-paedias	1980 Australia 17.9 + Canada, UK, Mexico, Italy = 45.8
	1983 Canada 30.6 + Australia 29.6 + UK, Italy, N.Zealand = 70.2
Textbooks	1980 Canada 37.5 + UK 13.5 + Australia, Mexico, China = 62.3
	1983 Canada 44.0 + UK 14.6 + Nigeria, Australia, Japan = 75.0
Technical/ Scientific	1980 Canada 21.9 + UK, Japan, Australia, Netherlands = 59.4
	1983 Canada 20.4 + UK 15.4 + Eire, Netherlands, Japan = 63.3
Books nspf.	1980 Canada 42.6 + UK 24.1 + Australia, Japan, Brazil = 79.4
	1983 Canada 46.3 + UK 15.4 + Australia, Japan, Netherlands = 77.1
Toy/ colouring	1980 Canada 42.9 + Australia 32.6 + N.Zealand, UK, Bermuda = 86.8
	1983 Canada 50.7 + Australia 34.1 + UK, Philippines, N.Zealand = 93.0

[1] shipments valued at $500 or more; nspf = not specially provided for
Source: adapted from US Department of Commerce/Bureau of the Census

Not surprisingly, when we turn to table 3.5, which identifies exports by destination country, we find Canada dominating the proceedings, although it is interesting to observe that the longer term view presented by this table indicates a significant movement away from Canada to other markets. The UK is one of these, although it peaked in 1980 when it accounted for such a large share of the 'Other' category. Australia has been remarkably consistent, and the West German market fairly buoyant, but market share losses have been sustained in Mexico, Brazil, Nigeria and the Philippines in recent years, causing the proportion of total exports accounted for by the ten main markets to decline.

TABLE 3.5   US EXPORTS OF BOOKS TO 10 LEADING COUNTRIES[1]

Unit: $ million	1977	1978	1979	1980	1981	1982	1983
Canada	149.0	146.6	178.1	191.3	221.5	237.7	242.3
UK	33.0	44.2	63.9	94.3	90.1	82.6	89.1
Australia	27.9	36.7	40.7	39.0	53.3	57.0	52.9
Japan	15.5	23.2	21.6	20.3	21.3	24.8	25.9
Mexico	4.4	10.3	11.0	14.7	15.7	15.5	4.4
Brazil	4.1	7.9	9.5	13.1	14.5	9.1	10.2
Netherlands	9.7	10.0	9.7	11.1	14.7	17.3	22.1
Nigeria	1.4	2.0	2.6	9.6	22.1	21.2	11.4
West Germany	3.7	5.2	7.9	8.5	9.6	11.9	11.7
Philippines	3.7	5.3	6.9	8.2	9.7	11.0	6.1
TOTAL	252.4	291.4	351.9	410.1	412.5	488.1	476.1

[1] prior to August 1979 data included shipments valued at $250 or more; post August 1979 data includes shipments valued at $500 or more
Source: US Department of Commerce/Bureau of the Census

The Nigerian results obviously reflect that country's economic problems in 1983, but that aside it is obviously exchange rate variations which are going to account for most of the variability over time. Some representative exchange rates are set out in Appendix table 6, and this shows, for example, the dollar declining in value compared to the £ between 1977 and 1980, but subsequently more than making good the lost ground. In relation to other major European currencies, the picture is very similar, the turnaround occurring in either 1979 or 1980. These exchange rates greatly favoured US exports up to 1980, causing, for example, certain UK publishers to switch production which was intended for the UK market to the USA; many US publishers to distribute in the UK through agents for the first time; and a sharp increase in trade in US remainders.

70

The past three years have seen the increasingly unfavourable exchange rate take its toll of US exports, which, after a year of stagnant real growth in 1982, fell back sharply in 1983. As we have seen, some countries were more affected than others, and also certain categories of books. The full implications of the 1983 results will not be easy to judge until at least one more year's figures are available, but the overall trends are fairly clear.

Between 1970 and 1980 the real value of US imports rose by 57%, compared to an increase in the real value of exports of 38%. Imports then fell away for two years, only to return to the 1980 level in 1983. Table 3.6 divides imports up by category. The 'other' book category is not merely much the largest, but is at an historically high level, whereas the next biggest category, foreign language books, shows a clear tendency to decline in importance, as do bible sales. The all-embracing nature of the 'other' book category inhibits further analysis, but table 3.6 listing import dependence by category is quite revealing. As can be seen, import dependence was exceptionally high in 1980, but had fallen in every case in the similar year of 1983. In 1980 the UK was the dominant exporter of other books to the USA, but by 1983 much ground had been lost to Canada. Predictably, most foreign language books appear in Spanish. The UK remains the major exporter of bibles, but again Canada has appeared out of nowhere to challenge for supremacy.

These factors are reflected in table 3.7, showing the origins of US imports by country. The UK had the field pretty much to itself up to 1980, only to be virtually caught up by Canada in 1983, with Japan also coming up strongly on the rails. In 1983, these three countries between them supplied 63% of all US imports, leaving the rest to fight over the scraps. The substantial imports from Japan and Hong Kong reflect the opportunities presented by low manufacturing costs in the Far East.

71

TABLE 3.6   US IMPORT DEPENDENCE BY CATEGORY[1] 1980 AND 1983

Unit: %

Bibles, prayer books	1980 UK 38.2 + France 17.8 + Belgium 10.9 + Israel 10.8 + Spain = 84.9
	1983 UK 29.1 + Canada 23.8 + Belgium 22.8 + W.Germany + Israel = 84.8
Books, foreign language	1980 Spain 29.8 + Mexico 25.2 + W.Germany 15.9 + France, Japan = 80.8
	1983 Spain 26.7 + Mexico 18.3 + W.Germany 13.2 + Japan, France = 73.8
Other books	1980 UK 39.2 + Canada 14.5 + Japan 13.2 + Hong Kong, Italy = 79.6
	1983 UK 27.8 + Canada 23.4 + Japan 17.0 + Hong Kong, Italy = 78.4
Toy books, colouring books	1980 Canada 25.7 + Singapore 19.0 + Japan 18.4 + Colombia 14.4 + Taiwan 10.4 = 87.9
	1983 Canada 31.4 + Singapore 20.7 + Colombia 14.1 + Japan + Taiwan = 82.0

[1] shipments valued at $250 or more

Source: adapted from US Department of Commerce/Bureau of the Census

TABLE 3.7   US IMPORTS OF BOOKS FROM 10 LEADING COUNTRIES[1]

	1977	1978	1979	1980	1981	1982	1983
Unit: $ million							
United Kingdom	64.4	88.0	99.9	103.5	90.2	85.0	93.3
Canada	11.5	15.6	23.6	39.9	39.2	47.5	81.2
Japan	18.4	30.6	31.9	37.1	44.6	46.9	59.2
West Germany	10.9	15.2	12.6	17.2	16.4	16.4	23.5
Hong Kong	5.0	7.4	10.7	17.6	15.5	19.3	18.7
Italy	12.4	17.6	24.0	16.7	14.1	15.5	16.8
Spain	10.9	12.7	15.7	14.8	15.1	16.6	15.9
Netherlands	5.0	8.5	7.9	9.4	8.7	9.5	10.9
Mexico	5.1	4.7	4.7	8.0	5.6	6.9	5.3
Switzerland	5.3	6.0	6.2	7.3	7.8	7.0	4.9
TOTAL	148.9	206.3	237.2	271.5	257.2	270.6	329.7

[1] Shipments valued at $250 or more

Source: US Department of Commerce/Bureau of the Census

TABLE 3.8   US IMPORTS OF BOOKS OVERALL[1] AT CURRENT AND 1976 PRICES

Unit: $ million

	1976	1977	1978	1979	1980	1981	1982	1983
Bibles & prayer books	6.1	8.5	8.8	6.1	5.9	5.3	7.6	7.2
	(6.1)	(8.0)	(7.7)	(4.8)	(4.1)	(3.3)	(4.5)	(4.1)
Books, foreign	19.6	22.2	25.2	25.5	30.1	27.0	27.1	25.7
language	(19.6)	(20.9)	(22.0)	(20.0)	(20.8)	(16.9)	(15.9)	(14.7)
Other books nspf[2]	3.8	3.8	4.7	3.5	4.2	7.2	10.3	12.1
wholly or in part the	(3.8)	(3.6)	(4.1)	(2.7)	(2.9)	(4.5)	(6.0)	(6.9)
work of an author								
who is a US national								
or domiciliary								
Other books	127.4	132.3	191.8	229.7	257.0	247.0	260.9	313.5
	(127.4)	(124.3)	(167.4)	(180.1)	(177.6)	(154.4)	(153.4)	(179.1)
Toy books &	1.0	1.7	1.9	4.0	9.3	8.4	9.0	9.3
colouring books	(1.0)	(1.6)	(1.7)	(3.1)	(6.4)	(5.3)	(5.3)	(5.3)
TOTAL	157.9	168.5	232.3	268.7	306.5	294.9	314.9	367.8
	(157.9)	(158.4)	(202.7)	(210.7)	(211.8)	(184.4)	(185.1)	(210.1)

[1] shipments valued at $250 or more

[2] nspf = not specially provided for

Source: US Department of Commerce/Bureau of the Census

United Kingdom

Table 3.9 contains the official trade statistics for the UK. Imports are slightly over-valued due to the 'cost, insurance and freight' method of counting. In money terms, exports have risen in value every year since 1970, but their performance in real terms has been very erratic. The peak year was 1978, which was a significant improvement on any preceding year, and the following year saw real exports drop sharply to a plateau which was maintained until there was a modest upturn in 1983, but this served only to restore the 1977 position.

73

TABLE 3.9   UK OVERSEAS TRADE STATISTICS IN BOOKS

Unit: £ million

	Exports		Imports		Trade balance	
	Money value	**Real value**	**Money value**	**Real value**	**Money value**	**Real value**
1970	46.3	46.3	20.8	20.8	25.5	25.5
1971	59.4	54.3	23.9	21.8	35.5	32.5
1972	69.2	59.0	27.4	23.4	41.8	35.6
1973	73.9	57.7	31.2	24.4	42.7	33.3
1974	84.0	57.1	42.5	28.9	41.5	28.2
1975	104.0	56.9	50.4	27.6	53.6	29.3
1976	136.1	63.7	58.1	27.2	78.0	36.5
1977	176.0	71.4	68.6	27.8	107.4	43.6
1978	206.5	77.4	88.1	33.0	118.4	44.4
1979	209.3	69.0	103.1	33.9	106.2	34.9
1980	237.6	66.2	124.1	34.7	113.5	31.6
1981	269.2	67.1	145.6	36.3	123.6	30.8
1982	287.8	66.3	162.4	37.4	125.4	28.9
1983	321.0	70.4	191.8	42.1	129.2	28.3

Source: Overseas Trade Statistics: Class 892.11

Imports have also risen steadily in money value, but in real terms the picture is quite different from exports because, after reaching a plateau in the mid-1970s, they took off in 1978, rose slowly but steadily from 1979 to 1982, then sharply again in 1983. Thus, whereas real exports rose by an apparently acceptable 52% between 1970 and 1983, real imports rose by just over 100%. The obvious consequence was that the real trade balance, which had risen, albeit unsteadily, from 1970 to 1978, fell very sharply in 1979, and continued to slide steadily in subsequent years, ending up a mere 11% above its 1970 level and comparable only to the rather disastrous year of 1974. Were this trend to continue for much longer then the UK would end up with a real trade balance of under £20 million, which few would have dreamt possible even ten years ago.

It is illuminating to look at the weight of imports and exports. In 1971 imports weighed 54% of exports. In 1975 it was 70%, but it fell back to its original ratio before shooting up to 82% in 1979. In 1981 imports actually weighed 4% more than exports, and have subsequently continued to weigh more. But as imports are worth much less than exports, this means that on a £ per kilo basis imports are currently worth much less than exports. The comparable figures for 1983 were £2.60 per kilo for imports, £4.55 per kilo for exports, a ratio of 57%. In 1977 it was 75%, and it has exceeded 70% in several years.

The UK is, therefore, clearly importing ever-larger quantities of cheap books. This is firstly because such books are increasingly printed overseas, and especially in the Far East and Italy (see table 3.10), and secondly because of a much increased inflow of remaindered books from the USA. It is also the case that imports of textbooks and the like from America are very heavy in relation to their price.

TABLE 3.10   UK EXPORTS AND IMPORTS: PRINTED BOOKS, BOOKLETS, BROCHURES, PAMPHLETS AND LEAFLETS

Unit: % breakdown

	Exports[1]					
	1977	**1978**	**1979**	**1980**	**1982**	**1983**
EEC	16.9	17.6	19.3	20.2	19.6	21.0
USA	20.6	20.8	20.2	18.5	17.5	18.5
Australia	15.0	15.0	15.1	11.3	13.1	13.8
Nigeria	13.7	11.1	7.8	12.7	7.3	3.2
South Africa	3.0	3.4	4.1	5.6	7.2	6.4
Netherlands	4.5	5.3	5.9	5.5	4.8	5.5
Ireland	3.5	3.8	4.9	5.0	4.8	5.1
Canada	6.1	4.8	4.5	3.7	3.8	4.4
New Zealand	3.2	3.1	3.7	2.9	2.8	3.3
Hong Kong	0.8	1.0	1.0	—	—	1.1
Italy	1.0	1.1	1.1	1.4	1.3	1.6
Japan	1.4	1.3	1.7	1.8	1.9	2.1
Spain	0.6	—	—	—	1.2	1.1
Others	15.2	18.1	17.7	18.3	20.8	20.0

continued...

Table 3.10 continued...

	Imports[1]					
	1977	1978	1979	1980	1982	1983
EEC	28.6	29.2	33.1	28.1	25.0	25.5
USA	38.6	37.7	36.5	39.6	42.1	40.5
Australia	1.0	—	—	—	—	—
Nigeria	—	—	—	—	—	—
South Africa	—	—	—	—	—	—
Netherlands	8.1	6.1	6.3	5.1	6.5	6.5
Ireland	1.0	—	—	—	—	—
Canada	1.3	—	—	—	—	—
New Zealand	—	—	—	—	—	—
Hong Kong	10.9	10.7	11.3	13.5	13.2	12.4
Italy	10.0	13.0	14.3	10.6	8.4	8.7
Japan	3.0	2.8	1.9	2.6	2.7	2.9
Spain	3.3	4.2	4.1	4.0	3.8	4.8
Others	12.3	15.4	10.3	12.2	13.2	13.9

[1] 1981 not available

Source: Overseas Trade Statistics

If one examines the geographic distribution of imports and exports according to overseas trade statistics, one immediately observes the high proportion of imports from countries which are used as sources of printing capacity by UK publishers. Hong Kong remains a popular location but Italy is well down from its 1979 peak (see section on printing). America remains the largest source of imports, but its share is vulnerable to exchange rate changes, so it is surprising that it is currently showing up so well. Presumably, it is cheap remainders which account for this as their prices are unlikely to be very sensitive to exchange rate variation.

On the export side the EEC has for some years provided a solid 20% of the total overseas market, just ahead of the USA. However, the early part of 1984 suggests an enormous increase in exports to America, in part a response to the exceptionally favourable exchange rate. Most other markets are reasonably consistent, but Ireland is surprisingly receptive to UK exports, and South Africa is buoyant as a result of big increases in spending power not being met by indigenous publishers.

The real collapse has occurred in Nigeria (and these data assume the exports have all been paid for). From a substantial 13.7% of the export market in 1977 Nigeria has begun 1984 with a 2% share. This is obviously a serious loss to UK publishers, and especially to those exporting school books and the like.

It is worth pointing out that were it not for Nigeria the export performance of UK publishers would really be quite respectable as the real value of exports rose in 1983, Nigeria withstanding. A rather less beneficial aspect is the continuance of overseas printing on a scale which is superficially incompatible with the UK's low exchange rate and low domestic rate of inflation.

It is also possible to examine exports in relation to book categories. The relevant data are based upon the raw Business Monitor data, but adjusted for inflation. These figures differ from those in the overseas trade statistics in a) coverage, that of Business Monitor being narrower; b) exports by booksellers no longer get counted by Business Monitor but appear in the other series; c) Ireland is sometimes regarded as the home rather than the export market by publishers; d) publishers sometimes count as an export, books supplied from an overseas subsidiary. Item d) cancels out a) to c) so that neither series is automatically bigger than the other.

Table 3.11 indicates the proportion of total receipts earned by exports. From 1971 to 1978 the proportion never fell below 35%, and this figure could be increased by up to 5% by taking into account exports by retail and wholesale booksellers (this information is no longer available). Since 1979, the position appears to have weakened markedly, but it is widely held that these figures are increasingly understated due to a rising number of books produced, sold and distributed by overseas subsidiaries set up or acquired, or by overseas companies in which a controlling interest is held. If this is correct then UK publishers' export drive has not slackened by anything like as much as the figures suggest.

It is evident from table 3.11 that certain categories of books such as school textbooks are far more dependent upon export markets than others. Fiction is no longer exported very much at all in hardback format, but is reasonably popular abroad in paperback format although, as table 3.11 indicates, well below its 1978 peak. The only paperback category to hold its own in real value in relation to 1978 is technical and scientific (1983 is not compatible with earlier years) and it is also the most

77

most resilient hardback category despite falling overall. However, the position is far worse for this category if a 1971 or indeed 1975 base year is used, a factor which is by no means uniform for all categories. Indeed, inspection of the totals shows that 1977 was the peak year of those analysed in aggregate, and the bottom line figure was 78.17 million in 1974, and 80.13 million in 1976.

TABLE 3.11   UK: PROPORTION OF TOTAL RECEIPTS EARNED BY EXPORTS

Unit: %

Category of book	1971	1975	1978	1979	1980	1981	1982	1983[1]
Hardback								
Bibles	75.3	60.8	62.1	55.2	60.4	58.0	19.7	48.2
School textbooks	38.7	41.9	39.8	40.3	43.4	43.8	39.4	40.4
Technical and scientific	51.4	54.4	43.4	41.8	42.7	40.2	40.6	41.3
Fiction, literature and classics	31.5	30.1	33.8	19.9	15.0	15.5	17.5	18.2
Children's	29.2	28.4	30.3	23.5	24.1	23.3	21.2	23.0
Other	32.5	26.8	28.8	26.0	26.0	26.7	25.8	24.2
Paperback								
School textbooks	44.0	44.7	47.4	46.9	54.8	52.7	47.2	47.1
Technical and scientific	38.2	37.3	44.1	43.5	22.1	21.5	20.1	26.4
Fiction, literature and classics	37.8	39.1	38.3	34.4	32.7	31.7	30.8	32.9
Children's	24.8	26.9	26.2	28.1	23.6	25.7	25.1	27.4
Other (incl. bibles)	21.0	20.1	27.3	25.9	21.5	21.5	24.2	24.5
Total	38.1	36.3	36.3	32.5	31.2	30.9	29.7	30.6
Royalties	52.6	58.7	49.1	49.6	72.1	56.7	56.7	53.5
TOTAL	38.6	37.0	36.7	33.0	32.5	31.8	30.7	31.3
Plus exports by principal retail and wholesale booksellers	43.2	40.5	40.6	37.1	n.a	n.a	n.a	n.a.

[1] not compatible with earlier years
Source: Department of Industry/*Business Monitor*

The difficulty is in deciding how much allowance to make for under recorded exports in aggregate, let alone in individual categories. The high exchange rate of earlier years obviously led to an increase in overseas production, and this is currently likely to be stemmed because the exchange rate is at an historic low. The only general conclusion to be drawn is, therefore, that the exporting situation isn't as bad as it looks, but is no longer as buoyant as it was in the late 1970s.

TABLE 3.12   UK EXPORT SALES AND RECEIPTS OF GENERAL PUBLISHERS AND PRINTERS

Unit: £ million at 1971 prices Category of book	1971	1975	1977	1978	1979	1980	1981	1982	1983[1]
Hardback									
Bibles	3.92	2.57	2.94	2.57	1.76	2.03	1.82	1.43	1.45
School textbooks	6.20	6.57	5.81	5.60	5.40	5.46	5.55	4.56	4.59
Technical and scientific	17.74	16.02	11.60	11.60	11.05	10.72	10.43	10.52	12.37
Fiction, literature and classics	7.25	7.08	7.39	8.07	4.29	3.58	3.52	3.74	3.37
Children's	4.40	4.38	3.88	3.97	3.10	2.90	2.72	2.36	2.68
Other	11.07	11.72	15.68	14.90	13.75	12.46	11.04	10.09	10.88
Paperback									
School textbooks	6.34	7.79	11.93	9.80	9.46	10.50	10.18	7.37	6.40
Technical and scientific	2.05	2.66	3.21	3.12	3.30	2.95	3.54	3.33	5.13
Fiction, literature and classics	7.02	9.61	9.81	10.46	8.58	7.34	7.57	7.39	8.11
Children's	1.08	1.66	1.36	1.32	1.49	1.00	1.07	0.94	1.22
Other (incl. bibles)	2.09	2.15	3.55	3.65	3.61	2.85	2.98	3.13	2.97
Total	68.81	72.21	77.16	75.06	65.79	61.79	60.42	54.86	59.47
Royalties	3.18	3.60	3.70	3.31	3.38	4.60	3.69	3.95	3.26
TOTAL	71.99	75.81	80.86	78.37	69.17	66.39	64.11	58.81	62.73

[1] not compatible with earlier years
Source: Department of Industry/*Business Monitor*

The Publishers' Association's own statistics collection scheme also collects information on exports. This appears as follows:

TABLE 3.13   UK: PA STATISTICS COLLECTION SCHEME — EXPORTS

Unit: £ million

	Mass-market paperback 1983	School 1983	Univer-sity 1983	Special-ised 1983	General 1983	TOTAL 1983
Western Europe	8.4	11.4	15.2	1.8	7.9	44.7
Eastern Europe	0.1	0.1	1.0	0.1	0.1	1.4
Indian sub-continent	1.4	0.1	2.1	0.2	0.8	4.7
Middle East/ N.Africa	1.2	7.6	2.6	0.5	1.3	13.2
Africa	6.3	6.7	5.3	1.6	4.3	24.1
Australia	15.0	1.7	2.8	1.6	9.3	30.3
New Zealand/ Oceania	2.5	0.4	0.6	0.4	2.2	6.1
Far East/ S.E.Asia	2.9	3.3	6.7	1.2	2.2	16.3
America/ Caribbean	6.2	5.2	16.5	3.8	12.9	44.8
Other	1.0	0.6	2.9	0.6	0.9	6.0
TOTAL	44.8	37.2	55.7	11.8	41.9	191.6

Note: a more detailed breakdown can be found in the Statistical Appendix

Problems of interpretation arise in adjusting the data to allow for inflation because of the two price indices used by the Publishers' Association for this purpose, but the general lessons to be learned from the exercise are 1) mass-market paperbacks, specialised and general books did well overall; 2) but mass-market paperbacks nevertheless did badly in non-EEC Western Europe, New Zealand/Oceania, West Africa (especially Nigeria) and Central/South America; 3) specialised books did badly in Western Europe, Central/South America and especially in West Africa where general books also did badly; 4) school books did well in Europe and the Middle East, and especially in the USA, but collapsed elsewhere; 5) university books did well in the USA and East/Central Africa, but generally performed poorly; 6) the significant growth markets were Australia and North America, whereas Nigeria was a disaster.

West Germany

Although West Germany does relatively little trade in relation to the size of its domestic market because of the restrictions imposed by the language problem, the domestic market is so large that the country is nevertheless a major trading nation. The main data for exports are as follows:

TABLE 3.14   WEST GERMAN EXPORTS, 1978-1982

	1978	1979	1980	1981	1982
Value of exports (DM million)	617	677	733	777	775
Value of exports at 1978 prices (DM million)	617	650	666	668	633
% total book sales	11.0	11.2	12.2	11.5	10.9

Source: Buchmarket/Euromonitor

As can be seen, progress in export markets essentially ground to a halt in 1979, and 1982 proved a major setback. Things would probably have been much worse were it not for the extremely low rate of inflation, 22% from 1978 to 1982 compared to 63% for the UK. Not surprisingly, German speaking Austria and Switzerland absorb over one-half of all exports. The major markets are as follows:

TABLE 3.15   WEST GERMAN EXPORTS[1] BY COUNTRY OF DESTINATION

Unit: %

	1978	1979	1980	1981	1982
Austria	25.3	28.1	26.3	25.6	27.1
Switzerland	25.4	25.0	25.6	25.2	26.1
Netherlands	9.6	8.9	8.9	8.7	8.1
USA	8.5	7.9	7.2	7.2	7.9
France	5.2	4.7	6.7	5.3	6.1
Italy	3.2	3.4	3.2	4.1	3.8
Belgium/Luxembourg	3.5	3.5	3.7	3.6	3.4
Japan	3.0	3.3	3.5	3.7	3.0
UK	2.6	2.3	2.4	2.3	2.2

[1] includes pamphlets
Source: Aussenhandel

No other major market shows so little variation over time, especially taking good and bad years together. Again, this may reflect the control exercised over German-speaking markets.

The level of import penetration in the German market is also fairly constant, as the table below shows.

TABLE 3.16   IMPORT PENETRATION OF THE WEST GERMAN BOOK MARKET, 1978-1982

	1978	1979	1980	1981	1982
Value of imports (DM million)	345.5	385.0	419.3	439.6	441.3
Value of imports (DM million) at 1978 prices	345.5	370.0	381.2	378.0	360.2
% apparent sales	6.5	6.7	6.9	6.7	6.3

The pattern is very similar to that for exports with 1980 and 1981 the peak years, and 1982 declining below the level of 1979. The trade balance is obviously very healthy, rising very gradually in real terms from DM

82

272 million in 1978 to DM 290 million in 1981, and only falling back to DM 273 million in 1982. The constancy of the trade balance, as we have seen, is rather unusual.

Imports come mainly from Switzerland and Austria as we would expect, but the USA and UK also have a significant toe-hold in the market, as shown in table 3.17 below.

TABLE 3.17   WEST GERMAN IMPORTS[1] BY COUNTRY OF ORIGIN

Unit: %	1978	1979	1980	1981	1982
Austria	22.1	22.1	21.6	21.5	21.5
Switzerland	19.7	19.0	20.6	21.1	17.5
USA	7.0	7.9	8.5	11.3	12.1
UK	7.5	7.2	8.5	8.3	8.1
Italy	11.1	13.4	10.1	9.0	6.9
Netherlands	9.4	9.7	8.1	8.4	6.9
France	4.4	3.8	4.1	3.2	. 5.2

[1] includes pamphlets
Source: Aussenhandel

The constancy of the aggregate total does, however, disguise some significant trade offs between countries. The USA is continuously increasing its market share whereas Italy is in corresponding decline, and the Netherlands is also struggling. Creeping up is Czechoslovakia with 2.7% in 1982, but there were some quite sharp changes in this recession year which may prove transient.

France

Imports of books into France showed strong growth in the second half of the 1970s. Subsequently the effects of the recession have caused imports to fall, although they appear to have stabilised at around 22% of the total book market. Inflation in France roughly doubled prices between 1975 and 1982. In real terms, therefore, school book imports have declined enormously, whereas imports of children's books have shown substantial growth. Encyclopaedias and dictionaries surged upwards in 1978 and have maintained their momentum at a more modest level. The origins of these imports are set out in table 3.19.

TABLE 3.18   FRENCH IMPORTS BY SUBJECT MATTER

Unit: million francs

	1978	1979	1980	1981	1982
Schoolbooks	12.21	12.03	12.10	12.29	19.44
Scientific and technical	37.13	34.36	44.83	43.59	28.99
Social sciences	35.44	27.81	37.57	39.64	44.10
Literature, history	367.61	397.07	484.03	465.98	501.27
Encyclopaedias	75.58	90.96	134.92	175.74	161.34
Fine arts	36.37	47.52	46.31	44.84	46.72
Children's	126.88	164.36	184.35	225.33	247.58
Practical books	129.08	159.40	174.98	190.09	185.71
Foreign language	91.25	105.22	125.23	141.05	162.12
Parts of books	104.25	147.68	138.85	137.23	157.57
TOTAL Money	1,014.89	1,186.41	1,383.21	1,475.68	1,548.84
at 1975 prices	775.91	819.34	840.85	791.24	742.85
% apparent sales	20.9	22.00	22.3	22.2	

Source: Direction Générale des Douanes

TABLE 3.19   FRENCH IMPORTS OF BOOKS BY COUNTRY OF ORIGIN

Unit: % breakdown

	1977	1979	1981	1982
Italy	28.6	28.9	27.2	24.0
Belgium/Luxembourg	17.1	17.2	16.5	20.1
Switzerland	16.8	12.8	13.5	11.7
Spain	13.3	13.7	15.3	8.9
West Germany	4.3	5.1	5.1	7.7
Netherlands	3.7	5.2	4.0	4.6
UK	4.5	4.1	4.5	4.6
All other	11.7	13.0	13.9	18.4
TOTAL	100.0	100.0	100.0	100.0
of which EEC	58.7	61.2	60.2	62.9

Source: Direction Générale des Douanes

Italy and Spain are normally favoured for printing facilities, so Belgium and Switzerland, with their significant French speaking populations, are the major source of imports in French originated outside France itself. West Germany, the UK and the Netherlands provide modest numbers of predominantly general literature books in foreign languages, Italy is used to print encyclopaedias, social science and practical books, and Switzerland used predominantly for general literature.

In aggregate terms French trade in books has long been very close to balance. In 1975, exports were worth FF 678 million compared to imports of FF 633 million, and this modest surplus was restored in 1981 after several years of modest deficit. Nevertheless, as table 3.20 shows, individual categories vary enormously.

TABLE 3.20   FRENCH EXPORTS BY SUBJECT MATTER

Unit: million francs

	1978	1979	1980	1981	1982
Schoolbooks	91.72	113.93	124.76	144.18	186.70
Scientific and technical	76.37	100.12	109.63	102.70	95.10
Social sciences	32.44	40.47	34.76	43.12	49.84
Literature and history	319.89	342.91	350.70	404.50	482.84
Encyclopaedias	66.69	81.95	99.98	114.08	120.69
Fine arts	7.44	10.71	8.76	9.82	11.48
Children's	21.50	24.40	27.33	30.14	25.32
Practical books	298.96	351.23	422.71	436.84	489.25
Foreign language	63.26	82.15	85.72	98.03	122.88
Parts of books	16.33	13.86	15.39	21.00	26.92
TOTAL	995.17	1,161.73	1,279.75	1,404.42	1,611.02
at 1977 prices	912.16	960.11	932.08	902.00	925.87

Source: Direction Générale des Douanes

In real terms, exports are up satisfactorily compared both to 1975 and 1977, although the peak year was in 1979. Thus the recession overseas has not bitten too badly into French exports. Certain sectors have not been very buoyant, such as fine arts (obviously a French taste judging by imports) and children's books, but exports of schoolbooks, literature, encyclopaedias and dictionaries, foreign language and practical books show no signs of flagging. The export market for children's books in French is surprisingly small although schoolbooks and especially practical books are popular. This reflects the nature of the export markets which are obviously greatly different to those of English language exporters.

TABLE 3.21   FRENCH EXPORTS BY COUNTRY OF DESTINATION

Unit: % breakdown	1979	1981	1982
Belgium/Luxembourg	25.9	25.6	23.9
Switzerland	12.5	13.6	15.3
Canada	10.3	10.5	9.8
Ivory Coast	5.4	5.1	7.3
Germany	3.0	2.1	4.2
Algeria	4.0	2.7	3.5
USA	2.3	2.3	2.9
Cameroons	2.0	2.4	2.6
Italy	3.0	2.9	2.5
Morocco	3.1	2.8	2.5
Spain	2.3	1.9	1.8
All other	26.2	28.1	23.7
TOTAL	100.0	100.0	100.0
of which EEC	31.5	35.0	33.3

Source: Direction Générale des Douanes

The EEC continues to provide a solid one-third of the market, although this is primarily Belgium and Luxembourg. Perhaps half as much again is accounted for by the ex-colonies, which, as pointed out elsewhere, damages to some extent their indigenous publishing. This market is bound to decline as the use of French steadily falls, being replaced either by English or indigenous languages. As the 'All other' total indicates, there are a large number of insignificant export markets which reflects the historically wide dispersál of the French language.

Japan

Exports are doing well in value terms, and have grown by 86% in real terms over the past five years, although at £46 million in 1983 Japan is not yet among the big league exporters, and exports constitute a rather low proportion of domestic production. The number of copies exported peaked in 1981, but the prices received have evidently risen sharply. The only major market is the USA, whose market share was 45% in 1979, which fell to 38% in 1980, but recovered to 42% in 1983. Australia, the UK and Korea fluctuate within the 4-8% range, and the EEC takes 15-20% overall. Imports in 1983 were worth £45.1 million, so trade is virtually in balance, although the real value of imports has declined sharply since the late 1970s, as has the number of copies imported. The USA originated 60% of Japanese imports in 1978, but only 40% in 1980, the present figure being 47%. Obviously the exchange rate has much to do with this, as has the fluctuating share of imports held by the UK, rising from 11% in 1978 to 22% in 1980, and currently down to 18%. West Germany provides another 15% and the rest are widely dispersed.

TABLE 3.22   JAPAN: TRADE IN BOOKS, 1978-1983

	1978	1979	1980	1981	1982	1983
Exports						
million yen at 1978 prices	9,030	9,010	12,412	14,073	15,495	16,793
Imports						
million yen at 1978 prices	23,023	21,238	20,570	16,244	17,664	16,296
Export copies (million)	22.9	24.2	41.2	48.3	48.0	44.7
Import copies (million)	20.3	19.2	17.1	17.1	14.7	13.8

Source: Japanese Trade Statistics

Australia

Australia is a major importer of English language books. These originate from the UK and USA. Table 3.23, below, lists total imports, in both money and real terms, for the past seven years (running July to June), divided up into hardback and paperback categories. Overall the total in money terms shows a steady, if erratic progression, but when expressed in real terms (adjusted by the consumer price index) it can be seen that a

87

sharp increase occurred in 1978/79 followed by an identically sized sharp reduction in 1980/81. Thus, over the full period, real imports remained to all intents and purposes unchanged.

TABLE 3.23   AUSTRALIAN BOOK IMPORTS (AT LANDED COSTS)

Unit: $A million	1976/ 77	1977/ 78	1978/ 79	1979/ 80	1980/ 81	1981/ 82	1982/ 83
Total:							
current prices	105.0	112.4	148.3	160.2	163.4	181.8	201.8
1976/77 prices	105.0	100.4	119.5	118.0	99.0	100.0	104.2
of which							
UK	44.6	53.9	71.1	74.4	73.4	73.0	81.0
USA	42.2	37.6	43.7	48.9	52.5	65.5	74.0
Asia[1]	18.2	20.9	22.3	23.2	26.3	31.2	33.3
Other	n.a	n.a	11.2	13.7	11.2	12.1	13.5
Paperbacks							
Total:							
current prices	41.1	47.5	58.2	64.3	65.2	68.7	77.1
1976/77 prices	41.1	42.4	46.9	47.3	39.5	37.8	39.8
of which							
UK	22.9	28.0	36.9	33.9	34.9	33.2	34.9
USA	13.7	13.0	16.5	16.5	17.7	21.7	27.0
Asia	4.5	6.5	8.3	8.3	8.0	8.9	9.7
Other	n.a.	n.a.	5.6	5.6	4.6	4.9	5.5
Hardbacks							
Total:							
current prices	63.9	64.9	78.9	95.9	98.2	113.1	124.7
1976/77 prices	63.9	58.0	63.6	70.7	59.5	62.2	64.4
of which							
UK	21.7	25.9	34.2	40.5	38.5	39.8	46.1
USA	28.5	24.6	29.3	32.4	34.8	43.8	47.0
Asia	13.7	14.4	15.4	14.9	18.3	22.3	23.6
Other	n.a.	n.a.	n.a.	8.1	6.6	7.2	8.0

[1] figures represent value of Australian publishers' imports of their own books printed in Hong Kong, Japan and Singapore

Source: Adapted from Australian Bureau of Statistics

In spite of this, the relative position of the UK and USA as exporters to Australia changed considerably. There was little to choose between them in 1976/77, but the following two years saw the UK establish a dominant position which was, however, progressively eroded during the subsequent three years.

In 1976/77, the US predominantly exported hardbacks to Australia, and the UK exported paperbacks. Subsequently, however, the USA lost part of its hardback market to the UK, leaving them equal pegging, and what at its peak was a 28% market share gap in favour of UK paperback exports has now been reduced to a mere 10%.

We have already noted that Australia is by a clear margin the USA's third largest export market, being a particularly significant importer of 'other' books, and, to a lesser extent, of encyclopaedias. US exporters also have certain parts of the educational book market fairly well sewn up. One must bear in mind, however, that the UK has had a considerably higher annual rate of inflation than the USA, and that the demise of the Traditional Market Agreement was highly favourable to US exporters. Furthermore, the UK is somewhat disadvantageously placed geographically for exporting to Australia. All in all, therefore, taking into account the exchange rate position, the UK has done well to maintain its share of the Australian market at such a high level.

Regional Survey
Having analysed the major trading nations, a number of general points can be made about other countries.

Western Europe

Austria: both exports and imports over 80% with West Germany as a result of common language. No other significant trade ties.

Belgium: 70% of exports and 80% of imports shared equally by Netherlands and France.

Denmark: over one-third of imports from the USA, followed by UK 15% and West Germany 10%. Exports predictably to Sweden 20% and Norway 15%. West Germany and UK also above 10% of exports.

Finland: exports of books in Swedish and Finnish have declined rapidly in percentage terms. The value of exports in other languages compared with production figures for the same category underlines the particular importance of re-exports. Both exports and re-exports are directed primarily at Sweden followed by the USSR. Norway and the UK are, however, steadily replacing Sweden. Imports account for some 10% of the domestic market and are generally increasing at a higher rate than exports. Finnish/Swedish language imports account for around 60% of the market, imported primarily from Sweden. The UK is a significant supplier of English language books, with 18% of imports, followed by the USA with 10%.

Greece: imports twice as much as the exports, but totals are insignificant. Two-thirds of imports come from the UK and 70% of exports go to Cyprus.

Ireland: insignificant exports go to the UK. Quite substantial imports from UK.

Italy: imports are growing steadily in volume and value. France, UK and USA of roughly equal importance, with West Germany (by their rather than Italian accounts) much the biggest source of purchases. Massive inflation is damaging export prospects, with France taking one-third followed by the UK at 15%, West Germany and the USA.

Netherlands: imports account for roughly one-third of all purchases, but year on year variations are quite large. Imports are mainly scientific books, which are frequently in English, giving the UK and USA an increasing share of the market, currently 34%. West Germany remains a significant source of imports, but on a declining trend. Exports account for over one-third of total sales, and of these one-third go to Belgium, although it was 45% for the years 1979-81. The West German market is important, but the UK and USA were the main replacements for Belgium in 1982.

Norway: Norwegian exports are minimal, and mainly in foreign languages. Imports have shown steady growth in real terms, and account for 12% of total sales.

Roughly half are in Norwegian, half in other languages. Sweden and Denmark predictably supply one-third, and the UK, its share declining, and West Germany, its share rising, roughly as much again.

Portugal: Portugal does little trade in books, and statistics are out of date. Exports, however, appear to be rising sharply in both volume and value terms. The Brazilian market has shrunk due to indigenous publishing, but Angola is once again taking the bulk of the exports. Imports, mainly in paperback, come almost entirely from Spain.

Spain: Because of its important Latin American markets, Spain ranks among the major book exporting countries of the world, with a high proportion of translations among its exports. It fulfils an important role as the intermediary between Latin America and the other book producing nations. Its imports have risen substantially since the early 1970s, one reason being the annual increase in the number of foreign (especially British) visitors requiring own language books. Statistics are out of date and unreliable, but over one-half of all imports come from the EEC, primarily from the UK, France and West Germany. Exports are buoyant because printing is so competitive, primarily to France and the UK within the EEC, and to Mexico, Argentina and Colombia in the Americas.

Sweden: Sweden exports 10% of its production by value, increasingly in foreign languages. Half of its Swedish language exports go to Finland, and most of the rest to Denmark and Norway. Norway also imports over one-third of books in other languages, and heads Finland as the major purchaser overall. Very little goes to English-speaking countries. Sweden is overall a net importer with imports accounting for one-quarter of all sales by value on a slightly rising trend. 60% of imports are in Swedish, up from 50% in 1975, and Denmark and Finland are major suppliers. The major exporter is, however, the UK, with 18% overall, followed by Belgium, Italy, West Germany and the USA. Many other countries hold small market shares.

Switzerland: from being a net exporter in 1972-74, Switzerland has become a net importer with a growing deficit. Over one-half of all imports come from West Germany, and 20% from France, reflecting the importance of official languages, with Italy third by a wide margin. France takes 35% (down from 44% in 1977) of Swiss exports, and West Germany 33%, the rest being widely dispersed. After several years of growth exports plummeted by over 20% in real terms during 1982, and by a further 10% in 1983, and are currently standing at a level roughly

91

one half of that attained in 1975, and well below 50% of that ruling in the early 1970s. It is interesting that this has occurred despite Switzerland having the lowest inflation rate of any advanced nation. It is the French market which has most notably collapsed; and one has only to examine the table of effective exchange rates in the Appendix to understand why this has happened.

Eastern Europe

Bulgaria: imported about 12% of books sold in 1980, largely scientific and technical and mostly from the USSR. Two-thirds of exports go to the Soviet Union, the rest widely dispersed.

Czechoslovakia: imports scientific, technical and medical books, but imports limited by lack of foreign currency. The UK gets about 30% of the foreign currency allocation. Exports are worth 50% more than imports largely due to purchase of high quality printing work.

Hungary: Hungary is a net exporter of books and pamphlets although the value is static in real terms. Imports come mainly from the Soviet Union (28%) and Czechoslovakia (16%) but the UK, surprisingly, comes third because English is now the second foreign language after Russian in secondary schools. Exports to the USSR (20%), Sweden (18%), UK (16%) and West Germany (12%).

Poland: minimal trade due to currency shortages. What there is, is mainly with the USSR.

The major trading nations are analysed individually above. In addition a number of general points can be made about the other countries.

The Americas

Canada: export sales increased significantly in real terms during the late 1970s, and outpaced sales to the home market to the extent that they constituted 32% of total production in 1979. This has now steadied at around 29% as real exports have declined gradually in recent years. The US buys between 70% and 80% of Canadian exports, the only other significant market being predictably France. Imports are much larger than exports, and rose by 15% in real value between 1978 and 1982 despite a minor dip in 1982. The share of these supplied by the USA rose from 76% in 1978 to 86% in 1982, gained at the expense of the UK (down 3%) and France (down 5% — is reading in French dying out?). Trade has thus increasingly become a cross-border affair from which the USA is the great beneficiary.

Argentina: trade statistics are years out of date. Imports greatly exceed exports and come 65% from Spain. Other imports and exports mostly traded with Latin and South America.

Brazil: no recent statistics, and trends very erratic in past, but undoubtedly the major trader in books in South America. Exports basically go two-thirds to Argentina, one-quarter to Portugal. Up to one-half of imports come from America, 15% from Spain.

Chile: minimal exports. Modest imports of around £17 million come 65% from Spain with some from Mexico, Argentina and USA.

Colombia: imports just under £20 million of which 57% come from Spain, 18% from Mexico and 13% from USA. Surprisingly, exports do not lag far behind at around £15 million as a result of exports throughout the Spanish speaking world, mainly Venezuela 20%, Spain 16%, Mexico 14% and Argentina 12%.

Ecuador: exports almost non-existent, imports of roughly £3 million come 42% from Spain, 17% from Argentina.

Mexico: trade was roughly in balance at a low level until 1978, but imports doubled the following year and the deficit has subsequently become ever larger. These imports have damaged home producers, and have come, predictably, 65% from Spain, with most of the remainder divided equally between North and South America. Over one-half of all exports go to South American countries and another 18% to Central America. Only 10% or so go to Spain.

Venezuela: minimal exports. Trade statistics very out of date but imports probably in £15-20 million range, 50% from Spain and 20% from USA.

Africa and the Middle East

Algeria: no recent statistics, and large annual fluctuations don't help, but imports may have been £7 million in 1982 with French share of 70%, although historic trends would suggest figure perhaps twice as large.

Bahrain: imports roughly £4 million in 1982 of which 35% come from UK, 9% the USA and the rest widely dispersed.

Egypt: exports and imports fluctuate wildly each year. Exports of roughly £4 million go mainly to Saudi Arabia, Algeria and Kuwait, but source of imports of roughly equal size unknown.

Ghana: no recent statistics. Imports rose sharply during 1970s, so perhaps £5/6 million in 1982. Two-thirds come from Hong Kong, rest from UK, USA and Malaysia.

Iran: no recent statistics. USA dominated exporters in 1970s, but this is hardly likely to be the case today.

Israel: imports worth roughly £7 million come 40% from USA, 20% from France (these have exchanged 15% of the market in favour of France since 1976), and 15% from UK. Exports at roughly £5.5 million do not lag far behind, 50% to USA and 15% to West Germany, one-quarter in the form of religious tracts.

Jordan: Exports roughly £0.5 million to USA. Imports of £2.3 million come from Lebanon 30%, UK 20% and the rest widely dispersed.

Kuwait: imports rising rapidly to a little over £10 million in 1982. Origins unknown.

Nigeria: no recent statistics. In 1978 UK supplied 75% of imports and the USA 5%, but the latter's export records indicate a major shift in recent years towards the USA.

Oman: trade insignificant. UK main source of exports.

Qatar: trade insignificant.

Saudi Arabia: imports roughly £45 million in 1982 according to domestic statistics, but only £11 million can be traced, divided equally between USA and UK.

South Africa: exports minimal, but substantial imports of roughly £33 million come 60% from the UK and 25% from the USA.

Tanzania: no recent statistics. Imports in 1982 perhaps £2-3 million of which over 60% come from UK.

United Arab Emirates: no recent statistics but current imports perhaps £7 million, of which a little under £1 million comes from the UK.

Asia and the Far East

China: trade in both directions has grown rapidly since 1977, but imports have grown much faster than exports and are estimated by US Intelligence at roughly £15 million. Origins of imports are unknown, but books in English are increasingly popular.

Hong Kong: Hong Kong does a roaring trade in books and pamphlets, as the figures below indicate.

TABLE 3.24 HONG KONG: TRADE IN BOOKS

Unit: $HK million

	1980	1981	1982	(£mUK) 1982
Exports	557.5	742.1	890.4	87.3
Imports	149.8	220.4	275.4	27.0
Trade balance	407.7	521.7	615.0	60.3

Exports grew by 60% and imports by 84% in money terms, representing substantial real growth in both cases. For some reason, however, the great bulk of these huge exports are difficult to trace in the trade statistics of countries other than the UK (17%), Australia (13%) and the USA (9%). Only £13 million of the missing £54 million are listed in the summary table, and although the USA and UK reckon to import more than Hong Kong reckons to export to them, one must presume that most of the rest is so widely dispersed that it plays no great part in any individual country's trade.

Imports are also something of a puzzle. The UK didn't record any exports to Hong Kong in 1982, although the usual figure was around the £3-4 million mark, and apart from the USA no other country records exports of any significance to Hong Kong.

India: Indian publishing is very heavily dominated by the home market. Exports in 1982 amounted to around £4 million, with £0.5 million going to the USA, the UK and Bangladesh, the rest being widely dispersed. US and Western European countries tend to concentrate upon books of academic interest in English, and there are small markets in Indian communities abroad who import general interest books in Indian languages. Imports amounted to roughly £11 million. This was three times the level of 1976, but the number of copies involved rose by only 15% as a result of a considerable loss of value by the rupee which caused the prices of imported books to spiral. In addition, however, a high level of remainder books, offering the Indian distributor very high discounts, has brought a large number of low-priced foreign books into the market.

The UK provides just under one-half of Indian imports, and the USA roughly one-third, much of the rest coming from Japan and Singapore.

Indonesia: Negligible exports, and imports of £2.7 million in 1982 predominantly in the form of scientific books. The USA supply two-thirds of the latter, and 50% of the general works. No other countries are significant.

Malaysia: exports of £1.6 million go 50% + to Singapore. Imports of roughly £11 million are several times greater than domestic production, and originate 35% from Singapore and 27% from the UK, the rest coming mainly from the Far East.

Pakistan: national trade statistics indicate imports to the value of £17 million in 1982, and exports doubling in money value in 1980/81 to the equivalent of roughly £25 million in 1982. No breakdown by country is available, and once again it is difficult to trace these flows by reference to other countries.

Philippines: negligible exports. Imports fluctuate considerably, and were worth £8.3 million in 1982. Aside from general books, the major import category is dictionaries and encyclopaedias. The USA supplies 60% of general books and the great bulk of all other books (worth £6.3 million according to US statistics). The rest goes to the UK and Far East countries.

Singapore: imports grew rapidly from 1978 to 1980, but have subsequently fallen in real terms. Exports were twice as great in 1978, but, after fluctuating wildly in real terms in subsequent years, were only 75% larger in 1982. Of the £17.7 million of imports in 1982, textbooks accounted for £4.5 million. Imports came mainly from the USA 30%, the UK 25%, Hong Kong and Japan 13% each. Exports of £30.6 million were very healthy. 32% go to Malaysia and effectively replace much of the Malaysian industry, 21% to Australia and 8% to the UK, in the former case supplying a considerable part of its printing requirements. Other European countries do not, however, print in Singapore on any scale. Roughly one-half of all exports are textbooks.

South Korea: mainly trades other than in the Korean language. Exports of £2.9 million in 1982 went almost entirely to Japan and the USA, and imports of £7.9 million from Japan, the USA and the UK.

Taiwan: imports of £7.8 million in 1982 came 41% from Japan, 33% from Hong Kong and 22% from the USA. Exports worth £3.8 million went 29% to Hong Kong and Japan, 18% to the USA, and 11% to Singapore.

Thailand: negligible exports. Imports worth £3.5 million come 45% from the USA and have risen sharply in real terms in recent years. No other country's trade is significant.

Oceania

Australia: has already been dealt with as an individual country study.

New Zealand: exports are minimal, almost all general books, and 70% to Australia. Imports are quite substantial, 95% general books, and have increased significantly in real terms other than in 1977 and 1981. The UK's share is down to 30% from 44% in 1978/79, whereas the Australian share has grown from 21% in 1978/79 to 32%. The USA has retained just under a quarter of the market, and the rest is mainly printing done in the Far East.

Conclusions

International trade in books is ultimately constrained mainly by factors which constrain trade in any commodity, namely per capita national income, expenditure patterns, and exchange rates. The previous table, plotting trade flows in a single year, necessarily presents a static rather than a dynamic picture. By examining the main trading nations in detail we have been able to relate the above factors together in a more dynamic way. Forecasting into the future is, however, a very hazardous business even for expenditure in aggregate, let alone for an individual commodity. No-one knows how quickly, and to what degree, individual countries are going to pull out of the recession of the early 1980s, nor is it at all easy these days to predict exchange rate changes. Furthermore, events such as the collapse of markets in countries such as Nigeria are always unexpected, even if obvious with hindsight.

Other considerations which affect trade are factors such as literacy levels in developing countries, and linguistic inter-dependence. Certain countries' market power originates from their production of a large proportion of the titles produced in specific languages. The English-speaking market is much the largest, but it contains two trading giants who have not as yet slugged it out for supremacy on the scale which was predicted in the 1970s. At the end of the day, therefore, one can only advise the prospective exporter to use the information in this section to identify where markets exist, their potential size, their current trading patterns, and to use exchange rate information to spot opportunities as they arise.

Chapter Four

MARKET TRENDS

The difficulties of calculating market trends from available statistical sources are all too well known to those who have attempted such an analysis for publishers or marketing organisations in the more advanced book markets of the world, and remain as fresh hurdles to cross for less developed book industries in later years.

In this chapter, a brief examination is made of the broad characteristics of market data published by official government departments or book trade organisations, highlighting the pitfalls of this information and the most useful conclusions that can be drawn from it. In order to accomplish this, four closely related, English-speaking markets have been isolated: the two countries that form the basis of all analysis in this study, the US and UK, and two other nations heavily influenced by both: Canada and Australia.

United States

Book sales, in $ million, at current prices, were as follows:

1972	1977	1978	1979	1980	1981	1982
3,018	5,142	5,792	6,332	7,039	7,843	8,243

The increase from 1972 to 1977 was 70.4%, and from 1977 to 1982 it was 60.3%. Over the full decade it was 173.1%. On the face of it, these represent considerable advances, but as usual adjusting for inflation produces a totally different picture. Between 1972 and 1977 prices rose by 44.9% which was rather little by international standards. From 1977 to 1982 the increase was 59.2%, and the increase for the decade as a whole was 130.8%. In real terms, therefore, there was a significant advance over the period as a whole, but it took place entirely during the first five years, the second five combining good, bad and indifferent years to end up significantly below where they began. The detailed picture, expressed in constant 1972 prices, appears in table 4.1.

TABLE 4.1   US: ESTIMATED BOOK PUBLISHING SALES AT 1972 PRICES

Unit: $ million Category	1972	1977	1978	1979	1980	1981	1982
Trade (total)	442	575	623	630	645	622	569
Adult hardbound	251	346	376	353	353	338	282
Adult paperbound	80	117	130	170	185	177	190
Juvenile hardbound	106	94	93	88	86	87	76
Juvenile paperbound	4	18	25	19	22	20	22
Religious (total)	118	173	177	171	178	166	164
Bibles, testaments, hymnals, prayerbooks	62	80	86	81	85	79	69
Other religious	56	93	90	91	93	87	95
Professional (total)	381	482	516	513	507	524	517
Technical & scientific	132	172	178	175	170	180	181
Business & other professional	192	198	214	215	216	226	223
Medical	57	112	124	124	122	118	113
Book Clubs	241	281	297	291	273	262	248
Mail order publications	199	274	282	282	288	300	254
Mass market paperback	253	374	390	350	332	338	346
Rack-sized	250	337	349	309	308	295	298
Non-rack-sized	3	38	41	41	44	43	48
University presses	41	39	40	39	41	40	39
Elementary & secondary texts	498	522	534	539	477	459	441
College texts	375	448	472	479	484	494	480
Standardized texts	27	31	33	36	34	29	29
Subscription reference	279	203	219	222	195	178	167
AV & other media (total)	116	104	97	85	85	77	62
El-hi	101	91	84	75	75	68	55
College	9	8	8	5	4	3	3
Other	6	6	5	5	5	5	4
Other sales[1]	49	44	33	35	34	35	32
TOTAL	3,018	3,549	3,713	3,671	3,573	3,522	3,347

[1] 'Other sales' category does not include any regular book sales but only sheet sales, domestic and export (except those to pre-binders), and miscellaneous merchandise sales.

Note: Figures for sales by industry segment in 1972 and 1977 are estimates of the Association of American Publishers, based on *Census of Manufactures* totals for these years. Figures for 1978 to 1982 are AAP estimates based on publishers' reports and adjusted to reflect the total size of the industry shown in the 1977 Census figures. When comparing AAP figures with Commerce Department figures it should be noted that the Commerce figures do not include data on most university presses or on audiovisual materials, while AAP figures exclude colouring books, Sunday school materials and certain pamphlets included by Commerce.

Source: Association of American Publishers

As the table shows, the prosperity of the early 1970s was not universally shared. Overall, the real improvement was 18%, but much better performances were recorded in religious, mass market paperback and trade books, although juvenile hardback among the latter did badly as customers switched to paperbound. Some sectors fared very badly, for example university presses, subscription reference and audio visual, all of which fell in real terms. The nature of the market hence went through a fairly significant adjustment process.

1978 was a further year of real growth with all sectors other than audio visual making advances, but from this point on it has essentially been a downhill progression despite a very modest upturn in 1981. Trade books appear to have held up well to 1980, but this was because of a transfer from mass-market to adult paperbound sales in the accounts, all in reality doing badly. Book clubs also fell back badly in 1980 as did El-hi, and in neither case did the following two years bring any respite, both closing well down on 1977. Trade books progressed satisfactorily until 1981, and despite a very poor 1982 ended just up on 1977, the gains being in the paperbound categories. All professional books did quite well, as did non-racksized mass market paperbacks and college texts, but mail order fell back sharply in 1982 after a very prosperous 1981, and subscription reference and audio visual both closed well down over the period as a whole. The period 1977 to 1982, therefore, also brought about significant changes in the market despite its static size in 1981 compared to 1977. The number of units sold rose modestly, indicating a switch to cheaper, paperbound books, a phenomenon common elsewhere in the world. Partly as a result, the market proved very resilient until 1982, showing no real signs of recession other than, perhaps, the decline in mail order. El-hi is inevitably a declining market because of the fall in school rolls, but higher education is holding up, and, on the above evidence, capable of absorbing price increases above the rate of inflation.

1982 was, almost inevitably, a recession year, but recent reports foresee a considerably brighter picture for 1983, with trade book sales especially buoyant.

The above data includes both retail sales and sales to institutions. However, data on consumer expenditure is also prepared annually by the Book Industry Study Group. Table 4.2 sets this out for the latest four years. As can be seen, nearly all categories showed strong gains in money terms during 1980, with trade books leading the way, but after adjusting for inflation the aggregate total fell marginally indicating that the prosperity

TABLE 4.2 ESTIMATED US CONSUMER EXPENDITURE ON BOOKS

Units: $ million/million units

	1979 Dollars	1979 Units	1980 Dollars	1980 Units	1981 Dollars	1981 Units	1982 Dollars	1982 Units	Dollars per unit 1981	Dollars per unit 1982	% change
Trade	1,629	327	1,984	389	2,219	396	2,278	409	5.60	5.57	-0.5
Adult hardbound	977	130	1,161	152	1,333	167	1,226	139	7.99	8.80	10.1
Adult paperbound	368	96	479	116	532	104	648	107	5.10	6.06	18.8
Children's hardbound	222	59	251	64	263	70	287	77	3.75	3.72	-0.8
Children's paperbound	61	43	94	56	101	55	117	85	1.83	1.37	-25.1
Religious	480	108	516	99	575	96	633	98	5.96	6.42	7.7
Hardbound	332	41	346	37	404	39	443	40	10.28	11.15	8.5
Paperbound	148	67	170	62	171	57	190	59	2.99	3.23	8.0
Professional	868	53	998	52	1,099	52	1,224	55	21.16	22.19	4.9
Hardbound	686	29	796	29	870	29	958	29	30.04	32.80	9.2
Paperbound	182	23	202	22	230	23	266	26	9.98	10.24	2.6
Book club	493	221	524	211	555	210	565	180	2.63	3.12	18.6
Hardbound	368	64	404	66	431	65	438	57	6.62	7.69	16.2
Paperbound	124	157	119	144	124	145	126	123	.85	1.02	20.0
Mail order publications	499	46	578	51	675	60	617	55	11.28	11.32	0.4
Mass market publications	1,073	527	1,208	534	1,398	564	1,549	583	2.47	2.65	7.3

continued . . .

Table 4.2 continued. . .

	1979 Dollars	1979 Units	1980 Dollars	1980 Units	1981 Dollars	1981 Units	1982 Dollars	1982 Units	Dollars per unit 1981	Dollars per unit 1982	% change
University presses	71	8	82	9	87	10	94	10	8.98	9.59	6.8
Hardbound	54	4	60	4	61	4	66	4	15.35	15.97	4.0
Paperbound	17	4	22	5	26	6	28	6	4.57	4.96	8.5
El-hi text	913	261	936	251	996	253	1,075	247	3.94	4.34	10.2
Hardbound	504	100	504	95	559	102	596	102	5.46	5.85	7.1
Paperbound	409	161	432	155	438	151	480	146	2.90	3.29	13.4
College text	926	92	1,075	96	1,210	98	1,339	98	12.33	13.67	10.9
Hardbound	716	60	805	63	909	64	998	63	14.31	15.92	11.3
Paperbound	210	31	270	34	301	35	341	35	8.79	9.65	9.8
Subscription reference	356	1	322	0	328	1	333	1	328.50	333.40	1.5
TOTAL	7,308	1,644	8,224	1,694	9,141	1,742	9,707	1,736	5.24	5.59	6.7
at 1977 prices	4,236.5		4,174.6		4,201		4,206				

Source: Book Industry Trends, BISG

was illusory. With prices rising by 14% during the year, the only categories to show up well on a dollar per unit basis were religious titles and paperbound college texts, whereas trade books came out very badly. 1981 recovered some, but not all, of the ground lost in 1980 with most sectors showing modest gains after allowing for inflation. 1982, regarded as a deep recession year, does not give that impression, if the industry's own data are to be believed, because real sales value rose just a fraction and unit sales fell just a fraction, which is an acceptable performance. With inflation under control at 6% it was easier for turnover to keep pace, but the picture is certainly an erratic one if individual categories are examined. On a dollar per unit basis, trade books declined overall, with adult books showing up well and children's doing disastrously. Paperbound professional books, mail order, hardbound university and subscription reference were the other categories to fare badly, but excellent performances were turned in by bookclubs, paperbound El-hi and college texts. Certainly unit losses, as in adult hardbound trade, were cause for concern, but taking the longer view rather than placing too much significance upon a single year, only paper-bound El-hi and book clubs show an ongoing tendency to decline, countered by the ongoing gains shown by trade and mass market publications.

United Kingdom

The basic source of data on turnover is the Business Statistics Office Business Monitor series. Until 1982, PQ489 covered General Printing and Publishing, and prior to 1972 coverage was of establishments in the UK having a turnover of £10,000 or more, whose main business activity was the printing and publishing of everything other than newspapers and periodicals. From the beginning of 1973, the criterion for inclusion was changed to one of employment of 25 or more persons, or, in the case of book publishers, to one of employment of 6 or more persons. At the beginning of 1978 the employment threshold for book publishers was also raised from 6 to 25.

Prior to 1973, coverage was thought to account for 70% of the employment of establishments classified to the industry, but between 1973 and 1978 the low reporting threshold for book publishers resulted in returns being 'substantially complete'. The under-reporting prior to 1973 is not normally regarded as significant, but the increase in the threshold size for reporting in 1978 unquestionably resulted in under-reporting of some

104

significance, arising both from the exclusion of establishments below the threshold size and from incomplete response from firms of the relevant size. In making comparisons between the pre-1978 and post-1978 data it is therefore necessary to make an allowance, in the form of a grossing-up factor, for the exclusion of establishments employing between 6 and 24 people after 1971. However, a problem then arises in determining what this grossing-up factor should be.

Business Monitor itself records a varying set of 'official' grossing-up factors, which, when applied to the original, unadjusted data, gives the second column figures in table 4.3 below. These were, however, generally regarded as too high. Euromonitor, in their annual Book Reports, produced the alternative figures listed in the table, and the Cranfield School of Management Report calculated, in a variety of ways, that a consistent make-up of 6% should be applied every year, producing the figures in the following column. The Publishers' Association, as a result of their own monitoring system, opted for a relatively high set of grossing-up factors, but became more conservative than Business Monitor after 1981 on the grounds that the under-reporting related primarily to the non-book part of the industry. In 1983, the PQ 489 series was terminated and divided up into parts, one of which is PQ 4753 Printing and Publishing of Books. Because the new series relates solely to books, the grossing-up factor should be more accurate than previously. Business Monitor reckoned to have covered 59% of the new industry's employment in 1983, yielding a grossing-up factor of 1.689 for a total turnover of £1,357.5 million.

TABLE 4.3 UK ESTIMATES OF PUBLISHERS' TURNOVER[1]

Unit: £ million (current prices)

	Unadjusted Business Monitor	Grossed-up Business Monitor	Euromonitor	Cranfield Report	Publishers' Association
1978	505	714	585	535	751
1979	561	808	655	597	844
1980	648	942	750	686	976
1981	714	1,171	890	757	1,077
1982	732	1,263	945	776	1,100
1983	804	1,357	n.a.	n.a.	n.a.

[1] excluding royalties

Source: Department of Industry, *Business Monitor*/Euromonitor/Cranfield School of Management/Publishers' Association

Grossing-up factors are too general to be applied to anything other than the annual totals, so the unadjusted data are presented in table 4.4.

TABLE 4.4   SALES AND RECEIPTS OF UK GENERAL PRINTERS AND PUBLISHERS

Unit: £ million Category of book	1971	1978	1979	1980	1981	1982	1983[1]
Hardback							
Bibles	5.20	10.09	8.83	11.01	11.50	11.40	12.50
School textbooks	16.03	34.35	37.08	41.20	46.34	45.74	50.28
Technical & scientific	34.49	65.27	73.16	82.20	94.96	102.46	124.40
Fiction, literature							
& classics	23.00	58.19	59.83	78.06	83.28	84.58	72.22
Children's	15.07	32.02	36.59	39.42	42.65	44.13	48.35
Other	34.06	126.09	146.76	156.95	151.39	154.84	187.22
Paperback							
School textbooks	14.41	50.41	55.82	64.24	70.59	61.83	56.57
Technical & scientific	5.37	17.27	21.01	43.61	60.10	65.62	80.80
Fiction, literature							
& classics	18.58	66.59	69.17	73.54	87.40	95.04	102.42
Children's	4.37	12.29	14.68	13.85	15.25	14.83	18.54
Other (inc. bibles)	9.99	32.53	38.56	43.43	50.71	51.08	50.47
Total	180.59	505.10	561.49	647.51	714.17	731.56	803.77
Royalties	6.04	16.33	18.89	20.87	23.82	27.58	25.32
TOTAL	186.63	521.43	580.38	668.38	737.99	759.14	829.09

[1] not compatible with earlier years

Source: Department of Industry, *Business Monitor*

The figures for 1983 are not compatible with those for earlier years. Although most of the categories are identical, the division of the original 'Other' category almost certainly resulted in a reallocation of items amongst the various other categories. This incompatibility is enhanced if the three sub-sections of the 'Other' heading (reference, academic and professional, and other adult non-fiction) are aggregated together, so I have joined the academic and professional to the technical and scientific category and the reference to the other adult non-fiction in order to produce a better fit. The precise hardback break-down is reference 71.06; scientific, technical and medical 70.17; academic and professional 54.23; and other adult non-fiction 116.16, and the paperback break-down is 9.55, 57.19, 23.61 and 40.92 respectively.

On the face of it, things don't look too bad at all if one measures turn-over at current prices. But most of the increase is simply the result of inflation, so table 4.5, below, expresses the current price data in terms of constant 1971 prices, that is it removes the changes due to inflation. This is done using the Retail Price Index, although a section below refers to the other price indices which could also be used for this purpose.

TABLE 4.5 SALES AND RECEIPTS OF UK GENERAL PRINTERS AND PUBLISHERS CONSTANT PRICES

Unit: £ million at 1971 prices Category of book	1971	1978	1979	1980	1981	1982	1983[1]
Hardback							
Bibles	5.20	4.14	3.19	3.36	3.14	2.88	3.01
School textbooks	16.03	14.08	13.40	12.59	12.67	11.56	12.09
Technical & scientific	34.49	26.75	26.41	25.11	25.97	25.89	29.92
Fiction, literature & classics	23.00	23.85	21.59	23.85	22.77	21.37	18.57
Children's	15.07	13.12	13.21	12.04	11.66	11.15	11.63
Other	34.06	51.68	52.98	47.95	41.40	39.12	45.03
Paperback							
School textbooks	14.41	20.66	20.15	19.63	19.30	15.62	13.60
Technical & scientific	5.37	7.08	7.58	13.32	16.43	16.57	19.43
Fiction, literature & classics	18.58	27.29	24.97	22.47	23.90	24.01	24.63
Children's	4.37	5.04	5.30	4.23	4.17	3.75	4.46
Other (inc. bibles)	9.99	13.35	13.92	13.27	13.87	12.91	12.14
Total	180.59	207.04	202.70	197.82	195.28	184.83	194.51
Royalties	6.04	6.74	6.82	6.38	6.51	6.97	6.09
TOTAL	186.63	213.78	209.52	204.20	201.78	191.80	200.60

[1] not compatible with earlier years
Source: Table 4.4 amended by author

Although the conversion of money to real values is necessarily done using the unadjusted Business Monitor data, the trends depicted would only be unrepresentative were the grossing-up factors significantly different for different categories, and there is no reason to think that is the case. The major trends are as follows:

1. Annual changes in real turnover since 1971 for the unadjusted Business Monitor series have been as follows:

    1972 +6.1%;   1973 −1.2%;   1974 +6.7%;   1975 −1.6%;
    1976 +1.2%;   1977 −0.3%;   1978 +3.2%;   1979 −2.1%;
    1980 −2.4%;   1981 −1.3%;   1982 −5.4%;   1983 +5.2%.

The series indicates strongly that the period from 1971 to 1978 was characterised by a step forward followed by half a step backwards. Although the industry was prone to seeing crises around every corner, the general trend was one of modest real growth. Between 1978 and 1982, however, it was downhill all the way, with 1982 the worst in memory. Fortunately, 1983 recovered some of the lost ground, making good almost all of the 1982 losses. The recent picture can be varied according to which measure of turnover one uses. These appear in table 4.6 below, expressed as annual rates of change.

TABLE 4.6   UK: ANNUAL RATE OF CHANGE IN PUBLISHERS' REAL TURNOVER

Unit: %

	Unadjusted Business Monitor	Grossed-up Business Monitor	Euromonitor	Cranfield Report	Publishers' Association
1979/78	−2.1	−0.4	−1.5	−1.6	−1.2
1980/79	−2.4	−1.2	−3.0	−2.8	−2.0
1981/80	−1.3	+11.2	+6.0	−1.1	−1.2
1982/81	−5.4	−0.3	−1.7	−5.5	−5.7
1983/82	+5.2	+2.2	n.a.	n.a.	n.a.

Somewhat surprisingly, given its aversion to the unadjusted Business Monitor figures, the Publishers' Association figures show an almost identical rate of decline, which results from the use of a fairly static grossing-up factor. The sharp increase in the Business Monitor's grossing-up factor in 1981 appears to be misleading, although Euromonitor also consider 1981 to have been a good year. Given these ambiguities, the only safe conclusion is probably that the industry was doing no better, and probably a bit worse, at the end of 1982 compared to the end of 1978, but that the upturn has at last arrived, although it may be too soon to be sure that it will continue.

2. Taking paperback sales as a proportion of total turnover we find that there was a steady increase from 29% in 1971 to just over 36% in 1977. It stayed at roughly that level for three further years (1980 = 36.9%) then rose to a new peak of 39.8% in 1981. The past two years have, however, seen a subsequent decline to 39.4% in 1982 and 38.2% in 1983, which may indicate that a proportion of over 40% cannot be sustained.

3. If we examine individual paperback categories through to 1982 (1983 has to be ignored on the grounds of non-comparability), we discover a major switch from hardback to paperback in the case of both school textbooks and scientific and technical books during the late 1970s, essentially as a response to the very high prices of hardbacks in these categories. Fiction etc., on the other hand, showed little change through to 1982. In the case of children's books, where both hardbacks and paperbacks were in fairly continuous decline, the rate of decline (39%) was faster for paperbacks between 1975 and 1982 than for hardbacks (31%).

4. Overall the relative changes for each category, hardback and paperback, were as follows:

TABLE 4.7   UK PUBLISHERS' TURNOVER AT 1971 CONSTANT PRICES

Unit: £ million

	Bibles	School text-books	Technical and scientific	Fiction and literature	Children's	Other	Total
1975	4	33	36	48	22	55	198
1978	4	35	34	51	18	65	207
1979	3	34	34	47	18	67	203
1980	3	32	39	47	16	61	198
1981	3	33	42	46	16	55	195
1982	3	27	43	45	15	52	185

The significant decline in the total during 1980 to 1982 is, of course, by no means unique to the book industry. Indeed it was far worse in some other industries. The book industry was most obviously affected by the general decline in real disposable income, and by the cuts in public expenditure insofar as they affected institutional buyers. The total peaked in 1978, as did most of the individual categories, although the ambiguous 'Other' category held out until the following year. The exceptions are children's books which reached a peak as early as 1975 (which they are still well below 9 years later), and technical and scientific which staged a recovery beginning in 1979 and which surpassed the previous record of £42 million, set in 1972, in 1982. This was caused by real growth in the paperback section of 320% between 1972 and 1982, an extraordinary achievement and one for which no simple explanation has been suggested.

5.   All hardback categories bar 'Other' declined between 1975 and 1982. This category is too ill-defined to provide an obvious explanation, but the inclusion of most reference books in this category was a contributory factor since their prices rose faster than for any other category during the bulk of the period.

6.   It is salutary to compare the changes in title output with the changes in real turnover over the period studied. It must be remembered that more books are commissioned in prosperous years, but they do not reach the market until two or three years have elapsed.

TABLE 4.8   UK PUBLISHERS' TURNOVER AND TITLE OUTPUT 1975-1983

Unit: %

	All books	New books	Turnover at constant prices
1975	+ 10.6	+ 11.9	− 1.6
1978	+ 6.7	+ 6.7	+ 3.2
1979	+ 8.2	+ 11.2	− 2.1
1980	+ 14.8	+ 13.8	− 2.4
1981	− 10.5	− 9.9	− 1.3
1982	+ 12.1	+ 12.6	− 5.4
1983	+ 5.7	+ 2.7	+ 5.2
1971-83	+ 57.0	+ 65.4	+ 7.7
1975-83	+ 43.3	+ 43.1	− 5.5
1978-83	+ 31.7	+ 32.0	− 6.1

1974 was quite a good year for real turnover, and 1978 quite acceptable, so the upsurge in title output during 1980 is unsurprising, as is the drop in title output during 1981 following the poor results of 1979. But why then so many titles in 1982 and 1983? Surely not in the expectation of higher profits! With title output showing every sign of having risen yet again in 1984 despite 1982's dismal turnover, it is a touch surprising that the welcome mat has been put out for, of all things, a sharp increase in the number of children's titles. We will return to the issue of overproduction elsewhere.

Canada

Canada is an interesting market because it is dominated by imports. The basic structure of the market, at publishers' selling prices, appeared as follows in 1981:

111

TABLE 4.9   CANADA: STRUCTURE OF THE BOOK MARKET 1981

Unit: $ million

Imports

Textbooks	English 142.2	French 10.9		
Tradebooks	English 350.7	French 82.3		
Other books	English 143.4	French 27.3	Other 0.7	
TOTAL	English 636.3	French 120.5	Other 0.7 =	757.5
		By exclusive agents		126.4
		By publishers		236.9
		By retailers/wholesalers etc.		394.2

Home Sales less *Exports*

Textbooks	English 60.3	French 9.5		
Tradebooks	English 125.4	French 21.3		
Other books	English 39.7	French 13.5	Other 0.5	
TOTAL	English 225.4	French 44.3	Other 0.5 =	270.2
			Total market	1,027.7

Source: Calculations from statistics Canada

Imported books accounted for 74% of total sales in Canada in 1981. Publishers in Canada particularly increased their sales of imported books, with a 7% increase on 1980 in real terms. Imports by exclusive agents kept pace with inflation. Publishers' domestic sales of their own books included an English component of 83.4%. The predominant commercial category was trade books which accounted for 56% of English language sales and 48% of French language sales. The proportions of imported books by language and commercial category did not differ greatly from domestic sales.

A longer term view of the market appears in table 4.10.

TABLE 4.10   TRENDS IN CANADIAN MARKET STRUCTURE 1977-1981

Unit: $ million	1977	1978	1979	1980	1981
Home production	225.8	261.9	305.6	360.7	382.1
− Exports	57.4	73.4	97.3	104.0	111.9
= Home sales	168.4	188.5	208.3	256.7	270.2
+ Imports	431.9	496.5	608.3	675.0	757.5
= Home market	600.3	685.0	816.6	931.7	1,027.7
at 1977 prices	600.3	628.4	686.8	710.7	697.7

Source: Statistics Canada

Despite breaking the $1 billion mark in 1981 the Canadian market actually shrank in real terms, although not severely in relation to the late 1970s. 1982 may, however, prove even more difficult. As indicated above, Canadian publishers bore the brunt of the recession in 1981 rather than importers, and almost one third lost money on book sales despite only modest increases in production costs. English publishers are more prone to foreign control, primarily from the USA and UK, but French imports were a higher proportion of the total in 1981 than they had been for many years.

It is not easy to convert sales at publishers' prices into retail prices because of the unusual distribution channels in Canada, but an approximation would be as follows:

TABLE 4.11   RETAIL VALUE OF CANADIAN BOOK MARKET

Unit: $ million	Retail sales		$ per capita	
	Current prices	Constant prices	Current prices	Constant prices
1975	444	444	19.5	19.5
1976	490	456	21.3	19.8
1977	551	475	23.7	20.4
1978	633	500	27.0	21.3
1979	755	547	31.9	23.1
1980	870	572	36.3	23.9
1981	959	561	40.0	23.4

Source: Statistics Canada/Euromonitor

113

In money terms this represents a consistently good performance, with a doubling of the total between 1975 and 1980, and at constant prices the performance was satisfactory until 1981.

Australia

Around 250 publishers operate in Australia, of whom perhaps 200 are publishers in the conventional sense of the term. Few are large scale by US or UK standards. Statistical compilation is a recent phenomenon, and is not altogether reliable for year on year comparisons because of changes in the sample groups. The basic data for 1979 to 1982 appear as follows:

	1979	1980	1981	1982
(1) Total sales in Australia $A million	258	288	317	339

This figure is arrived at by grossing-up the returns of ABPA members (119 in 1982) to allow for incomplete coverage of the industry (1982 grossing-up factor = 1.25).

	1979	1980	1981	1982
(2) Retail book sales $A million	450	502	551	590

This is row (1) grossed-up to allow for an average bookseller discount of 42.5%.

This represents a 31% rise in money terms over the period, but after adjusting for inflation the series reads ($): 450, 480, 480, 463, so the market showed very little real growth other than in 1980.

In 1982, after adjusting for exports and imports, Australian books increased their share of the market, obtaining just over one-half for the first time. Too much faith should not, however, be placed in this conclusion because of changes in the firms sampled in successive years. Some light can be shed on the relationship between Australian and imported books in the wake of the demise of the Traditional Market Agreement by examining market share by nationality of ownership.

TABLE 4.12   AUSTRALIAN MARKET[1] SHARE BY NATIONALITY OF OWNERSHIP

Unit: %

	1980			1981			1982		
	Educa-tional	General	Total[2]	Educa-tional	General	Total[2]	Educa-tional	General	Total[2]
Australia	14	21	18	19	32	27	24	30	28
USA	57	30	41	48	28	35	31	28	29
UK	29	43	37	33	40	37	45	41	42
Other	0	6	4	0	1	1	0	1	1

[1] includes exports

[2] includes rights income, of which roughly 70% is earned by Australian publishers and 25% by UK publishers

Source: Australian Book Publishers' Association

The changing mix of firms sampled each year has probably depressed the true US market share in 1982. On the other hand, US publishers accounted for 66% of Australian book exports in 1982, and the shares of the Australian domestic market in 1982 were UK 44%, Australia 29%, USA 26% and Other 1%. It therefore seems reasonable to interpret the figures to mean that Australian imprints are making increasing inroads into their domestic market, essentially at the expense of US imprints. This tendency, and the buoyancy of the UK market share, has occurred almost entirely because of changes in the educational market, very little change having occurred in the general market. In many ways, this is unexpected because there is less volatility in educational book buying, where imprints can earn a reputation for quality, than in general publishing. Evidently, the demise of the Traditional Market Agreement did not stimulate all US imprints to try harder.

Some of the difficulties in comparing data based on differing samples have been overcome by the use of smaller control groups which are identical every year. Data is available for 1978-1982 for a cross-section of 18 firms, accounting for roughly 30% of all the turnover and 50% of all new and reprint titles.

TABLE 4.13   ABPA 18 FIRM CONTROL GROUP SALES

Unit: $A million

	1978	1979	1980	1981	1982	1982[1]
Australian educational	16.7	18.9	21.5	25.7	29.0	(19.8)
Australian general	10.9	13.2	11.9	11.8	14.7	(10.0)
Imported educational	18.8	20.2	21.9	23.8	22.6	(15.4)
Imported general	28.0	29.9	29.2	31.3	41.7	(28.5)
Total domestic sales	74.4	82.2	84.6	92.7	108.1	(73.7)
Exports	2.9	3.1	3.1	3.0	3.4	(2.3)
Total sales	77.3	85.3	87.7	95.7	111.5	(76.0)
at 1978 prices	77.3	74.2	73.0	72.6	76.0	

[1] at 1978 prices

The picture presented in current price terms is, as usual, rather illusory. Once inflation is allowed for, it immediately becomes obvious that there were three poor years for the control group from 1979-81, and that even 1982 was a bit worse than 1978. The same conclusion is true for general books, whether Australian or imported. Exports suffered in real terms, but the biggest transition was the switch from imported to Australian educational books.

The ABPA is also able to provide a second control group, consisting of the 55 of the 119 firms analysed above which submitted returns for 1981, 1982 and 1983.

Comparison with the previous table shows Australian publishers in an improved light, with general book sales as buoyant in real terms as educational, and exports holding up well. Taking the three series of real turnover together it would appear that 1982, which was a poor year for the market as a whole, was a holding year for the bigger control group yet rather prosperous for the small control group. As these are mainly larger, established, firms, this must help protect them from the impact of recession.

TABLE 4.14   ABPA 55 FIRM CONTROL GROUP SALES

Unit: $A million

	1980	1981	1982	1982[1]
Australian educational	28.4	35.4	41.7	(34.2)
Australian general	41.8	52.8	60.2	(49.4)
Imported educational	32.8	35.5	35.2	(28.9)
Imported general	54.7	62.7	72.0	(59.0)
Sale of rights	0.2	0.2	0.1	(0.1)
Total domestic sales	157.9	186.6	209.2	(171.6)
Exports	12.0	15.7	15.6	(12.8)
Total sales	169.9	202.3	224.8	(184.4)
at 1980 prices	169.9	184.3	184.4	

[1] at 1980 prices

An individual set of statistics is available for 8 mass-market paperback publishers for the period 1978-1983, accounting between them for some 85% of all paperback sales in Australia. For the period 1981-1983, a 15 firm sample, including the original 8, is also available.

TABLE 4.15   AUSTRALIA: CONSOLIDATED PAPERBACK STATISTICS FROM 8 COMPANIES

Unit: $A million

	1978	1979	1980	1981	1982[2]	1983[2]	1983[3]
Retail sales gross	69.4[1]	86.0[1]	97.6	102.6	128.4	136.5	(84.7)
Less returns (%)	22.0	25.8	35.8	23.6	30.4	30.8	
Retail sales net	54.1	63.9	62.7	78.4	89.3	94.5	(58.6)
of which							
Adult	49.7	58.8	57.2	71.0	81.0	84.6	(52.5)
Children's	4.4	5.1	5.5	7.4	8.3	9.9	(6.1)

[1] excludes Sphere; [2] not completely compatible with earlier years; [3] at 1978 prices
Source: Australian Book Publishers' Association

117

The great variability in the rate of returns makes analysis difficult, although it may possibly have found its level at around 30%. As this is well above the figure for 1978/79 the effect, once inflation is allowed for, is to transform a substantial rise in the real gross figure between 1978 and 1983 to a very modest rise of 8% in the real net figure. Not surprisingly, unit sales reflect this, as table 4.16 shows.

TABLE 4.16   AUSTRALIAN UNIT RETAIL SALES FOR 8 COMPANIES

Unit: millions[1]	1978	1979	1980	1981	1982	1983
Adult	17.8	17.8	15.1	16.9	17.1	16.6
Children's	2.5	2.3	2.4	2.6	2.6	3.0
TOTAL	20.3	20.1	17.5	19.5	19.7	19.6

[1] turnover value ÷ average retail yield
Source: Australian Book Publishers' Association

A similar picture appears if one examines the 15 firm sample.

Gross and net retail sales, adjusted for inflation, are as follows:

TABLE 4.17   AUSTRALIA: GROSS AND NET RETAIL SALES, ADJUSTED FOR INFLATION (15 FIRM SAMPLE)

Unit: $A million	1981	1982	1983
Real gross retail sales	107.2	122.6	117.6
Real net retail sales	81.7	85.6	81.8

Source: ABPA

1981 and 1982 were good years, as table 4.17 indicates, showing an excellent recovery from the 1980 recession and, although there was inevitably a dip in 1983, the market is proving remarkably resilient.

Consumer expenditure on books is not itemised separately in the national accounts statistics but is included with papers and artists goods. Assuming that 75% of books are sold to the general public, a fairly crude estimate of retail book sales for 1982 comes out at $A 500 million, a figure which would indicate a modest rate of real growth since 1977. Expenditure per household was roughly $A 110 in 1982, again indicating modest real growth despite the imposition of a 2½% sales tax at the beginning of 1982.

Chapter Five

BOOK DISTRIBUTION

Of all the problems faced by the book publishing industry that of distributing the product is widely regarded as the most intractable. The most obvious explanation as to why distribution should be more difficult in the case of books compared to most other consumer products is to be found in the sheer variety of the product on offer. Between them, the UK and USA list nearly one million books as officially in print. The total number of books available in English alone must, therefore, lie between 1½ and 2 million, and if other languages are added in, the grand total is truly astonishing.

Naturally a large proportion of this total are hardly ever demanded, but this 'advantage' is more than offset by the fact that a single copy only may be wanted, almost anywhere in the world, and somehow the product has got to reach the customer. Standing in its way are a whole variety of obstructions. Relatively few books go directly from publisher to customer whether nationally or internationally. Mostly they have to travel along a route involving intermediaries such as wholesalers and retailers and, in the case of international trade, to be associated with form filling, currency regulations, import restrictions and possibly censorship. These various factors at best cause delays, and at worst cause chaos.

Although one may well feel inclined to the view that such problems simply should not occur, the temptation is understandably to try to rationalise the distribution process in order to improve speed and accuracy. One way of achieving this is to restrict the type of book (often done for political reasons) to be allowed free access to a market. Another, in international trade, is to limit the aggregate value of what is allowed free access irrespective of content. Another is to require that items do not travel singly but in bulk, possibly being gathered together at either the exporting or importing end where borders are to be crossed. Consolidation has the obvious advantage of cost reductions in transit and of improved control over where the item is at any point in time, but it inevitably creates delays.

Consolidation is likely to be associated with some kind of wholesaling facility, and this will be true whether trade is national or international in its scope. But no wholesaler can remotely hope to cope with the full range of titles on offer, so his role will often involve a process of selection which, by its very nature, must deny some element of choice to the customer. All this amounts in total to reasonable reductions in cost and some improvement in efficiency and security of delivery, to be set against restrictions of choice and delays in delivery. This would suggest that there is no magic wand which can be waved in order to make all distribution problems disappear. There are, in particular, certain additional problems which tend to arise when less developed countries are involved. The most obvious of these concerns is the need for such countries to pay for their purchases in a currency acceptable to the vendor. Many such countries simply don't have enough foreign currency to spare for imports of books, and some that traditionally were satisfactory in this respect, can, like Nigeria in recent times, rather suddenly prove extremely reluctant to pay up.

Shortages of foreign currency may result in import restrictions, although these may equally well arise in order, for example, to protect home producers. The biggest drawback to such quotas is that they are usually indiscriminate, and thus have an unpredictable impact upon prospective suppliers. However, even when books do enter such countries there are still problems to overcome. Although communications facilities are reasonable in major urban areas, they are likely to be inadequate elsewhere. As a result the product may never reach the market, either because it is mislaid, damaged, stolen or simply stuck at one point in the distribution chain. Climatic conditions are themselves unconducive to long shelf life in many countries, and may indeed harm the product before it reaches the shelf if, for example, warehousing facilities are inadequate.

Sectors of Distribution

In the sections which follow we will be examining a number of facets of distribution systems. If one examines changes in distribution systems over time one may be struck in particular by the declining role of the stockholding bookseller. Everyone, it seems, wants to cream off the profitable parts of his business, leaving him with the awkward and unprofitable parts. Were it not for resale price maintenance, analysed elsewhere, the survival of the species in many countries would be endangered. A number of general trends have proved damaging to the stockholding bookshop. In the first place, for example, there has been the emergence of book clubs, prospering either where bookshops are thin on the ground, or where increases in literacy have been accompanied by a desire on the part of the newly literate to have their decisions about reading matter largely taken on their behalf by the clubs. Secondly, there has been the introduction of books into department stores and super-markets where only a limited selection of fast moving titles are held in stock, and display and promotional techniques are years ahead of those used in. traditional bookshops. Thirdly, there has been a reduction in institutional sales, either because of budget reductions or because publishers have refused to provide the discounts necessary to make such business profitable. Finally, there have been difficulties in setting up dis-tribution systems which get books from publishers to booksellers cheaply and efficiently. This list is by no means exhaustive, but it does give some indication of the major forces at work in the retail market for books today.

Wholesaling

The heart of the book distribution problem in developed countries lies in the transmission of too many orders of too little value between large numbers of publishers and retail outlets. The immediate solution which presents itself is to set up an efficient wholesaling operation, and it is therefore hardly surprising that many developed countries chose that route from an early stage in the development of the trade. It must be borne in mind that a distribution system's efficiency does not necessarily reflect the efficiency of individual publishers and booksellers. Another way of expressing this point is to say that if UK publishers operated in the content of the West German distribution system, then books would arrive in the hands of booksellers as rapidly as do the books of West German publishers. The trouble is that efficiency requires discipline, and if such discipline was not introduced at an early stage in the development of a distribution system it becomes ever harder to introduce at progres-sively later stages. The essential reason for this is that if development occurs on an individualistic rather than communal basis, each participant increasingly comes to believe that his contribution is perfectly sound whereas the problem lies in every other participant's inefficient individu-alism.

The biggest contrast lies between the general continental pattern and that in the USA and, in particular, the UK. In the latter case there was indeed some attempt to set up an efficient wholesaling service between the wars, when Simpkin Marshall held stocks of all important publishers' lists sufficient to service single-copy and small-value orders from booksellers. Unfortunately, publishers were unwilling to offer attractive discounts, and the company folded in 1955. Subsequently, no replacement has emerged on a similar scale, and in the absence of a national wholesaler most large publishers set up their own warehousing complexes. This in turn destroyed the potential of such a wholesaler since publishers were doing so much business direct from their own warehouses. From the viewpoint of each individual publisher, this was the correct path to take in the pursuit of self-interest, but the results for the system as a whole were deplorable. The system does not preclude a role for wholesalers, indeed a number currently exist and operate efficiently on a limited geographic scale. In addition, as discussed elsewhere, the beginnings of the introduction of technology such as teleordering cannot help but improve distribution. Nevertheless, the two day delivery time which is quite common on the continent is still regarded as unrealistic in the UK.

It is interesting to look at an example of a continental operation at this stage, because it is becoming noticeable that there are always dangers lurking ready to undermine even the most efficient of distribution arrangements. The Centraal Boekhuis (CB) was founded nearly 160 years ago in Amsterdam, but is currently sited at Culembourg within easy reach of Belgium and Germany. It is a private company jointly owned by publishers and booksellers. It both acts as a stockist for part of the lists of major Dutch publishers, and for the entire list of smaller publishers. Roughly 85% of the lists which it handles can be supplied directly from stock, most of the rest being in the process of reprinting. In recent years the major publishers have accounted for an increasingly large proportion of CB's total turnover. In particular a publisher conglomerate, UDC and Elsevier, represents 30% of total turnover.

In addition to its other functions CB always acted as a small order supplier to booksellers, who initially sent their bulk orders direct to publishers. But the 48 hour service maintained by CB promoted a higher order frequency, each order being smaller in size, and increasingly less business was transacted direct with publishers. Booksellers benefited from this arrangement because CB did not penalise small orders whereas most publishers did, but the drying up of bulk orders from booksellers inevitably reduced the publisher's overall profit margin because it had to grant a higher discount to CB than would have been accorded to individual booksellers, and simultaneously reduced the economic justification for publishers' existing costly warehousing facilities.

124

In principle, this made it seem sensible for UDC and Elsevier to transfer back to their own warehouses, leaving CB in the lurch. The alternative was to reduce the structure of discounts.

Ironically, the fulfilment of the bookseller's dream in the UK, namely a rapid delivery system without penalties, apparently sows the seeds of its own downfall because it begins to look like the fulfilment of the publisher's nightmare of high overheads and heavy discounts. When business booms the nightmare is put off, but the coming of recession soon eats into publishers' profits and inclines them to transfer part of the suffering back on to the other parts of the distribution system.

At the end of the day, what these examples show is that there is no unique solution to the ideal relationship between publisher, wholesaler and retailer. Nevertheless, they do indicate certain respects in which existing systems clearly are not ideal. Superficially there are enormous attractions in a system whereby the publisher sells to the retailer at a lower discount than he would be forced to allow to a wholesaler. Equally the retailer then ends up with a bigger discount than the wholesaler can afford to allow to him. The retailer gets his periodic gossip with the publisher's representative, and can make his returns direct to the publisher. Against this, however, must be set the errors and delays which inevitably accompany a system in which so many individual participants have so many individual contacts. Logically an intermediary is needed if these latter difficulties are to be overcome, but intermediaries have drawbacks. A publisher is only interested in selling his own books, whereas a wholesaler is indifferent whose books he sells. The publisher and bookseller see themselves as part of a cultural system, whereas the wholesaler is in it for the money.

In many European countries the driving force has been rather different. If the customer wants the product the objective is to get it to him as quickly and efficiently as possible. The book business is ultimately about doing business. But if the customer is not buying enough, who is to bear the burden, publisher, wholesaler or retailer? None is likely to volunteer. Perhaps it all boils down to a choice between speed of delivery and size of discount. If a bookseller wants a small order to be fulfilled very quickly he may have to become reconciled to some sort of small order surcharge. On the other hand an innovatory system may be required with the following objectives in mind: to do away with small order surcharges; to provide an acceptable service (i.e. slower than Dutch, faster than the UK); to organise a central order consolidation system which minimises

125

stock holding; to do all these things without radically changing existing practices or requiring new technology. A solution does exist in principle which meets these objectives[1] although it has to be said that it requires both a teleordering system, SAN's and ISBN's, and, here's the rub as they say, an awful lot of subscribers to the system. The countries with the bits of the system they need such as the UK are too individualistic, so there aren't enough subscribers. The countries which can organise the subscribers don't have the system sufficiently well developed. Something along the lines of the recently introduced American Booksellers Association's Booksellers Order System may therefore prove an acceptable staging post. BUS electronically receives the bulk booksellers' orders which are passed on to publishers. They then invoice BUS which invoices booksellers without any small order penalties. It is too early to say how well this will work out in practice.

Chain Booksellers

Traditionally the stockholding bookshop was an independent operation, with perhaps the odd branch or two but no more. One consequence of this was to maintain market power in the hands of the supplying publishers at a time when the retailing of other commodities was becoming concentrated in the hands of a number of chains, and the power being transferred from manufacturer to retailer. In recent years, however, the book industry has at last begun to show signs of moving in the same direction, partly as a consequence of the evident unprofitability of the typical independent bookshop.

In the United States, for example, the 1977 Census discussed above also shed light on the rapid growth of bookstore chains. Sales of multi-unit bookstores rose 133% from 1972 to 1977 compared to 110% for industry sales as a whole, and sales of firms owning 51 or more units rose 212%. The two largest firms, Waldenbooks and Dalton, have subsequently continued to increase their market share. In 1980 Waldenbooks earned a revenue of $260 million from 650 stores, and expected to own another 100 stores by end-year 1981. Dalton earned a similar revenue from 435 stores, and anticipated owning 600 by end-year 1981. Altogether the 9 largest chains expected to acquire another 300 stores between them by end-year 1981, although the two leading chains dwarfed all the others in terms of numbers of outlets.

[1] see H. Mackennan's article in the *Bookseller* (June 30th, 1984)

126

One obvious consequence was that individual proprietorships, although they represented more than half of the total number of bookstores, were already doing less than 20% of the turnover by 1980. An American tendency which will doubtless be reflected elsewhere in developing countries during the 1980s is for corporations to take over the larger outlets. No doubt the end result will approximate the old rule of thumb that 80% of the business goes through 20% of the outlets.

The position in the UK bears some resemblance to the US position. Once again there are two dominant retail chains, W.H.Smith and John Menzies, although these have moved a long way away from a specialist bookselling operation (a W.H.Smith store will now typically have one floor in three devoted to books). In 1982, W.H.Smith owned 425 stores, and Menzies 260, of which a number are station bookstalls. However, Smiths not only own some 350 stores mostly located in High Streets, but they also own a stockholding bookshop chain Bowes and Bowes. The success of these two groups as compared to the rather dismal performance of the independents has, not surprisingly, set other groups off in the same direction. Typically, however, these are more akin to stockholding bookshops than to a typical W.H.Smith operation, and tend to be associated with a wholesaling function which can act as a powerful central buying unit for the chain. Websters and Hammricks are examples of this development, but it is fair to say that the current rate of expansion is fairly slow and regionally concentrated. Other groups which are expansion minded are also unlikely to have acquired a chain of more than 20-30 shops by the end of the decade, and again are regionally concentrated, but these obviously represent quite large chains in relation to the overall market. Their development is ultimately constrained by the limited number of ideal sites for a bookshop. It is clear that, whereas a stockholding independent can survive other than in the High Street provided there is no chain outlet in the latter, the chains need to locate in central positions, and this in turn means that they need a very high turnover to succeed. Although best seen in terms of US and UK experience, the logic of these developments is universal among developed countries. The imbalance of power in the market place in favour of publishers cannot last for ever, just as it has not lasted in other retailing operations. The only obvious reservation which is bound to be expressed concerns the consequences for the independent outlets, since these may find that the terms offered by publishers are inferior to those offered to chains, and insufficient for survival. Furthermore, the appearance of a chain outlet in the same vicinity is likely to be very damaging. Unfortunately, the disappearance of the small retailer is likely to be a consequence of the growth of chains, but it has to be said that this is very much in line with retailing trends in general.

Non-bookshop Outlets

Stockholding bookshops hold a representative sample of the whole spectrum of book categories. Non-bookshop outlets do not, but rather concentrate upon mass-market paperbacks, low priced reference books/ dictionaries, hobby and leisure books, and remainders. The characteristics which make these attractive categories for such outlets are their relatively fast stockturn, and their reliance upon impulse buying. Customers must buy what is in there in stock, so there is no need for a high level of staffing nor many other expenses incurred by the bookshop. By the same token, the price range of the stock is at the lower end of the spectrum, reflecting the disposability of many items bought on impulse. Remainders are particularly attractive in this respect as, despite their low prices, they are often expensively packaged books, so they appear to be exceptional value for money. Despite this the retailer does very well from such sales because of the low buying-in prices which he himself pays.

Such outlets are regarded as a threat by stockholding bookshops. Into the same category would come book-clubs and certain direct purchasing agencies. These are discussed in more detail below. Another recent development, this time in America where there is no rpm (retail price maintenance), is the proliferation of discount bookselling chains. These obtain best-sellers at big discounts off list prices and, by moving into a neighbourhood on a big scale, attract a significant share of the market away from established outlets. This being America, certain lawsuits are currently pending on the grounds that the scale of the discounts cannot be justified in terms of cost savings to publishers, and are therefore illegal. Such practices would, of course, not be feasible in countries where rpm is in force.

Remainders

The use of books as loss-leaders is sometimes practised in countries without rpm. However, even if rpm is a force, it is perfectly legal to sell remainders at any prices the retailer so chooses. We have discussed elsewhere the increasing tendency for publishers to toss titles into the marketplace on a speculative basis, and the increasing returns resulting

128

therefrom. Such returns, and any unsold stock, must either be destroyed or sold to a remainder dealer as a job lot at knockdown prices in order to generate cash-flow. Because buying-in costs are so low, the potential profitability of selling at well below retail prices is often better than that available to established bookshops trading at full retail prices. Furthermore, because of the nature of the business, customer accessibility is essential, and High Street locations are far commoner for such outlets than for stockholding bookshops, thereby generating at least a partial expectation among the general public that full price sales are tantamount to exploitation. Remaindering is not, however, the key to a fortune, particularly since some quite prominent remainder firms do go bankrupt. This may result from over-indulgent advertising, a shortage of suitable products, adverse exchange rates if remainders are imported, or simply a reluctance to spend on books of any kind in a recession. However, the continued presence of remainder merchants in prominent sites is a thorn in the side of bookselling associations everywhere.

Book Clubs

There are two main sorts of book club. The first, generally known as 'simultaneous', offer a book club version of a published title within a short time period of its original publication. The two versions will normally appear to be identical, although the book club insignia will normally be added to the author/publisher information on the dust-jacket, the title page and, perhaps, the binding. The second, generally known as 'reprint', offer titles which have been in print for a significant period of time. The club version will reprint the original text, but bind it in the club's own format and quite possibly use cheaper raw materials, so the two versions, if examined together, will appear visibly different. Because sales of the original version are less obviously affected by the reprint version its rights will be sold to the club at a very high discount.

A book club can offer its titles in a variety of ways; the main ones are set out below:

1. Members receive a catalogue, generally monthly, which contains a recommended choice. This has to be actively rejected or it will automatically be sent. Any book listed in the catalogue may be ordered at any time, but the overall commitment is of the so many books per year form rather than a one per time period form.

2.   Members receive a regular catalogue from which to select a given number of books in the course of a year. No club selection is specified.

3.   Club selections are sent, sight unseen, at regular intervals, often with no facility to return unwanted titles.

4.   Members must order a minimum number of books, or pay at least a minimum sum, as a condition of joining. Further purchases are entirely at the member's discretion.

5.   Members pay a joining fee which covers the receipt of a number of titles during the year, generally these will be club selections with no element of choice allowed.

6.   Members pay a joining fee which covers the receipt of a number of titles during the year which can be chosen at random from catalogues sent to the members. Joining fees are non-refundable.

Book club editions are always sold at a discount off retail price, often a quite substantial discount. This reflects a number of savings in relation to normal trade practice. In the first place there is no retailer involved, nor wholesaler, and although postage has to be paid by the club, which isn't by any means insignificant, this is invariably charged to the member's account. Secondly, a simultaneous club edition allows the publisher to increase his print run significantly and hence to achieve economies of scale which can be passed on to the club. Thirdly, where the club edition is a reprint, the rights may be bought from the publisher very cheaply, and the production process may be chosen to produce a poor-quality version of the original. Finally the club edition may have been purchased very cheaply as a publisher's remainder.

Because the member pays postage the potential savings are necessarily much reduced. Postage may be related to the parcel's weight, expressed as a percentage of the book's price, or expressed as a rate per book sent. The typical 25% discount will probably end up closer to 15%, but for cheaper books the discount may be almost entirely wiped out.

Because members often fail to appreciate the effects of postage they may well join clubs in order to obtain what they perceive as cheap hardback books. However, the main reason for joining is the nature of the

130

introductory offer which generally offers huge discounts and cheap postage. These offers occasionally constitute loss-leaders, but in most cases they simply represent the club's unsold stock of titles resulting from an over-optimistic print-run, or remainders specially bought in for the offers.

The losses associated with introductory offers are one reason for the heavy preliminary costs incurred in setting up a book club. In addition there are the costs incurred in buying a list of suitable prospective members and of mail shots to these, most of which are wasted. Heavy general advertising and promotion is required, and the costs of obtaining and holding stock, and the preparation and making of catalogues, escalate rapidly. It is unlikely for these reasons that a book club can hope to show a decent profit in much under five years, and if during that time the market goes into recession the club may prove a radically different proposition from the licence to print money which is the image fostered by other parts of the book trade.

The most obvious difficulty in running a club is that a large percentage of the membership resigns every year. Some, quite sensibly from their point of view, move from club to club in order to take advantage of the joining offers. Others simply run out of choices which interest them. The consequence is that a club must attract at least as many new members as it is losing in order to make any headway at all, yet those who join, only to depart at the earliest opportunity, offer no prospects for longer-term profits.

Unlike a traditional publishing operation, which is rarely strong on marketing, book clubs must market effectively or die.

In the UK the typical breakdown of the price of a club hardback is:

Payment to publisher	30%
Advertising/promotion	30%
Gross margin	40%

Again, for illustrative purposes, advertising and promotion expenditure by book clubs and by publishers can be compared for the UK:

	Clubs/mail order (£000s)	Publishers (£000s)
1975	1,620	1,231
1976	2,050	1,862
1977	2,773	1,984
1978	4,352	2,146
1979	4,877	3,323
1980	5,802	4,732
1981	7,754	6,249
1982	7,299	7,398

As can be seen, only very recently has expenditure by publishers matched that by clubs. However, this is ongoing expenditure and has to be added to any losses incurred by clubs in attracting members which may itself take a full year's membership to recover.

This expenditure obviously brings into focus the whole question as to whether it does or does not rub off on the rest of the book trade. Book club supporters argue that their expenditure necessarily increases the size of the overall market for books, especially given the reluctance on the part of publishers to promote their products at all extensively. Secondly, by increasing publisher's print-runs for simultaneous editions they reduce their unit costs and allow them to be sold more cheaply to the trade. On the other hand, members of the trade are increasingly drawn to the conclusion that clubs really prefer to force up the trade prices of their selections so that their money-off approach looks more attractive, with serious implications for trade sales. Many publishers are also changing their tune somewhat, arguing that whilst it is logical for a book club to demand an ever bigger discount in return for a guaranteed increase in the size of the print run, there must come a point where publishers' profitability will actually decline rather than increase, especially since most clubs expect publishers to do most of the storage. Furthermore high discounts leave very little for authors. A 10% royalty doesn't amount to much when it is based upon a net 20% of the retail price. Many authors are, therefore, declining the opportunity to appear in a book club edition, which was unheard of until fairly recently.

The Leisure Circle Approach:

Although the great majority of book clubs tackle their marketing in the manner described above, the Leisure Circle offer an interesting example of an alternative approach. The club is owned by the West German Bertelsmann Group, and its main method of generating members is through door to door canvassing using self-employed agents working on commission. Whereas the main book clubs often aim their promotional material at the top socio-economic groups, the Leisure Circle aim further down market, and hence are not in direct confrontation with other clubs. In effect the club seeks to tap the great army of irregular book buyers, rather than the more limited number who already spend money regularly on books. Quite a high proportion of membership is female.

Leisure Circle also operates through Club Centres, of which there are around 300 in West Germany, in some cases operating within the confines of a traditional bookshop. These are well established in France, Austria, the Netherlands and Italy, but have proved a failure so far in the UK. The great virtue of such centres is that they avoid postal charges and allow members to take a look at the product rather than relying upon a catalogue. As a result, turnover per member is predictably higher than for traditional clubs, but it is interesting that the latter have not chosen to follow suit.

It is rather difficult to draw any definite conclusions about the role of book clubs, simply because they are ultimately a mixture of good and bad consequences which vary in intensity from country to country. On the plus side are deals which make good money for both publishers and authors, and where club publicity boosts bookshop sales; are deals which reduce the retail price of the books; are deals which result in the publication of books which would not have been published without the deal. On the minus side are deals which earn very little for either author or publisher; are deals which result in higher retail prices; are deals which damage trade sales. Certainly there is a question mark both over their role in life and their economic viability. In the former case this particularly affects countries where resale price maintenance is in force because book clubs can easily be perceived as undermining its existence. The more jaundiced members of the book trade tend to see clubs as a sophisticated exercise in cut-price selling which has little to do with their original, nobler objectives. In the latter case it is certainly disturbing that, despite the massive discounts, clubs do not necessarily make a profit, for some damaging side-effects are bound to occur. This suggests

133

that the money sunk in unprofitable club operations could have been put to better use elsewhere in the system.

However, until such time as every town and village possesses a stock-holding bookshop, many prospective book buyers must rely upon clubs as an alternative distribution channel. No doubt the trials and tribulations which clubs face in a number of countries will eventually result in an acceptable equilibrium position being reached which satisfies the various book trade participants. In most countries, however, it is unlikely that this will be the case. Although one cannot, for example, put any kind of categoric figure upon the percentage share of the market which is excessive for the book club sector, it would certainly appear to be excessive in countries such as the Netherlands and Sweden. The obvious danger lies in the ability of the clubs virtually to dictate which books will sell in large quantities and which will not, and the general level of prices at which books are to be sold. It is unlikely that countries which have yet to develop book clubs to this degree will do so in the foreseeable future. Nevertheless the running battle between clubs and other outlets is liable to flare up periodically because there does seem to be some tendency for the clubs to bend the rules, often deliberately, in order to establish a new status quo more favourable to themselves.

We cannot expect to return to the days when, as in the UK prior to 1968, clubs were obliged to meet quite onerous conditions. The pressure from the USA, as ever antithetical to regulations, especially with respect to simultaneous editions, was bound to see to that. But simultaneous publication was not to be the end of the road. UK experience is representative of what can happen. In 1968 simultaneous clubs were first permitted to function. Originally the discount off net price was limited, but this no longer holds good; the format was to differ from the trade edition, but is now often identical; the number of choices to be made was regulated, but now clubs do much as they please; the trade was to be informed in advance of titles to be produced as club editions, but now little if any advance warning is given; the number of books to be offered cheaply to entice members was limited to 12, but is now 18; reprint clubs had to wait a minimum time after first publication, but now often issue their choices early.

Under the circumstances the danger is that the public will come increasingly to view club books as a straightforward, but cheaper, alternative to obtaining topical bestsellers from bookshops. Bookclubs won't make too much headway in the UK simply because libraries are cheaper than any form of purchase, but in countries where good bookshops and libraries are scarcer on the ground the sorts of practices set out above will ensure that bookclubs will never be accepted as a gentlemanly way to sell books.

Mail Order

Mail order is especially significant in the USA. Independent estimates, based upon the total mail order market, suggest that the total sales of books by this method may be 2 to 3 times as large as suggested in the Association of American Publishers' statistics. Bearing in mind that there are roughly 20,000 bookstore outlets it may appear surprising on the face of it that mail order should be such a thriving business. However, America is a vast country, and many bookstores hold in stock only a small proportion of available titles. Hence potential customers for relatively specialized titles may be unable to obtain them efficiently and quickly other than via the mail order method. Obviously a bookstore can order such titles for a customer, but he first of all needs to know of their existence, and that is where a mail order company scores heavily because it can obtain lists of people working in specific occupations and direct mail order shots at these target markets.

The use of mail order is obviously enhanced by a wide dispersion of population and a lack of stockholding bookshops. Equally it is inhibited by a good library system where expensive titles can be consulted at little or no cost by occasional users. Under such circumstances the very high proportion of sales which are mail order/direct to public in a country such as West Germany are somewhat surprising, and perhaps suggest that the potential of these methods has yet to be fully exploited in similar countries where historically such methods have been little used.

It is interesting in this context to examine a recent skirmish in the UK where direct selling is, like book club selling, regarded as anathema by stockholding bookshops. The basic justification put forward by the publishers is the same as that used in the case of book clubs, namely that many customers who learn of offers through direct mail publicity then go to their local bookshops to obtain the books. The publishers argue that established methods of reaching potential customers are woefully inadequate, and that even direct mail shots cannot hope to generate a response of more than 10%, a 1% response being the outcome in many cases, so it is hardly a case of destroying the bookshops' potential markets. A responsible publisher will in any case point out that postage and packing has to be charged for direct sales, and that the titles can be obtained from bookshops.

Evidence put forward by direct mail publishers indicates that it is by no means uncommon for the bulk of orders to be directed through trade outlets, and that even where the bulk of orders come direct to the publishers, those directed through bookshops tend to follow rather than precede the direct selling campaign. It must be borne in mind that mail order often relates to educational/professional titles where much of the buying is done by institutions through normal trade channels.

Given the relatively low response rate, the cost per title sold of direct selling may well be a factor inhibiting the spread of this practice. One must remember that the basic method itself is freely available to any organisation, bookstores included, who are willing to buy the lists of target markets which are commercially available, and to spend the necessary sums on postage. The fact that they generally prefer not to do so may well reflect their prevailing view of the riskiness of such operations. Nevertheless, it hardly makes sense for outlets which refuse to take the risk to complain subsequently that it damages their business, for if this were really the case they would be foolish not to participate in direct selling themselves.

In addition to straightforward distribution of books direct from publisher or bookseller, the term mail order is generally used to include publishers who offer their own titles in a continuity series, that is a series with a common theme. The customer agrees to buy the first title in the series and subsequently gets sent further titles in the series, usually on an automatic basis, with the right to cancel the subscription at any time. In the USA companies such as Time-Life and Grolier derive most of the revenue from such continuity series. Generally their books contain a good deal of illustrative material and are aimed at the sort of people who do not customarily browse in bookshops. Prices are kept within modest bounds by the tendency for those who subscribe to take additional books in the series, although it is roughly as expensive to obtain subscribers as it is for a bookclub, despite the absence of big premium offers. A book club does at least have a guarantee of a minimum subsequent purchase, whereas the continuity series subscriber may even return the original volume as unsuitable or may buy no other books in the series. Test marketing is, therefore, a sensible, if expensive, strategy, and the heavy

136

costs involved tend to make this an area of publishing dominated by a relatively small number of very large firms. Not unexpectedly, mail order selling generally is liable to suffer badly in a recession because it is easy for subscribers to cancel an order to save money. There is also no opportunity for impulse buying on which bookstores depend so much.

Distribution Systems

It is a fairly obvious truism that only countries with a high level of consumer expenditure on books need sophisticated book distribution systems. Such systems are, therefore, confined to parts of Europe, North America and Australasia; in other parts of the world, very little information is known about how books are distributed. Even in the highly developed markets it is not easy to be precise about how books reach buyers because such information generally requires a detailed survey to be conducted, and there is no uniform definition of outlets in use. The table below attempts to summarise the proportions of sales which go through different distribution channels, but it must be borne in mind that, for example, the distinction between supermarkets, food outlets and drugstores is necessarily blurred at the edges.

The rest of this distribution study concentrates upon the US and UK experience, before briefly reviewing book retailing in other selected markets around the world.

United States

The last official survey of the US retail trade was in 1977, when bookstores' sales totalled $1.84 billion, which in that year represented about 45% of the retail market for books. Unfortunately, in the survey's analysis of the distribution of sales by particular goods, books are included with magazines and newspapers. Nevertheless it is possible to rework the data to produce the distribution of sales by outlet set out in table 5.1.

137

TABLE 5.1   DISTRIBUTION OF BOOKS, WORLDWIDE SURVEY

% breakdown

	Year	Book shops	Department/ other stores	Super-markets	CTNs[1]	News-stands	Book clubs	Mail order	Direct to public	Direct to SLI[2]	Distrib-utors	Instal-ment sales	State book-seller
Belgium	1980	45	5	3			20		7				
Denmark	1982	72					—19—	5					
Finland	1981	48						14			11	22	
France	1982	—39—					3			2	34		
Ireland	1980	55	12	2	20		1		2				
Italy	1980	28	2				6½	7½				48	
Netherlands	1982	48[3]	6				27	8					
Norway	1980	60	5				17						
Sweden	1980	30	9				—35—	12					
Switzerland	1980	55	23							14½			
UK	1982	60	7	2	10		8		5				
W.Germany	1981	61½	7½				7½	6½	11½				
Bulgaria	1982	76											
GDR	1979	25											75
USA	1981	47	5	7			8	10	19				
Canada	1980	—23—					3	1			14		
Australia	1980	33	15	10	30		10						
New Zealand	1981	65	12	12	10			8					
Japan	1981	75	8				—5—						
India	1980	45					30						
S.Africa	1980	68					5			12			
Brazil[4]	1979	20½				21	1½	3		24	16½		

[1] confectioners, tobacconists, newsagents; [2] schools, libraries, institutions; [3] including kiosks; [4] % of volume

Source: Own calcuations from national sources

The 1977 survey indicated that there were some 12,720 bookstores operating in the USA in 1977, controlled by roughly 10,600 separate businesses. 81.4% of these were single unit businesses, and these accounted for 52% of bookstore sales. On the other hand the 7.4% of businesses with over 51 outlets accounted for 17% of total sales. Between 1972 and 1977, the major growth area had been chain stores, and their continued growth beyond 1977 increased their share of the market to roughly 55% by 1981. In that year the total number of outlets had grown to 17,708 and by 1983 it had grown to 19,580. The table below indicates the type of outlet in both years, with some comparable data for Canada to illustrate how the distribution system can develop in different ways even in neighbouring countries.

TABLE 5.2   BOOKSTORES IN NORTH AMERICA

	USA				Canada	
	1981	%	**1983**	%	**1983**	%
Antiquarian	993	5.6	1,086	5.5	86	4.3
Mail order (antiquarian)	594	3.3	631	3.2	22	1.1
College	2,703	15.3	2,857	14.6	144	7.3
Department store	1,201	6.8	948	4.8	109	5.5
Drugstore	22		21		4	
Educational	98		112		20	
Exporter-importer	28		30		1	
Foreign language	94		17		38	
General	5,409	30.5	5,757	29.4	984	49.7
Gift shop	95		110		9	
Juvenile	133		154		29	
Law	63		67		3	
Mail order (general)	313	1.8	361	1.8	14	0.7
Medical	102		119		3	
Museum/art gallery	228		n.a.		n.a.	
Newsdealer	129		131		6	
Office supply	48		62		2	
Paperback[1]	754	4.3	767	3.9	35	1.8
Religious	2,576	14.5	3,664	18.7	205	10.4
Remainders	18		21		4	
Rental	4		4		0	

continued...

139

Table 5.2 continued...

	USA				Canada	
	1981	**%**	**1983**	**%**	**1983**	**%**
Science-technology	61		71		8	
Stationer	148		143		24	
Used	494	2.8	724	3.7	48	2.4
Other	1,400	7.9	1,723	8.8	180	9.1
TOTAL	17,708		19,580		1,978	

[1] excludes paperback departments of general bookstores, department stores, stationers, drugstores or wholesalers handling paperbacks

Source: American Book Trade Directory

The 21,558 stores of various types in 1983 shown in Table 5.2 are located in approximately 6,300 cities in the United States, Canada, and regions administered by the United States. All 'general' bookstores are assumed to carry hardbound (trade) books, paperbacks and children's books; special effort has been made to apply this category only to bookstores for which this term can properly be applied. All 'college' stores are assumed to carry college-level textbooks. The term 'educational' is used for outlets handling school textbooks up to and including the high school level. The category 'mail order' has been confined to those outlets that sell general trade books by mail and are not book clubs; all others operating by mail have been classified according to the kinds of books carried. The term 'antiquarian' covers dealers in old and rare books. Stores handling only secondhand books are classified by the category 'used'. The category 'paperbacks' represents stores with stock consisting of more than an 80% holding of paperbound books. Other stores with paperback departments are listed under the major classification ('general', 'department store', 'stationers', etc.), with the fact that paperbacks are carried given in the entry. A bookstore that specialises in a subject to the extent of 50% of its stock has that subject designated as its major category.

The number of bookstores in America rose by over 10% between 1981 and 1983, a commendable performance. Of these the majority were general stores, followed at a considerable distance by religious and college bookstores. No other categories had as much as 10% of the total. The number of department stores stocking books fell sharply, but the really significant reduction was in the number of foreign language book-stores. On the other hand, there was a pleasing increase in the number of juvenile bookstores (rather surprising in the light of sales of children's books), as well as a lot more office supply, religious, used book and non-specific bookstores.

The Canadian distribution is very different, with 50% of all book-stores being general, a figure slightly down on 1981. There are only half as many college bookstores as in America and mail order bookstores are uncommon. Religiosity is also evidently less popular than in the USA, and rather few stores specialise only in paperbacks.

The percentage of the market accounted for by bookstores, excluding the vast numbers of college and religious outlets, was roughly 2 points higher in 1981 (47.5%) compared to 1977 (45.5%), largely as a result of growth among the chains. Possibly because of improved access to these outlets the share of the market held by department stores fell one per-centage point during the same period. On the other hand supermarkets managed to gain a half percentage point despite their concentration upon mass-market paperbacks which were not a growth area.

There are an appreciable number of stores dealing in mail order, a phenomenon by no means unknown elsewhere as table 5.1 indicated, but the overall scale is far larger than in any other country. This form of selling is quite resilient, maintaining its share of the market intact over the past decade or so. Interestingly the same is not true of book clubs which were level pegging in 1977, but two percentage points down by 1981.

Somewhat surprisingly the American Booksellers Association does not review its members' fortunes every year, but rather conducts a far rang-ing survey on a periodic basis. One was conducted in 1977, and another in 1981[1]. The latter survey elicited 320 responses, which is slightly less than the UK sample despite the much larger market size. The most obvi-ous feature in common with the UK is the avowedly unprofitable nature of the business combined with no shortage of people willing to soldier on regardless. The 1977 survey revealed that roughly one-half of the sample were unprofitable when judged against what might reasonably have been expected of them, yet this had apparently become an even more promi-nent feature of bookselling by 1981.

[1] see *American Bookseller,* January 1982

It is possible to examine how the recession has affected distribution channels in the USA by reference to table 5.3.

In money terms the picture is quite rosy, but in practice the real value of consumer expenditure fell sharply in 1980 and has yet to rise back to its 1979 level. The brunt of this recession has not, however, been felt by general retailers, college and other stores, but entirely by libraries, schools, and sales direct to customers. The first two categories understandably reflect the tight budgetary situation of institutions, so the real blow has been the unwillingness of consumers to spend their disposable income on direct purchasing. The picture is not so bad in volume terms as these are well up on 1979 levels, but the switch to cheaper types of books has obvious consequences for publishers.

United Kingdom

For a good many years now a core group of stockholding bookshops in the UK, known as the Charter Group, have been subjected to a thorough analysis which forms the heart of this section. The Group are more important than their numbers suggest as they account for a substantial part of the retail bookshop trade. In return for improved discounts from publishers the Charter bookseller must bring his shop up to a laid-down standard, train his staff, and maintain a proper bibliographical service.

It should be borne in mind that price competition is not permitted for the great majority of books. Since it is unusual for Charter booksellers to be found within a short walk of one another there is very little direct competition. This not surprisingly results in the stability of the larger bookshops, but there is considerable movement at the smaller end of the size spectrum, not as a result of competition but rather as a result of poor profitability. It is easy to become a bookseller, but not so easy to remain one for long.

The results, which appear in Diagram 5.1, are so poor that many critics are prone to level the accusation that they are fiddled by creative accounting. It is very difficult to pass judgement on such an issue, but it does have to be recognised that the figures are taken from audited accounts, so the creativity is presumably no greater than for any other trade, and must be considered by the tax authorities. The proportion of businesses making a loss is certainly on the high side.

142

TABLE 5.3 CHANNELS OF US BOOK DISTRIBUTION — ESTIMATED CONSUMER EXPENDITURE

Unit: $ million

	1979		1980		1981		1982		Million units			
	Money	1979 prices	Money	1979 prices	Money	1979 prices	Money	1979 prices	1979	1980	1981	1982
General retailers	2,542	2,542	3,028	2,651	3,497	2,773	3,754	2,806	682	736	785	814
College stores	1,231	1,231	1,437	1,258	1,625	1,289	1,792	1,339	189	197	201	204
Libraries & institutions	605	605	660	578	683	541	751	561	72	73	66	62
Schools	1,177	1,177	1,222	1,070	1,268	1,005	1,330	994	319	308	293	283
Direct to consumer	1,659	1,659	1,769	1,549	1,950	1,546	1,938	1,448	320	315	326	293
Other	93	93	108	95	118	94	141	105	61	63	70	79
TOTAL	7,308	7,308	8,224	7,201	9,141	7,248	9,706	7,253	1,644	1,694	1,741	1,735

Source: *Book Industry Trends*

143

TABLE 5.4   UK BOOKSHOP PROFITABILITY AND COSTS

	1972	1975	1980	1981	1982
Completed questionnaires	352	355	347	346	326
% sales:					
Retail	50.5	53.0	60.1	57.0	38.7
Library	9.4	9.3	8.2	7.1	5.0
Book agents	0.6	0.5	0.4	0.4	0.2
Schools	9.4	6.1	4.2	3.5	4.1
Other goods	30.1	31.1	27.1	32.0	54.0
Gross profit[1]	26.3	27.8	29.2	29.4	29.8
Total expenses[1]	21.6	23.5	27.3	28.6	28.8
a) Wages/salaries[1]	12.7	14.1	16.8	15.9	15.8
b) Rent/rates[1]	2.9	2.9	3.9	4.7	4.8
c) Other working expenses[1]	6.0	6.5	6.6	8.0	8.2
Net (trading) profit[1]	4.7	4.3	1.9	0.8	1.0
Stockturn per annum	4.7	4.0	3.8	3.5	4.3
Sales per person employed (£'000)	9.0	13.7	28.9	32.4	37.5
Sales per sq.ft. floor space (£)	41.9	58.0	116.0	110.0	123.0
% write down of book stock			39.3	38.8	39.5

[1] all expressed as % of total sales
Source: Charter Economic Surveys

Only one in three small businesses (turnover less than £82,000) made a profit in 1982-3, and the medium/large businesses (turnover roughly £200,000 to £400,000) seem to be doing increasingly badly. The ability of the largest companies to remain profitable may, perhaps, be accounted for primarily by their management expertise.

The outlets are not identical from year to year. In 1982, for example, there were 49 outlets not appearing in 1981, and 69 outlets in the 1981

Diagram 5.1.

% Making a loss

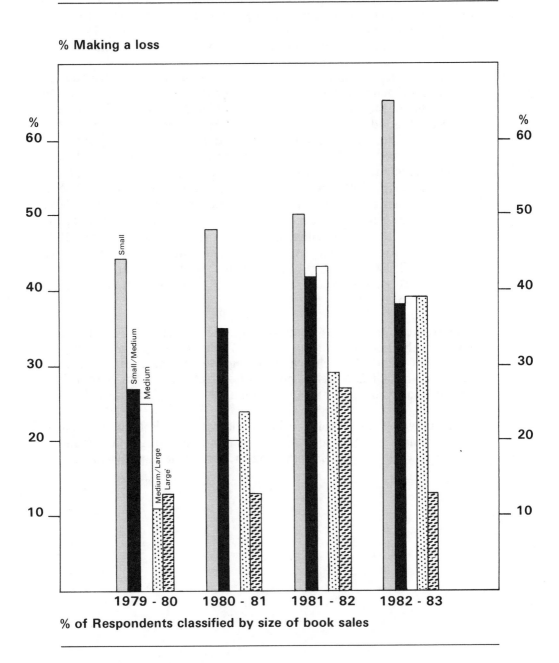

% of Respondents classified by size of book sales

Source : Charter Economic Survey

sample did not report data for 1982. Unfortunately, the 1982 figures are distorted by the arrival of one very large firm with a large non-book turnover. Excluding that firm results in a column sequence of 325; 55.0; 7.1; 0.3; 3.1; 34.5, which is much closer to the previous year's data.

Over the decade examined stockholding bookshops have evidently become more dependent upon retail rather than institutional sales. On the other hand, there has been no consistent tendency to switch into sales of non-book goods although these have been rather more prominent in recent years. Gross profit margins have gradually improved as publishers have been forced to allow higher discounts, if only to keep outlets in business, but net trading profit has fallen in virtually every year as expenses have shot up. Both wage costs and rents/rates have contributed to this rise in expenses in most years. Clearly the most sensible way to offset rising expenses is to improve stockturn, but here again the table suggests that the opposite has happened, with stockturn falling steadily (the 1982 result may be caused in part by changes in the sample). The sales figures show superficially healthy improvements, but after adjusting for inflation sales per person are rather better than in 1975 but sales per sq. ft. of floor space rather worse.

Bankruptcies are not as common as these figures might lead one to suppose, although the allegedly genteel nature of the trade may endure a tolerance of what would elsewhere be regarded as unacceptable rates of return. The book trade itself is not short of explanations for the continuation of poor results, and it is to this matter that we must now turn.

The following paragraphs review basic retailing data for the major European markets and a selection of the more interesting markets in the rest of the world for which details on the retail trade are available.

Western Europe

Belgium: There are about 6,000 outlets selling books in Belgium. These include 300 specialist bookshops, 5,000 newsagents of which perhaps 3,500 stock a substantial number of books, and 700 large stores including department stores and supermarkets.

Denmark: The number of retail outlets selling books, stationery and magazines has fallen quite sharply in recent years from over 2,200 in 1974 to only around 1,600 today, but this decline in outlets is due principally to closures of the smaller outlets, so the proportion of book sales passing through these outlets has fallen very little. About 700 outlets are engaged primarily in the selling of books, the largest being in Copenhagen. Book club and mail order sales are a relatively significant force in the market.

Finland: Recent figures show a large decline in the number of bookshops in Finland. Bookshops proper, and branches of bookshops totalled almost 500 at the beginning of the 1970s, but there were only 300 in 1980 and their share of the market had predictably declined. On the other hand, the number of small bookshops and agencies had grown in number, and totalled 233 in 1980.

France: In general, the marketing and distribution of books is carried out either by the individual publisher's own sales department or by a distributor, known as the 'diffuseur'. The latter may himself be a publisher who distributes other publishers' books as well as his own, or an independent distributor who does not depend on any particular publisher for his business but may handle the distribution for any publisher. 'Diffuseurs' operate through a variety of different outlets, including wholesalers who, with only around 10% of publishers' turnover, have never been a very significant force in the distribution network, and currently account for 35% of publishers' turnover. The principal 'diffuseurs' include Hachette, les Messageries du Livre, Sodis and Odeon-Diffusion.

On the retail side there are some 25,000 outlets selling books, of which less than 5,000 are mainly concerned with the selling of books and stationery. Bookshops currently account for approximately 40% of book sales, and these bookshops are heavily concentrated in Paris where the largest shops are found, accounting for up to a third of total sales of general literature. The largest bookshops in terms of turnover are les Presses Universitaires de France, le Furet du Nord and FNAC

147

(Fédération Nationale d'Achat des Cadres) which in the Paris branch alone has annual sales of over half a million copies.

Traditional bookshops are now, however, being challenged by the growth of supermarkets and hypermarkets, channels which are quite distinct from normal bookshops. Their growing importance is mainly due to their concentration on mass market best-sellers and children's books, which together account for 50% of book turnover in hyper-markets.

Although declining in significance, direct sales through door-to-door selling still accounts for 9-10% of publishers' turnover, the books offered being mainly expensive editions such as encyclopaedias. Mail order selling continues to represent a growing share of publishers' turn-over, over 13% in 1982, with publishers involved in this method of selling including France Loisirs (Presses de la Cité), Livre de Paris (Hachette), Laffont, Rombaldi, Reader's Digest and Tallandier. Book club member-ship in France is currently around 4 million, the largest club being France Loisirs with 5.5% of the total book market in 1979.

Italy: Some 75 million books are sold annually in Italy. There are 530 firms of distributors, and over 20,000 booksellers of which 10,000 are bookstalls, 500 are stockholding bookshops, and the rest stores of vari-ous kinds. Book clubs have done well in recent years, but the unusual feature of the market is the huge share taken by instalment sales.

Netherlands: The distribution channels in the Netherlands have changed very little in recent years, indicating that the surge in book club sales has reached an equilibrium. The number of stockholding bookshops declined during the 1970s to a total of 750 whilst book clubs boomed, partly through a process of merger. However, this merger activity should now largely be at an end.

Norway: There are about 615 bookshops in Norway, most of which are concentrated in the more heavily populated southern regions. Roughly 20% of them are to be found in Oslo. Such shops have long enjoyed the bulk of sales, but, as is true elsewhere, other outlets such as department stores seem set to muscle in on the market. Outlying areas offer good opportunities for book club sales, which are correspondingly high and may well have further growth potential.

148

Spain: There are currently 500 or so bookshops, only 50 or 60 of which are fully stocked. 3,500 stationers shops sell books, and there are some 11,000 further points of sale.

Retail booksellers are the main channel of distribution of books in Spain, though some country areas are poorly served in this capacity. There are a number of door-to-door salesmen ('Corredores') representing publishers and/or wholesalers, and they tend to deal mainly in books in the higher price ranges such as encyclopaedias. There are also several hundred 'Distribuidores' or wholesalers (some of which specialise in the distribution of foreign titles) who deal with the bookshops. Some large publishing houses own their own wholesaling operations.

There are an increasing number of specialist bookshops in Madrid and Barcelona, and a large number of 'ordinary' bookshops sell stationery, greeting cards, etc. Most kiosks deal only with newspapers and magazines, but some are licensed to sell books, a large percentage of which are paperbacks. Book clubs are growing in membership and importance, the two principal ones are offshoots of the German publishing groups Bertelsmann and George von Holzbrinck.

Sweden: The abolition of resale price maintenance has reduced the share of the market held by stockholding bookshops. Discounting has helped department stores and food outlets to take a larger share of the market, and book clubs and mail order sales have also done well.

West Germany: Books are sold through nearly 10,000 outlets in West Germany. Perhaps 3,500 are technically bookshops, the rest being department stores, food outlets, kiosks and consumer markets ('Verbrauchermarkt'). The structure of distribution has barely altered for the better part of a decade, which is at odds with experience in other parts of Europe, and it is especially noteworthy that stockholding bookshops have held on to over 60% by value of the retail market.

Eastern Europe

Bulgaria: The State Corporation Knigorazprostranenie is responsible for a chain of bookselling organisations in the capital and throughout the country, and also owns warehouses and transport. It supplies over 1,600 bookstores in the country, including 'Universal Bookstores' which deal with all types of literature and comprise 81% of the total number, and specialised bookstores, selling, for example, technical or medical books. There are, in addition, large stores called Homes of the Book (over 3,500 square metres in extent), planned for every large town, although only a few were in existence in 1982, 'Pavillions' (kiosks) and the recently established organisation 'Friends of the Book'. This includes voluntary workers who distribute books in schools, factories and other institutions. Currently they number over 25,000 people organised in 3,000 clubs, and are increasing steadily. Bookstores account for roughly 75% of retail sales, and the other organisations for 25%.

Czechoslovakia: Distribution is centralised under the state distribution organisation Zahrancini Literatura and the national enterprise Kniha Hlarniho Mesta in Prague. Books are distributed according to the size and turnover of the bookseller.

East Germany: The 800 state booksellers account for 75% of retail turnover, and are relatively free to make their own purchases subject to a centralised budget. The other 25% of turnover is accounted for by the 1,400 private sector booksellers.

Hungary: There are some 500 bookshops excluding railway kiosks and selling points in factories. There are several specialist shops dealing with foreign language publications and a number that sell only scientific and technical works.

Poland: The Booksellers' Union (Zjednoczenie Ksiegarstwa) is the body responsible for book distribution in Poland. Its book warehouses buy books from the publishers and sell them to the retail bookshops of Dom Ksiazki (House of Books) which operates a national chain, and to other distributors. The Ruch enterprise runs a network of kiosks as well as its 64 press and book clubs, and books are also sold through rural trade co-operatives such as Samopomoc Chlopska (peasants' self-help). Orwan Pan sells books published by the Polish Academy of Science.

Rest of the World

Mexico: Most sales to the public are through bookshops, although there are some clubs and a small amount of trade through department and general stores. In 1975 there were around 1,100 retailing booksellers and a further 136 wholesalers selling books direct to the public.

Brazil: The 1979 distribution channels listed in the table had changed quite appreciably compared to 1976. In the latter year agents were recorded as distributing 48% of books. By 1979 this was down to 16½%, and news-stands were doing 21% of the volume of business compared to only 2½% in 1976. However, distributors rather than publishers directly would have been responsible for much of the business done by news-stands.

Israel: Virtually all sales of books are through bookshops who buy through wholesalers. There are very few general stores selling books, and book clubs are in their infancy. There is one old established book club, but book clubs have not yet caught on to any great extent.

Kenya: Internally, textbooks are distributed under the Kenya School Equipment Scheme organised by the Ministry of Education. There were 205 bookstores and other selling points in 1980, some 163 being in towns, especially Nairobi. The textbook centre in Nairobi alone accounted for 20% of total turnover of the book market.

India: Distribution is probably the biggest stumbling block to the development of the retail market. Bookshops are only found in the large cities while many provincial towns must rely upon the local railway station bookstall. Most publishers attempt to organise their own national distribution as there are few bookstore chains in operation.

Pakistan: There are few wholesalers: publishers supply books directly to retailers as well as, in many cases, selling books themselves. Bookshops are concentrated in Karachi and Lahore, while many of the smaller towns and villages have shops selling only textbooks which, in practice, constitute the sole mass market for books.

Bangladesh: The domestic book market is fairly large and the number of booksellers, although unknown, is considerable. However, few of them keep substantial stocks and most are concerned with retailing textbooks and 'Bazaar Notes'. There were 12 good sized bookshops in 1982, mostly in Dacca, and some with networks in the country districts. There are no wholesalers, and booksellers from outside the capital very often buy discounted stock from Dacca bookshops.

China: All books within China are distributed and sold by Xinhua Book Store through its network of 5,800 state bookshops plus roughly 59,000 bookselling stalls or counters attached to rural supply and marketing co-operatives. A National Conference on urban book distribution, held in 1982, urged an increase in the number of collectively owned book-stores and stalls.

Taiwan: There were well over 20,000 retail outlets in Taiwan in 1979 selling books, stationery and music. A feature of the book trade is the development of the 'Book City' which acts almost as a book super-market. Some Book Cities rent stalls to different publishers. Others are owned by publishers but sell other publishers' books.

Japan: In 1982 Japan had over 78,000 stores selling books and station-ery, but sales through bookstores accounted for roughly 60% of gross sales of books and magazines. Bookstores are currently showing real growth, turnover of stock is good at 3.9, and so is the ratio of gross profit to sales at 21.3% although part of this stems from non-book sales. There are three bookstores with a massive turnover, but convenience stores are beginning to accumulate a big enough market share to threaten smaller bookshops, and this may reflect the low value of the average purchase at £1.67.

Australia: About 75% of sales are to the general public, and 25% to the institutional sector. Of the latter 70% are educational books. Bookshops account for 40% of sales overall and about one-third of retail sales to the public.

TABLE 5.5   RETAIL STRUCTURE IN AUSTRALIA 1980

Unit: % Retail only		All sales			
			Educational	General	Total
Bookshops	33	Bookshops	24	45	40
Newsagents	30	Other retail	5	32	20
Department stores	15	Direct mail	1	20	15
Mail order	10	Institutional	70	3	25
Book clubs	10				
Other	2				

Australia lends itself to direct selling because of the distances involved and the lack of bookshops in rural areas. All told there were only 4,362 est-ablishments selling books, newspapers and stationery in Australia in 1980.

New Zealand: There were 750 booksellers operating in New Zealand in 1977-1978. Most were small, single location establishments. Many books are ordered directly from overseas countries by New Zealanders and do not consequently pass through any type of retail channel. These may account for as much as 20% of the total market.

Distribution in Less Developed Countries

Developed countries, with their high per-capita incomes and very high levels of literacy, have developed sophisticated distribution systems for books. Such systems cannot be utilised in less developed countries not least because of their expense. On the whole, for example, there is rarely any justification for a wholesaling operation given the scale on which distribution occurs, and it is by no means unknown for publishers to double up as booksellers.

Bookshops as such are rare, being mostly located in the relatively affluent urban centres, and elsewhere the trade may be predominantly in second-hand texts sold on street stalls. In the rural areas there is unlikely to be anything even on that scale. The problem, therefore, is how to distribute small numbers of books to a widely dispersed audience. There is no single answer to this question. One possibility is to set up a huge agency network such as the Home Library Club system in India. An alternative, favoured in Mexico, is to use schools as distribution centres using schoolteachers as agents. Ideally libraries would play a role, but the evidence presented elsewhere suggests that this is more of a hope than of an expectation in the majority of cases.

Bestsellers and Returns

Possibly the most significant relationship which publishers in developed countries need to take into account is that between rights income, bestsellers and returns. Although the obtaining of income from the sale of subsidiary rights is an old-established phenomenon, it is only in fairly recent times, with the appearance of mass-market paperbacks, that the sale of rights has become a life or death matter for many publishers. The potential markets are huge. A bestseller title in America will sell several million copies, and in a major European market several hundred thousand. The potential profits from a bestseller are far too large for a publisher not to want to join in the fray.

153

A publisher who can market a title in hardback which receives public acclaim can obtain subsidiary rights income in three principal ways: firstly from the sale of paperback rights; secondly from the sale of book club rights; and thirdly from the sale of television rights. It is the last of these which is increasingly significant. In America, bestsellers in extended film format are regularly churned out; whereas in the UK the preference is for a multi-instalment version to be presented over a period of weeks. Hence a hardback house which doesn't get its titles spotted as potential bestsellers is in real trouble because it is a simple fact of life that only a small proportion of hardback titles actually achieve that status, whereas most of the rest lose money. Of course a bestseller can attain that status without first going through a hardback printing, or alternatively both editions may come out simultaneously. Subsidiary rights to a hardback imprint may not, therefore, necessarily be involved. Nevertheless, paperback imprints need bestsellers just as much as hardback imprints, either because, having paid out a whacking advance for the paperback rights, the money has got to be recovered through sales volume, or simply because few mass-market paperbacks are held in stock for more than a few weeks and only those that are make any kind of profit.

The real problem is knowing a bestseller when you see it for the first time. Sometimes it is easy. A TV company may decide to do a series based around a book or an author, and this is certain to send viewers out into the bookshops. Sometimes it is all a question of the 'hype' element, although hypes are not always successful, and very costly when they aren't. Sometimes it simply happens out of the blue, and the publisher, short of stocks and unsure why it has happened, needs do no more than keep enough copies entering the distribution system.

But if spotting winners is ultimately rather a hit and miss affair, what is the most sensible strategy for a publisher to follow? The answer in practice (few publishers give any thought to its theoretical soundness) is to pump out more and more titles on the grounds that if, say, one hundred titles per year attain bestseller status, you stand a better chance of some being yours if your share of total output is 10% compared to a share of only 5%. The trouble is that all the other publishers are playing the same game, hence, among other consequences, the ever rising number of titles. Provided the overall market is buoyant this may not prove particularly unsatisfactory, but in a recession year it is little short of disastrous. Increasingly, the bestseller is not adding to aggregate sales, but simply transferring them from other mass-market titles, and this in turn harms the development of new authors, very few of whom feature in the bestseller lists.

This also ties in with the channels of distribution, because of the issue of returns. Many books, and especially mass-market paperbacks, are sold on a sale or return basis. It is critical, therefore, for a publisher to get his titles held as stock items rather than as ephemera which are returned by the bookseller very quickly. Obviously a stockholding bookshop will tend to be conservative in its returns, whereas newsagents, railway bookstalls etc. will constantly want new titles to promote before the public. Equally it is clear that this affects different kinds of books, and the table below, which is based upon current UK experience, but which is very much in line with experience elsewhere, illustrates this.

TABLE 5.6   UK: RETURNED BOOKS BY VALUE

Unit: % gross sales	Home sales		Export sales		Total sales	
	1982	1983	1982	1983	1982	1983
Mass market paperbacks	14	15	13	15	14	15
General books	6	5	3	2	6	5
Specialised books	3	4	2	2	2	3
School books	3	2	2	4	2	3
University publications	4	4	4	5	3	4
All books	7	7	5	6	6	7

Source: Publishers' Association Statistical Bulletin

The figure for mass market paperbacks is almost certainly too low because in 1982 4 of the leading 11 paperback imprints reported returns of over 20%, and only 1 of under 10%. The general view in the UK, and elsewhere, was that only sales by established authors were at all good. One response has been to print fewer copies at a time, but more frequently, so as to reduce the potential scale of surplus stock. A critical relationship is between sales from stock and sales of new titles since returns are part of the latter magnitude. Hence if sales from stock are poor the ratio of returns to total sales is certain to rise, and this is increasingly the nature of the problem in developed markets. This in turn discourages the holding of stock, and returns may be made so quickly that many new titles never really get a chance to get established. The only items held in

155

stock tend to be bestsellers, so they increasingly dominate the market, and this tempts paperback houses to offer to distributors packages of bestsellers and weaker titles on an all or nothing basis. Thus, at the end of the day, few new imprints, if any, can hope to break into the ranks of well established paperback houses, and the latter in their turn find themselves bidding ever higher sums for bestseller rights and facing increasing mountains of returns.

Technology and Distribution

Many of the drawbacks to book distribution can be laid at the door of the human element. Labour is expensive, unpredictable and error-prone. This obviously suggests that technology presents opportunities to overcome these deficiencies. The original solution widely favoured by publishers was to set up their own warehousing complexes, often some distance away from major conurbations, and develop computer invoicing systems. In certain cases special book delivery systems were instituted. But the individualistic approach has one major disadvantage, namely it makes it increasingly difficult for communal solutions to be devised.

Technology, on the whole, bears greatest fruits when applied commercially. In the sections below we will refer to a few areas where the common approach has not been damaged by the actions of individual publishers. The first of these are International Standard Book Numbers (ISBNs). The use of ISBNs is essential, not merely because identification by author or title can lead to considerable confusion if even minor inaccuracies occur, but also because a standard numbering system is ideal for computerised operations. The great virtue of the ISBN system is its sheer simplicity, substituting as it does a limited number of digits for a possibly lengthy and confusing author and title identification. The system in the UK, although still not as fully utilised as it should be, is a good example of what should be done in this respect.

The ISBN identifies the publisher. A similar system can be used to identify the customer. Any purchasing outlet can be given a standard Account Number, and this can be applied on a worldwide basis.

A third application is that of Machine Readable Codes. This ideally involves the combined use of two machine-readable technologies which

156

are already fairly commonplace for other products, namely bar codes and optical character recognition (OCR). This latter part is, of course, extractable by a person doing paperwork, but the real virtue of the system lies in the ability of a machine to extract data off a book cover, or indeed catalogue, advance jacket or advertisement in order to feed a computer database. For example, a library can track them down if they are not returned. A bookshop can record the loss of each item from stock as it is sold and trigger off an order for a replacement automatically. This should much reduce reordering delays and hence allow a small stock per title to be held without disappointing potential purchasers.

This latter point ties in with the electronic transmission of orders, known commonly as teleordering. This was developed in Germany where most bookshops record their orders on to a tape inside their computer terminals. These are linked to a wholesaler's computer by phone, and the orders can be read off by the latter at any time of the day or night. The computer then prints out the invoices, and this is used as the basis for looking out, packing and despatching the order direct from the wholesaler's stock.

The bookseller identifies his orders using stock numbers obtained from an ultrafiche catalogue supplied by the system's operators. This yields exact details concerning the customer, the title, the size of the order, and an order identification number. If working smoothly this eliminates mistakes in picking from stock and in invoicing incorrectly, and generally reduces the volume of queries which can arise at any stage of the ordering process. Potential savings are obvious. Fewer errors means less time spent on rectification and fewer returns of orders incorrectly executed. The order gets set up once, and never gets rewritten, or changed from one format to another, so eliminating expensive duplication of effort. If the original order is incorrectly specified there can be no quibbling about who is responsible for errors.

In an ideal world every country would develop a widespread national system, and the national systems would subsequently be joined up into a compatible international system, so any participating bookseller would order from any participating stockist anywhere in the world.

Such a vision is still far off. Indeed developing national systems is no small feat. In the first place the economies available can only best be achieved where, as in Germany, the warehousing system processes most of the orders. In a country such as the UK a large proportion of the orders must go to individual publishers, and this involves more work and is more prone to error. Every participant must buy and maintain his computer terminal and must learn to use the system efficiently. This cost must be set against the savings generated by speedier supply, reduction in errors, more accurate invoicing and reductions in staffing. Such savings are clear cut when a relatively small number of warehouses deal with the bulk of the orders, but more ambiguous if orders have to be passed on to publishers in much smaller quantities by some kind of clearing house. This inevitably creates the Catch 22 situation whereby individuals are reluctant to incur expense until they know a national system is running smoothly, yet a national system cannot be set up until enough individuals join the system.

These distinctions also have implications for the single order problem. Where a warehouse can supply the great bulk of a retailer's needs they can be bulked together and despatched by the most economical form of transport. Where, however, a clearing house has to send large numbers of very small orders to individual publishers these can only be despatched at a relatively high cost per item. Logically, a publisher must budget for transport costs, but he does so on the assumption of a bulk delivery. Hence single copy orders require an additional unbudgeted cost to be incurred. The publisher generally takes the view that that is the retailer's fault, and transfers the additional cost to the retailer either by reducing his discount or by imposing a surcharge. In principle this surcharge then becomes the responsibility of the customer who ordered the book, but he doesn't generally have to pay extra for ordering other kinds of products not held in stock, and, especially in countries where resale price maintenance is in force, he generally regards the cover price as sacrosanct and refuses to pay over the odds for what he sees as the retailer's inability to hold an adequate stock.

The publisher then responds that the retailer should bulk up his orders if he doesn't want to incur surcharges, as the only other alternative is to budget for higher transport costs in the first place and put up wholesale prices, thereby possibly pricing some of the titles out of their markets. In any event why should those who don't create the problem expect to subsidise those who do.

Many retailers would respond that they don't get enough orders for smaller publishers to make delaying a single order worthwhile. Customers won't wait all that long for an order to come through. The customer could be advised that no surcharges will be levied if he waits for his order to be bulked up with others, although the effects of this are unpredictable. Equally it could be made clear that all orders must incur a surcharge, which will discourage orders but ensure that they are not fulfilled at a loss.

All this suggests that there is no simple answer to the small order problem, and it therefore inevitably remains an ongoing cause of discontent between publisher and retailer. It does, however, suggest at least one justification for an improved wholesaling operation.

Chapter Six

LIBRARIES

Purchases of books by libraries of all kinds have always formed an important part of the overall market for books. Institutional expenditure on books in various countries are dealt with elsewhere in the text, and the core of this chapter is concerned with the size of the book stock and the acquisitions rate around the world, rather than with the costs of acquisition. There are, nevertheless, some general issues about the budgetary position of libraries which need to be aired at this juncture, and as usual this is done in the context of specific countries which are representative of what is happening elsewhere. The discussion of the summary table which is contained in the Statistical Appendix indicates the disproportionate role played by libraries in the USA and UK, and these are therefore examined in some detail to bring out the kind of trends which are also apparent in other countries with less developed library systems.

Regional Survey

In the summary table, in the Appendix, it has been necessary to limit individual entries to categories of libraries which contain five million volumes. The effects of this admittedly arbitrary process are plain to see. In the case of Africa there is not a single country listed, and the entire continent's libraries, with the exception of South Africa, which is not listed by UNESCO, contained only some 10 million volumes in 1979, far less than the British Library by itself. Of these 10 million, 1 million were held in Algeria, 2 million in Egypt, 1 million in Ghana, 1.25 million in Nigeria, 1.75 million in Tunisia and just under half a million in Tanzania and Zambia. Obviously, the statistics are not comprehensive, but one can relate this stock to the 600 libraries listed and derive a figure of some 15,000 books per library, and an acquisition rate of under 1,000 books per year per library. Compare this latter figure to the annual average acquisition of 80,000 volumes by each of the 760 public library systems in the UK, and one can hardly but conclude that a ratio of 1:80 leaves much to be desired. Libraries may traditionally be regarded as captive markets by publishers, but it is obvious that no individual publisher is going to capture very much in Africa.

The South American picture is not as good as one might expect. Brazil, which is not, for some reason, listed by UNESCO, held 12.5 million volumes in 2,330 libraries in 1977. Argentina's record was also reasonable; French Guiana's collection was extensive although apparently barely growing at all; and Peru in 1980 held 4 million volumes in 520 public libraries. Nor does Asia exactly sparkle, with the exception of Japan which far exceeds all the others put together, and which has a system comparable to the top rank in Europe. India shows up well on the educational side, but it has a huge population so there aren't that many books to go around. Hong Kong's 1 million volume stock looks respectable, but there are nearly 1 million registered borrowers. However, that is better odds than face Indonesia's 3 million borrowers who must choose from a stock of 500,000 volumes. Malaysia's 400,000 borrowers have access to 2.5 million volumes which is much better, but it is clear that widespread choice is not the order of the day in Asia, even assuming that it is possible to get to a library in the first place.

North America contains two substantial book stocks as the table shows, but Mexico is also worthy of mention both because of the number of its libraries (2 national, 485 public and 250 higher education, each in aggregate containing over 2 million volumes) and because of the 3.5 million borrowers registered at its public libraries.

Information on Oceania is too sparse for proper analysis, but the information on Europe is quite extensive, so it is illuminating to make some comparisons. The UK's reported public library stock was 131 million in 1980, growing at an annual rate of 13 million, which puts it, slightly surprisingly, in a class of its own. France can only rustle up 50 million and 3 million respectively and West Germany 62 million, so it is Poland at 94 million and 7 million respectively, and Romania with 61 million and 3 million which are running the UK closest, not other countries in the West. 7 million borrowers are registered in Poland and 4 million in Romania, so it may be either that books are too expensive to be bought on any scale, or that most are available only through the library system. With Bulgaria and Czechoslovakia both on the 50 million and 3 million mark respectively, it would appear that library systems are better developed, and more extensively used, in the Eastern bloc rather than the Western; certainly, the USSR has more books in its public libraries than the USA. Clearly, the public libraries are the key element in the system, since whereas users in educational and specialist libraries are increasingly happy to access information in non-book form, public libraries are used almost entirely for the borrowing of books.

United States

The most up-to-date information on US libraries is available in the 36th edition of the *American Library Directory,* published in 1983. This contains the following data about the number of libraries.

TABLE 6.1   US LIBRARY DATA 1983

Public libraries (including branches)	14,968
Academic libraries	4,900
Armed forces libraries	483
Government libraries	1,591
Special libraries	4,281
Law libraries	430
Medical libraries	1,552
Religious libraries	839
TOTAL	29,044

The number for comparison with the UNESCO figure for public libraries was 8,822.

The three national libraries spent a total of $210 million in 1978, of which just under 50% went on wages and salaries. At that time, the collection consisted of 80 million items, of which UNESCO listed only 20 million as the bookstock, although this was nevertheless the biggest in the world (no national figure being available for the USSR). However, one can learn much more about library provision in a country by looking at its public libraries, and these have been chronically underfunded in America other than during the period 1957-1967. One explanation for

163

this is that, because the library is built on the concept of self-improvement and free access to information, it is perceived to be an elitist institution designed by the ruling elite for the benefit of the masses. But the masses remain indifferent to library provision, causing it to be assigned a low social priority. The only prosperous period dated from the 1957 Library Services Act, which both signalled the acceptance by the Federal Government of a role in making information available through the public library, and also required that states receiving funds set up a state library agency with a long-range plan for library provision. Money was plentiful because the economy was booming, but libraries remained a low priority area. Hence, when the budgetary situation tightened after 1967, this exposed the basic conflict between ability to finance and the rapidly improving ability to provide services resulting from the application of technology in the library context.

Once budgets require reductions to be made the difficulty is in determining where to cut and by how much. Unlike, say, an academic library, a public library has general and ill-defined objectives, with the result that budgetary issues are often tackled in a piecemeal, one-off manner. What is needed is to look at communities as markets for the services provided in order to determine which services are justifiable in economic terms; which require a subsidy; how much subsidy should be provided overall; and by whom it should be provided. There is a big danger in dividing up such extra resources as may become available in accordance with historic provision.

If one turns to academic libraries in America one discovers that over the past thirty years the ratio of library expenditures to the total expenditures of academic institutions has fluctuated in a clearly identifiable way. In 1950, the ratio was 3.3%, first falling to 3.0% in 1960, then rising to a peak of 4.1% in 1970. However, the subsequent decade saw the ratio fall back to 3.6% with no sign of a subsequent upturn. The small variation from year to year is interesting because it shows that there is no absolute standard of provision in operation.

If an institution obtains more money it simply continues to give virtually the same proportion to the library budget. The decline in the percentage allocated has obviously caused difficulties over the past decade, and this has to be taken in conjunction with a general decline in the availability of capital to fund infrastructure improvements. The inevitable result has been a reduction in the amount of expenditure per student, adjusted for inflation, and in the number of staff per student. Given that

164

demographic changes are likely to reduce the number of potential students, and hence an institution's gross income, in coming years these tendencies are likely to accelerate rather than the reverse. The interesting question is how this is likely to affect the allocation of expenditure to materials, staffing, and other categories. Historically the ratio was 60%, 30% and 10% respectively, and although there has been some tendency for the first category to reduce in favour of the second, the historic ratio tends sooner or later to be re-established.

Then then raises the issue of whether to spend the materials budget on books or periodicals. In 1970, books took 62% and serials 34%, but by 1976 this had changed to 44% and 50% respectively. Recently a reversal has taken place as some kind of equilibrium is evidently sought. However, this does not bode any too well for book publishers because, in the first place, one is effectively saying only that library expenditure on books will maintain its share of a total institutional budget which is rising slowly, if at all, and secondly that this is occurring in the context of (a) inflation and (b) an increasing number of publications. Although general inflation is less of a problem than it has been in recent times, book prices have typically risen faster than prices generally, with the consequence that a library is forced to purchase an increasingly smaller proportion of what is on offer. If one takes a retrospective view of library purchasing one is drawn to the usual conclusion that 20% of the purchases provide 80% of the total use, so budgetary cuts need only remove books which are very occasionally opened. The trouble is that no-one knows in advance which 20% of potential purchases are going to be the high-use items.

Shifting money from other parts of the library budget to the book budget offers no real solution. The share of the budget covering such matters as inter-library loans really needs to increase rather than the reverse as an increasingly smaller proportion of books in print are held by an individual library. The rest is almost all staff costs, and unless a library is willing to discard old stock faster than it acquires new stock, there is unlikely to be a reduction in the amount of work to be done, but rather the reverse. Computerisation offers opportunities to increase productivity, but the cost of software and the rapidity of technical change in the computer field may well cause costs to rise rather than fall.

United Kingdom

The library service in the UK has long been the envy of much of the rest of the world. This is not necessarily good news for publishers because it implies an internationally high ratio of books borrowed to books purchased.

The following table indicates the scale of provision.

TABLE 6.2   LIBRARIES IN THE UK

	Number of service points	
	March 1979	March 1982
Central and branch libraries		
open 60 + hours per week	107	86
open 30-60 hours per week	2,554	2,471
open 10-30 hours per week	1,234	1,381
Part-time (open less than 10 hours per week)	1,063	827
Mobile libraries	709	691
Hospitals and homes etc.	10,131	11,346
TOTAL	15,798	16,802

Source: CIPFA

There has been a tendency in recent years for fewer libraries to be open beyond normal working hours, and for more to be open over shorter periods. Mobile libraries, which were seen as an economic solution for difficult, under-serviced areas, have also shown a decline in numbers since 1978.

The total bookstock held by public libraries currently stands at just under 140 million volumes, of which over 12% are reference rather than lending books. The table below is a little incomplete due to the omission of certain local authorities, but is strongly indicative of the nature of the library bookstock.

166

TABLE 6.3   UK PUBLIC LIBRARY BOOKSTOCK BY TYPE 1982

Unit: million copies (as at March 31st)

Lending books	101.1	
— adult fiction		37.1
— adult non-fiction		43.5
— children's		20.5
Reference books	16.5	
TOTAL (all authorities)	137.1	

Source: CIPFA

Local authorities purchase the majority of books, and both their recurrent and capital spending on libraries has been declining in real terms for a considerable number of years. As a result the spending on libraries as a proportion of total local government spending has fallen to less than 1.5%. But this has to be combined with the fact that whereas expenditure on books constituted 23.3% of total library spending in 1967-68, it had become 21.5% by 1972-73, and 17% by 1977-78. The current figure is less than 15% as table 6.4 shows.

TABLE 6.4   UK PUBLIC LIBRARIES' ACQUISITIONS EXPENDITURE

Unit: £ million

	1978-79	1981-82
Books	43.1	52.6
Newspapers and periodicals	1.8	2.6
Sound recordings	1.7	2.1
Other	0.4	0.5
Total acquisitions	47.0	57.8
Other costs	186.4	294.8
Total expenditure	233.4	352.6
Books as % of total	18.5	14.9

Source: CIPFA

The fact that expenditure cuts tend to fall disproportionately upon book funds mirrors US experience. The Department of Education and Science consider an efficient and comprehensive library service to mean the addition each year of 250 books per 1000 population. The implication that many of these would have to be extremely cheap is fairly clear if one examines how much money is available on a per capita basis.

TABLE 6.5   UK EXPENDITURE ON BOOKS PER CAPITA

Unit: £

	1978-79	1979-80	1980-81	1981-82	1982-83
London boroughs	1.04	1.20	1.23	1.35	1.43
English counties	0.63	0.71	0.74	0.78	0.86
English metropolitan districts	0.70	0.79	0.86	0.95	1.06
Welsh counties	0.63	0.70	0.67	0.71	0.86
Welsh districts	0.75	0.72	0.78	0.76	0.90
TOTAL	0.71	0.80	0.86	0.91	0.99

Source: CIPFA/own calculations

168

These figures are at current prices. Adjusting for inflation results, for example, in an 18% reduction in the total for 1982-83 compared to 1981-82. Some places are obviously better stocked than others, although commuters borrow very heavily from the well provided libraries of London boroughs.

This rather dismal set of information may well be less ominous for countries where book purchasing is much more common in relation to book borrowing. But in the USA, for example, where this is the case, the library market still represents a very important market for trade books, professional books, university press books and books published in short print runs generally. The latter are often produced solely in hardback format, although libraries are increasingly switching to paperback editions, not solely to save money, but because what the public wants to borrow is often dictated by fashion, with the result that many books become unpopular after a relatively short shelf-life. All this is rather bad news for certain types of publisher, and in the longer term the library situation is bad news for publishers generally because children need to acquire the reading habit at an early age, and access to books in libraries is the only economic way for many parents to foster such habits.

Libraries in the Developing World

The most fundamental point here is that, whereas in developed countries publishers have traditionally relied upon the libraries to provide a solid market for books in hardback format, this facility has clearly not been available in developing countries. Thus the development of a proper library system in such countries has implications not merely for the spread of literacy, but also for the development of indigenous publishing. It is often useful to consider libraries as part of a system of book distribution if the alternatives are poorly developed. It is also important that the bookstock in libraries is tied in to the educational system; there are very few educational libraries as such in developing countries, and book purchasing is limited largely to secondhand textbooks. Such libraries as exist must, therefore, help to fill this gap in the educational system, and also provide opportunities for those outside the formal educational system to acquire knowledge for themselves. To this end, care must be taken to acquire a stock suited to the literacy levels of potential users. In Latin America in the 1960s, a study showed that over fifty per cent of the

169

population were still at a learning stage with respect to reading, and only two percent could read complicated texts. This situation has now improved, but it is worse in other parts of the world. Some fairly rough calculations suggest that only some 6% of literate adults in Latin America bother to read books, and, what is more worrying, only around 7% of schoolchildren show any inclination to do so.

This suggests that a priority for the library system in developing countries is to devise ways of encouraging children to read while at school, and to continue reading after leaving school. The most urgent need in pursuit of this aim will depend upon an individual country's strengths and weaknesses. All are predictably short of libraries, and all are short of books. Some are short of trained librarians and some of training facilities. Some existing libraries provide a good service, others a service that is inadequate. Some have a library structure which connects up the parts in an efficient manner, others have virtually no structure at all. All are backward with respect to the application of technology.

It would be foolish to imagine that anything short of a major investment programme is going to resolve many, if any, of these problems. To this end a favourable tax regime which fostered the setting up of institutional libraries would undoubtedly help. At the end of the day, it has long been recognised in developed countries that economic progress is heavily dependent upon the educational system, and the educational system is heavily dependent upon the availability of knowledge in book form. Libraries play a crucial role in this process, and it is cheap in the short run, but expensive in the long run, to starve them of resources.

Chapter Seven

READING AND OWNING BOOKS

Surveys on book readership have been conducted in a number of countries, and this chapter summarises some of their main findings. Before doing so, however, it is interesting to examine the popularity of books from a different viewpoint, namely the relationship between consumer expenditure on books and consumer expenditure on other leisure activities.

Consumer Expenditure

The popularity of different leisure activities is obviously determined by national characteristics, and one is therefore mainly interested in how spending on books compares to spending in total, to spending on other reading matter, and to spending on the other activities popularly assumed to attract people away from books, such as cinema and TV. Three major markets are examined below, namely the USA, the UK and Japan. The best performance is recorded in the UK where book reading has proved far more resilient than is commonly believed. In America, where expenditure on books constitutes an almost identical proportion of total consumer expenditure to that in the UK, books have also done well, but not so well in relation to other reading matter. In Japan, on the other hand, trends are relatively gloomy.

United States

The US Bureau of Economic Analysis produces annual data on personal consumption expenditures for recreation. This appears as table 7.1, in the form of real index numbers.

TABLE 7.1   US: PERSONAL CONSUMPTION EXPENDITURES

Unit: real index numbers

	1975	1977	1978	1979	1980	1981	1982
Books and maps	100	106	119	120	114	115	115
Magazines/newspapers	100	102	106	104	99	95	92
Radio/TV/records	100	107	109	111	104	103	98
Cinema admissions	100	142	156	148	121	119	130
Theatre/opera	100	116	132	136	140	145	143
Spectator sports	100	107	110	109	102	95	96
Commercial amusements	100	108	116	110	110	123	128
Total recreational	100	108	113	112	107	109	108
% personal consumption	6.7	6.6	6.6	6.6	6.4	6.5	6.4
Book % personal consumption	0.39						0.39

Source: US Bureau of Economic Analysis. *The National Income and Product Accounts of the United States,* 1929-1976; *Survey of Current Business,* July '82, July '83

Recreational expenditure in America has declined somewhat since its 1978 peak, although consumption in total has fared a little better. One of the few sectors to have ignored this trend has interestingly been theatre and opera. All forms of reading are down on the late 1970s, but books and maps have proved more resilient than newspapers and magazines, and have done better than recreational expenditures in general.

In view of these trends it is interesting to note that a survey of household participation in leisure time activities in 1983 did not include reading as such an activity.

United Kingdom

If we compare the series for the three types of reading material in the table below, we can see that not merely has the books series risen while the other two have fallen, but their relative position has changed by the better part of 100%. There was something of a lull for book expenditure in the mid-1970s, but the table certainly disproves any allegations that reading is a declining pastime in the UK. Indeed, expenditure on books is a steadily increasing proportion of total consumer expenditure. Certainly, people in the UK are increasingly glued to their TV screens, but this has eaten into time previously spent reading newspapers and magazines and going to the cinema, rather than into the time spent reading books.

TABLE 7.2 UK CONSUMER EXPENDITURE AT CONSTANT 1975 PRICES

Unit: Index numbers (1969 = 100)

	1975	1976	1977	1978	1979	1980	1981	1981 £mn
Books	135	135	135	142	147	149	150	562
Magazines	82	77	77	79	80	80	80	375
Newspapers	89	86	86	85	85	84	83	1,279
Cinema	59	50	48	56	52	47	40	142
Other entertainment	132	144	161	168	173	168	161	1,338
Misc. recreational	157	155	156	162	171	178	182	3,285
Radio/TV	186	205	210	220	231	233	238	1,501
Total consumer expenditure	114	114	114	121	125	125	125	151,042
Books % total		0.32					0.37	

Source: National Income and Expenditure *Blue Book*

Japan

The overall situation in the Japanese consumer market is one of rising consumption and expectations, increased leisure time and growing expenditure on leisure. However, spending on reading has not increased in line with other leisure items. In 1980, 43 hours of leisure time were available per week, up from 29 hours in 1970. Of these 4.17 hours were spent reading newspapers, books and magazines. The expenditures involved in various leisure activities were as follows:

173

TABLE 7.3   JAPANESE CONSUMER EXPENDITURE AT CONSTANT 1980 PRICES

Unit: Index numbers

	1980	1981	1982	1983
Radio/television	100	92	92	81
Sports goods	100	102	113	119
Package tours	100	99	105	100
Admissions fees	100	104	117	127
Books/other reading	100	100	99	96
TOTAL	100	99	103	104

Whereas total real spending, after a dip in 1981, recovered well by 1983, reading activities did not. Watching and playing sport is evidently in vogue. Sitting at home evidently is not, and it is a small consolation that radio and television expenditures are falling rapidly compared to reading.

Expenditure on books constituted 36% of total expenditure on reading in 1983.

TABLE 7.4   COMPOSITION OF JAPANESE READING EXPENDITURE 1983

Unit: %

Newspapers	51.0
Magazines	7.0
Weekly magazines	1.2
Dictionaries	0.5
Other books	35.3
Other reading	5.0
TOTAL	100.0

Source: Statistics Bureau, Prime Minister's Office

Readership Surveys

One might have expected readership surveys to be conducted in all book markets. After all, there's nothing like knowing who your potential customers are, or even if you have got any in the first place. Unhappily, there are rather fewer than one might expect — which is understandable for less developed countries, but less so, for example, for the USA — only one is conducted every year (in the UK); and the questions asked are different from survey to survey.

One question which one would like to have answered is, what proportion of the population reads books on a regular weekly basis. The only available answers appear to be Finland (19% in 1979), Spain (36% in 1978), West Germany (40% in 1980), Denmark (41% in 1976), Switzerland (45% in 1980) and the rather implausible Italy (83% in 1981). From this admittedly weak sample one is driven to conclude that in developed countries a target of 40% should be aimed at by publishers. In the UK, a fairly constant 45% of a sample surveyed have been reading books at the time of interview in a series of annual surveys conducted during the 1980s.

One would also like to know both what proportion of the population reads books in a given year, and how many they read, and also what proportion of the population buys books and how many they buy. Again the only answers to these questions appear as tables below. Certain countries, such as the UK, are omitted because no question is asked to elicit these answers, although in the latter case data is plentiful concerning purchases during a specific month.

TABLE 7.5   HOW MANY BOOKS READ?

Unit: % population										
Country	Year	Category	None	1	2	3-5	6-10	11-15	16-20	20 +
Finland	1971	Male	31.5	6	24		14		10	13.5
		Female	30	6	24		14		11	14.5
		All	30.5	6	24		14		10.5	14
France	1979	Male	23		28		15	8	7	9
		Female	21		29		17	11	6	7
		All	22		28		16	10	6	8

Continued...

Table 7.5 continued...

Country	Year	Category	None	1	2	3-5	6-10	11-15	16-20	20+
Norway	1980	Male	22		12		31		17	19
		Female	22		11		29		18	20
		All	22		11		30		17	19

HOW MANY BOOKS PURCHASED

Country	Year	Category	None	1	2	3-5	6-10	11-15	16-20	20+
Finland	1971	Male	54	2		11	7	6.5		9
		Female	53	2		11	7	7		10
		All	53.5	2		11	7	7		9.5
France	1979	Male	41		21		14	8	6	6
		Female	38		25		15	6	5	6
		All	40		23		14	7	5	6

Turning to individual country surveys, the majority of examples presented here are, not surprisingly perhaps, from European countries. And, even amongst examples from 'the rest of the world', the major surveys available are from Australia, New Zealand and Canada, markets which are heavily influenced by US and UK publishing trends.

Unfortunately, it has not always been possible to obtain details regarding sample composition, but the following surveys have been conducted by, or on behalf of, recognised and reputable bodies in each of the relevant national book industries.

Europe

Finland: A survey in 1979 indicated that 24% of adults did not read at all, and a further 31% read very little. Females tended to read more than men, but rather more of the heavy readers were men. The proportion of non-readers rose with age, and most heavy readers were aged under 40, which should represent good prospects in future years if the reading habit is maintained into old age. Frequency of readership predictably declined sharply down the socio-economic scale, and in line with reductions in population density.

176

The most popular book category was general novels, followed by thrillers/detective stories and books relating to work and studies. The first category, presumably including romance, dominated female reading and reading by the under 35s, whereas the second category was much more popular amongst men as were war books. The under 25s especially liked thrillers and titles obtained off bookstalls, whereas religious books became increasingly popular as age advanced. Children's books were largely a female preserve and very popular up to the age of 35 (it doesn't say whether this was reading for the benefit of adult or child!)

TABLE 7.6   FINLAND: READERSHIP SURVEY 1979

How many books have you read in the last year? (%):	None	1-5	6-10	11-30	Over 30
Male	22	31	16	20	11
Female	25	33	15	15	12
15-29 years	10	27	17	25	20
30-39 years	25	26	17	21	10
40-49 years	28	40	14	9	8
50-59 years	31	33	15	14	7
Over 60 years	35	35	13	11	4
Upper class	3	10	18	28	41
New middle class	10	23	21	26	18
Old middle class	20	36	16	23	5
Farmers	34	39	14	10	3
Skilled labour	23	33	15	17	11
Unskilled labour	37	36	8	10	8
Large cities	13	22	23	20	23
Other cities	22	27	13	19	9
Rural densely populated areas	26	23	15	16	20
Sparsely populated areas	31	36	13	14	4
ALL	24	31	15	18	11

Source: Central Statistical Office

TABLE 7.7   FINLAND: TYPE OF BOOK READ 1979

What type of book have you read in the last year? (%):

	All	Male	Female	15-24	25-34	35-64	Over 65
Books relating to work & studies	35	38	33	57	46	18	—
Other non-fiction	27	31	23	35	35	15	11
Memoirs, biographies	29	25	32	31	27	30	27
Thrillers, detective stories	38	46	33	65	42	23	13
War books	29	41	18	34	31	27	19
Children's books	22	14	29	29	31	11	9
Other novels	52	40	63	62	58	43	35
Poetry, plays	15	10	20	19	15	14	11
Social, opinion books	13	15	11	15	18	9	5
Religion	16	9	21	7	11	20	34
Bookstall literature	23	22	23	47	22	13	3

Source: Central Statistical Office

France: The last major survey was conducted in 1979. 49% of all adults regarded book reading as a major leisure time activity. This represented 42% of men but 55% of women. The 18-49 age group particularly enjoyed reading; the popularity of reading rose with the educational level of respondents.

As the survey didn't elicit information about what kind of books respondents actually read, the only information to go on are the expressed preferences for certain genres. Female preferences were for novels, classics and books on health, whereas male preferences were for detective stories, scientific books, documentaries and science fiction. Teenagers preferred detective stories, comic books and science fiction. Those aged 30-50 liked history books.

The table below indicates the number of books read during the previous year, divided by sex and age cohort. School books and university books were not included in this survey. The table shows that women are slightly more likely to be regular readers, but also slightly more likely to be non-readers. Heavy readership is very much concentrated in the 18-24

178

age cohort, after which reading falls off with age, although moderate levels of reading are maintained to the age of 50. As older people have more time to read one must presume that they are discouraged in France either by their level of literacy or by the lack of a widespread public library system.

TABLE 7.8   FRANCE: READING AND OTHER ACTIVITIES 1974

Which activities do you most enjoy? (%):

	Reading books	Reading newspapers and magazines	Watching television	Listening to music	Cinema	Theatre
Male	42	45	58	36	26	7
Female	55	39	51	45	29	15
15-17 years	35	19	30	74	62	4
18-24 years	51	36	37	56	57	12
25-34 years	51	40	45	49	43	13
35-49 years	51	43	54	38	19	15
50-64 years	46	52	67	31	9	10
65 years +	49	46	73	22	5	7
TOTAL	49	42	54	41	27	11

Source: Sofres

TABLE 7.9   FRANCE: TYPE OF BOOKS PREFERRED 1979

Which genre do you prefer? (%):

	Novel	History	Detective	Health	Scientific	Documentary	Comic books
Male	24	37	32	15	24	18	16
Female	55	36	23	33	5	11	13
15-17 years	41	26	38	10	9	9	49
18-24 years	47	23	30	26	19	13	35
25-34 years	44	33	24	29	17	21	18
35-49 years	43	41	26	28	16	17	12
50-64 years	32	44	30	22	15	14	5
65 years +	34	40	24	20	14	9	1
TOTAL	40	37	27	24	16	15	15

	Classics	Science fiction	Poetry	Philosophy	Art	Encyclopaedias	Religion
Male	10	14	8	9	7	8	5
Female	17	9	10	8	9	8	6
15-17 years	12	28	9	4	4	11	4
18-24 years	18	26	18	16	7	6	2
25-34 years	13	18	10	10	11	11	4
35-49 years	17	6	6	10	11	11	6
50-64 years	9	6	9	5	8	5	9
65 years +	12	2	4	5	6	6	6
TOTAL	14	12	9	9	8	8	5

Source: Sofres

TABLE 7.10   FRANCE: NUMBER OF BOOKS READ DURING PREVIOUS YEAR

Unit: % reading	None	1-5	6-10	11-15	16-20	21-30	31-50	50+
Male	23	28	15	8	7	6	4	5
Female	21	29	17	11	6	6	3	4
15-17 years	9	39	20	11	6	3	7	4
18-24 years	10	26	19	9	13	10	5	6
25-34 years	18	29	18	9	5	7	5	4
35-49 years	22	32	17	13	6	4	2	3
50-64 years	29	24	14	10	4	3	3	8
65 years +	32	27	13	6	6	8	1	4
TOTAL	22	28	16	10	6	6	3	5

Source: Sofres

Of more significance to the book trade of course are statistics referring to book purchase rather than reading, as this directly affects the profitability of the trade. The survey revealed a considerably lower purchase rate, with 40% of adults not purchasing, a proportion which not surprisingly increased with age as the elderly are less literate and often less able to afford to purchase books. Less than half of those aged 65 years or more purchased in the 12 months prior to interview.

TABLE 7.11   FRANCE: NUMBER OF BOOKS PURCHASED DURING PREVIOUS YEAR

Unit: % buying	None	1-5	6-10	11-15	16-20	21-30	31-50	50+
Male	41	21	14	8	6	3	2	1
Female	38	25	15	6	5	4	2	—
15-17 years	34	34	12	8	6	3	1	—
18-24 years	28	24	20	8	5	5	5	2
25-34 years	31	27	14	7	7	5	3	2
35-49 years	34	27	17	8	5	4	2	—
50-64	47	16	13	6	6	2	2	1
65 years +	59	18	10	4	3	1	—	—
TOTAL	40	23	14	7	5	3	2	1

Source: Sofres

In addition, 12% of households were found not to own any books at all, predominantly those containing the elderly (24%), agricultural workers, and situated in villages with less than 2,000 inhabitants. A further survey by the Ministry of Culture in 1981/82 showed that 20% of the population owned no books at all, although this was an improvement on the 27% figure for 1973. Interestingly, hardly anyone owned just a few books. Even in groups such as farm workers, where ownership was least common, a minimum of 20 books was the normal pattern. This would tend to suggest that the key factor is starting the ownership habit, rather than trying to sustain it. Since literacy levels tend to improve with each succeeding generation, the future prospects for book ownership in France should be optimistic provided the effort is made to inculcate the ownership habit among school children.

Norway: As indicated in an earlier table, book readership is almost identical for males and females. Again, there is some tendency for those who read at all to read a lot, although this is less marked than in France. The 16-24 age group is especially prone to reading in large quantities, but although reading declines with age, as normal, this is also less marked than in, for example, France. Reading rises with the level of education, with most graduates reading in large quantities, but it is surprisingly little affected by income. Only the very rich show any marked tendency to read more avidly than other income groups, which suggests that the habit of reading is well established in Norway at an early age and is not all that much affected by the individual's circumstances in later life.

TABLE 7.12 NORWAY: NUMBER OF BOOKS READ 1980

How many books have you read in your spare time in last year? (%)

| | Total reading books | Number of books read | | | | | |
		1-2	3-4	5-9	10-19	20+	Total
All	78	11	13	17	17	19	100
Sex							
Male	78	12	14	17	17	19	100
Female	78	11	13	16	18	20	100
Age							
16-19	88	7	12	22	19	27	100
20-24	85	9	11	21	16	28	100
25-44	80	12	12	16	19	21	100
45-64	74	12	16	15	16	15	100
65-79	72	13	15	16	14	14	100
Education							
Second level, first stage	65	12	14	13	13	14	100
Second level, second stage	83	12	14	17	19	21	100
Further university	94	8	11	23	23	29	100
Household income							
0-39,900 kroner	74	11	13	17	16	17	100
40,000-59,900 kroner	69	10	11	16	17	15	100
60,000-79,900 kroner	74	12	14	13	14	21	100
80,000-99,900 kroner	76	13	15	14	17	17	100
100,000-119,900 kroner	80	11	15	18	17	19	100
120,000-139,900 kroner	83	14	12	17	20	20	100
140,000 kroner and over	85	10	13	21	19	23	100

Source: Publishers' Association

Spain: In the national survey of cultural activities carried out in Spain by the Ministry of Culture in 1978, it emerged that 22% of households owned no books at all. A further 37% of households owned fewer than 25 books, whilst only 17% owned more than 100. It can reasonably be concluded, therefore, bearing in mind that most households contain more than the individual, that book ownership is not a very well established custom in Spain. Given that exactly one-third of the population claims never to read at all, and almost as many again to read very infrequently, it is perhaps surprising that Spain has such a flourishing book industry.

TABLE 7.13   SPAIN: HOUSEHOLD OWNERSHIP OF BOOKS 1978

Unit: % households owning	
Less than six books	15.6
Between six and 25	21.6
From 26-100	24.4
From 101-500	12.3
More than 500	4.3
None	21.8

Source: Ministerio de Cultura/La Realidad de Espana

TABLE 7.14   SPAIN: FREQUENCY OF READING A BOOK 1978

Unit: % population	
Read a book every day	18.2
Read occasionally during week	11.2
Read a book one day per week	7.0
Practically never read a book	30.3
Never read a book	33.3

Source: Ministerio de Cultura

Children's books, for long a neglected sector of the Spanish market, have greatly improved in both quantity and quality in the last decade and in 1979 accounted for around 12% of titles and 20% of copies. A detailed enquiry into children's cultural habits and activities carried out by the Ministry of Culture in 1980 showed, nevertheless, that nearly a quarter of Spanish children between the ages of six and thirteen possessed no 'books and tales' at all.

TABLE 7.15   SPAIN: % OF CHILD POPULATION OWNING BOOKS 1980

Unit: % 6-14 year old population owning books	
No books	23.8
Less than 10	41.1
Between 10-20	18.1
More than 20	16.4
Do not know/no reply	0.6

Source: Ministerio de Cultura

There was only minimal difference between the sexes as far as ownership was concerned. A large percentage (40.8%) claimed never to read a book, while only 11.2% read one every day. Adventure and science fiction is the favourite subject of both boys and girls, with straightforward fictional narrative the only other category claiming more than 10%.

TABLE 7.16   SPAIN: PREFERRED SUBJECT MATTER OF CHILD POPULATION 1980

Unit: % 6-13 year olds

	Boys	Girls	Total
Narrative fiction	19.1	30.3	25.1
Adventure and science fiction	59.9	49.0	53.9
History and biography	9.9	9.4	9.7
Plays	0.3	0.5	0.4
Poetry	1.3	2.0	1.7
Other	9.5	8.8	9.2

Source: Ministerio de Cultura

185

Switzerland: According to a survey in 1980, 45% of the Swiss population had read a book during the previous 8 days. The proportion reading other kinds of material was considerably higher, so the reading habit clearly extends throughout Swiss society. However, when it comes to books the Italian region of Switzerland does much less reading than the French and German regions; rural areas much less than urban; males (41%) less than females (50%); and lower social classes much less than higher.

TABLE 7.17   SWITZERLAND: READERSHIP SURVEY 1980

Have you read a book over the last eight days? (%):

All	45
Region	
French part	47
German part	45
Italian part	35
Locale	
Urban	51
Rural	37
Sex	
Male	41
Female	50
Social Class	
AB	74
C1	46
C2	44
DE	43

Source: Analyses Economiques et Sociales

TABLE 7.18   SWITZERLAND: COMPARISON OF LEISURE PURSUITS 1980

Which of the following have you done over the last eight days? (%):

Read a book	45
Read magazines	74
Read newspapers	91
To watch television	86
Go to cinema	14
Go to theatre	6
Go to a dance	15
Listen to radio	92

Source: Analyses Economiques et Sociales

United Kingdom: Every year an extensive book readership survey is conducted by Euromonitor. The 1983 survey produced an array of 25 tables covering current readership, subject of book being read, methods of obtaining books, book purchasing, prices paid, source of purchase, subjects of books bought and the reasons for purchase. The main findings concerning readership are presented in table 7.19. The proportion claiming to be reading a book has not altered for a number of years.

The proportion of men currently reading a book, having dipped slightly in 1982 to 38%, has regained its previous level of 42%. The proportion of readership among those aged 55 or older continues to rise, and is now significantly higher (by 8%) than the percentage of readers in the 16-34 age group. Readership among ABC1 respondents (which averages 58%) is significantly higher than that claimed by C2DEs (average 37.3%). The rise in AB readership is particularly marked since 1981, with 7 percentage points more of that group now claiming to be current readers than was the case two years ago. The South, London and Anglia achieved a readership of around 50%. Readership is at its lowest level in Lancashire and the Midlands/Central area. Anglia and Midlands/Central both showed a rise on last year's figures — Anglia's quite a sharp gain at 8 percentage points higher than in 1982 — while the other six regions either fell slightly or remained at the same level.

TABLE 7.19   UK: BOOK READERSHIP AND PURCHASE BY CATEGORY OF READER/BUYER

Unit: %

	1980		1981		1982		1983	
	Reading	Buying	Reading	Buying	Reading	Buying	Reading	Buying
TOTAL	45	27	45	26	45	35	45	29
Men	42	27	42	24	38	36	42	28
Women	47	27	48	27	51	35	49	30
Age								
16-34 years	43		43		43		42	34
35-44 years	44		42		44		47	35
45-54 years	46		46		42		42	26
55 years or more	46		47		48		50	20
Social class								
AB	61		60		61		67	44
C1	55		54		55		53	38
C2	40		36		36		38	25
DE	35		39		39		37	19
Location								
South	51		55		52		50	33
London	51		51		51		49	36
Wales West/South West	43		38		46		44	25
Yorkshire/North East	47		42		45		45	28
Border/Scotland	45		42		44		43	24
Lancashire	36		42		42		41	28
Anglia	49		40		41		49	29
Midlands/Central	38		42		39		41	27

Source: RSGB/Euromonitor

188

The age pattern of readership in the UK is perhaps its most unusual feature. It is accounted for in part by the extensive public library system with which residents become familiar at an early age, and which is used extensively by retired people. In terms of subject of book being read romantic fiction has become increasingly popular, but is an exclusively female preserve. Thrillers are in decline. Historical fiction is a female preserve, but history a surprisingly male preserve. Women show a very strong preference for fiction, only biographies showing up well in the non-fiction categories. Men enjoy crime and adventure fiction, but are surprisingly heavy readers of non-fiction.

Table 7.20 allows us to compare buying and reading habits. Book buying is more volatile than reading, with 1982 an exceptionally good year for the former. Sex differences are not clear-cut. The 35-44 age group was the most likely to have bought a book or books during the month prior to interview, thereafter the level of purchase declined quite sharply with age. Purchase proved predictably a function of social class, and was higher in high income/class regions of the country.

TABLE 7.20   UK: SUBJECT OF BOOK BEING READ

Unit: %	1980	1981	1982	1983	Male	Female
Number of readers	891	893	894	907	400	507
Fiction						
Romance	14	16	17	18	1	31
Crime/thriller	14	15	16	12	14	11
Historical	12	10	7	10	7	13
War/adventure	5	7	5	5	8	3
Modern novel	6	6	8	9	7	10
Classic	3	3	4	2	2	3
Science fiction	2	3	2	2	4	1
Horror/occult	2	2	2	2	3	2
Western	3	1	1	1	3	0
Children's	0	*	*	*	*	*

Continued...

189

Table 7.20 continued...

	1980	1981	1982	1983	Male	Female
Fiction continued...						
Humour	1	1	1	1	2	1
Other	3	3	3	4	3	5
All fiction	65	68	65	67	55	80
Non-fiction						
Encyclopaedia/atlas/ dictionary	—	—	—	*	1	*
History	5	7	6	7	12	3
Biography	7	6	8	8	7	8
Educational	6	3	4	3	5	2
Business/technical	2	2	1	1	3	*
Gardening/DIY/leisure	3	2	2	2	3	1
Travel/guides	1	1	1	1	2	*
Religion	2	1	3	2	2	2
Sport	1	1	1	1	2	0
Arts/crafts	1	*	1	*	*	*
Cookery	*	*	*	0	0	0
Other	6	7	7	6	8	3
All non-fiction	34	31	34	32	44	19
Don't know/can't remember	1	1	1	1	1	1

Note: *less than 0.5%
Source: Euromonitor/RSGB

West Germany: Book readership appears to be a fairly popular leisure activity, with 40% of the adult population reading books on a regular basis and 20% not reading. Readership is generally higher among the young, as is normally the case in other European countries. A Euromonitor survey conducted in 1980 identified travel books, humorous books and politics/current affairs as the most popular types of non-fiction, while in the fiction category preferred subjects were romance and the serious novel. In terms of type of book most recently purchased and read, business and technical, romance and the serious novel featured most prominently.

TABLE 7.21   WEST GERMANY: BOOK READERSHIP AND PURCHASE 1980

Unit: %

	Type of book preferred	Type last read	Type last purchased
Non-fiction			
Biography	39	7	5
History	48	9	7
Domestic science/DIY	31	3	3
Politics/current affairs	44	8	7
Religion	16	4	3
Sport	26	3	3
Educational/encyclopaedia	29	7	13
Business, technical	32	11	11
Arts	30	3	5
Humour	51	7	4
Travel	55	7	9
True adventure	38	3	3
Fiction			
Romance	46	14	12
Historical	36	4	3
Thriller/mystery	44	10	6
War	15	2	2
Classic	25	3	4
Occult/science fiction	17	3	2
Western	16	1	1
Serious novel	46	9	10
Humour	53	6	5

Source: Euromonitor Survey

Slightly over half of books purchased were hardback, the split between hardback and paperback being most evident in the non-fiction category with particular reference to religion, arts and history.

Rest of the World

Australia: A book readership survey was conducted in 1977 by the Australian Council. The findings were as follows:

TABLE 7.22   AUSTRALIA: BOOK READING AND PURCHASE 1977

	% reading regularly	% buying in last 6 months
TOTAL	70	60
Age		
15-19	79	80
20-29	72	60
30-39	72	68
40-49	71	64
50-64	67	48
65+	65	35
$A income		
0-6,000	60	45
6-9,000	59	56
9-11,000	78	68
11-18,000	72	65
18,000+	83	76
Students	97	
Professional	88	
Clerical	85	
Skilled trade	62	

Source: ABPA

Reading did not tend to fall off much with age, but book buying showed a marked decline. The effects of variations in occupation and income were much as expected.

Canada: A major survey of book readership was carried out in 1978. It covered trade books in English speaking Canada only, so it is not fully compatible with other surveys, although the sample size was much larger than the normal 2,000 so the results are more accurate as well as more narrowly defined. Book readers were defined as those who reported spending some time reading a book in the past six weeks. Of the adult English language population 58% were book readers, and only 7% claimed not to read at all. The main conclusions were as follows:

1. The percentage of each age group who are book readers starts at 78% for those 15-16, and declines steadily as age increases to 42% of those 70 years and over.

2. Women are more likely to be book readers then men. While 52% of men are book readers, 64% of women are.

3. Participation in book reading is higher for those with some post-secondary education than those with less educational background.

4. Participation in book reading varies for men and women with different occupations. The figures vary from 80% for teachers and 76% for those in medical occupations, to 44% for those in blue-collar occupations.

5. Participation in book reading varies from region to region; 50% of the population of Atlantic Canada, 57% on the Prairies, 59% in Ontario and 66% in British Columbia.

6. Residents of cities over 100,000 are somewhat more likely to participate in book reading than those in cities under 100,000 (62% vs. 55%), and both are more likely to read books than rural dwellers (51%).

7. Reading is a major leisure time activity for adult Canadians. It ranks behind television viewing, visiting, radio listening, and relaxing but ahead of a surprising variety of other activities such as listening to records, sports, hobbies and arts activities.

8. There are large variations in the audiences for the various major categories of fiction and non-fiction books. Men and women have quite different tastes, so for instance 21% of men are regular readers of history/social science (compared to 9% of women); 12%

193

of women are regular readers of medical, health and child care books (5% of men); 17% of men are regular readers of science fiction (7% of women); 28% of women are regular readers of romance (2% of men); 26% of women are regular readers of novels generally (16% of men); 6% of women are regular readers of poetry (3% of men).

9. Fiction accounts for 65% of all the books read by women book readers, and 53% of those read by men.

10. History/social science titles account for 17% of all books read by men book readers (9% for women); biography 10% of all books for men (14% for women) and other non-fiction categories 19% for men (15% for women).

Israel: According to a 1979 survey 73% of the population had read a book during the previous month, compared to 40% in 1975. Of those who read, roughly 30% (15% of the population) read at the rate of more than one book per week. Females (55.4%) were more likely to read than men (49.7%) and teenagers (80%) much more likely than any other age group. Unlike many other countries reading increased somewhat among pensioners. Those from a European/American background, or native born, tended to read much more than those from an Asian/African background.

TABLE 7.23   ISRAEL: READERSHIP SURVEY 1975/1979

Unit: % reading in previous month		1975	1979
	All	45.1	52.6
	Male	43.9	49.7
	Female	46.3	55.4
Age			
	14-17	74.1	80.0
	18-29	51.9	55.7
	30-44	36.6	46.2
	45-59	36.0	46.1
	60+	37.1	50.2

Continued...

Table 7.23 continued...

	1975	1979
Origin		
Israel	55.4	68.1
Asia/Africa	31.2	38.2
Europe/America	56.4	62.3
Type of locality		
Jerusalem, Tel Aviv, Haifa	46.0	59.6
Old towns and built-up areas	44.8	53.5
New towns and built-up areas	36.2	38.1
Villages	46.7	48.5
Kibbutzim	58.2	72.1

Source: CBS

TABLE 7.24   ISRAEL: NUMBER OF BOOKS READ PER MONTH 1975/1979

Unit: % of book readers

	1975/6	1979
One only	32.2	30.4
Two to three books	40.6	40.0
Four or more books	27.2	29.5
TOTAL	100.0	100.0

Source: CBS

Japan: A 1976 survey indicated that reading books was the third most popular way of spending leisure time. Females were a little more likely to read regularly than males, but whereas females read very heavily between the ages of 15 and 24, and rather little after the age of 40, males read fairly consistently throughout the age span, although slightly more between the ages of 20 and 40 than in other age groups. A subsequent survey in 1980 revealed that around 35% of the population read at least one book per month.

TABLE 7.25   JAPAN: READING AND OTHER LEISURE ACTIVITIES 1976

Level of regular participation (% persons):

	Males	Females
Gardening	24.4	26.8
Playing 'Pachinko'	22.9	2.5
Reading books	9.0	10.5
Listening to music	8.5	6.7
Seeing movies	8.2	5.6
Flower arrangement	—	13.3
Watching sports	8.0	2.9
Playing musical instruments	6.4	5.2
Dressmaking/knitting	—	6.5

Source: Statistics Bureau, Prime Minister's Office

TABLE 7.26   JAPAN: READERSHIP SURVEY 1976

Unit: % regular readers

	Males	Females
Total	9.7	10.5
Employed	9.1	10.0
—15-19 years	8.8	18.4
—20-24 years	10.6	18.9
—25-39 years	10.0	11.4
—40-59 years	8.7	7.2
—60 and over	6.6	3.3
Unemployed	12.7	11.1
—15-19 years	14.3	23.0
—20-24 years	23.1	21.9
—25-39 years	19.5	12.1
—40-59 years	7.4	8.8
—60 and over	6.5	3.3

Source: Statistical Office, Prime Minister's Office

TABLE 7.27   JAPAN: NUMBER OF BOOKS READ PER MONTH 1980

Number of books per month	%
None	54
1	21
2	8
3	3
4	1
5	1
6	—
7	1
Unknown	11
TOTAL	100

Source: Publishers' Association for Cultural Exchange

New Zealand: Findings on book readership in New Zealand were published in a 1976 survey published by the New Zealand Book Trade Organisation. 57% of those surveyed claimed to have read a book during the previous month, comprising 53% males and 63% females. Purchasing was heaviest in the 25-34 age group at 69%, although this group reckoned to read rather less than the age cohort on either side. Only the over 55s claimed to buy much less than they read.

Heavy purchasing by females in their twenties was not surprisingly associated with children's books. Only fiction purchases comprised a comparable proportion of female book purchasing. Males, on the other hand, bought hobby and reference/study books rather than children's books.

TABLE 7.28   NEW ZEALAND: BOOK READERSHIP SURVEY 1976

Unit: %

	Reading a book in previous month	Purchasing a book in previous month
All	57	58
Male	55	53
Female	57	63
15-24 years	63	62
25-34 years	55	69
35-44 years	59	64
45-54 years	53	55
Over 55	52	45

Source: New Zealand Book Trade Organisation

TABLE 7.29   NEW ZEALAND: TYPES OF BOOKS PURCHASED 1976

Unit: %

Females		Males	
Children's	27	Fiction	29
Fiction	26	Hobbies, 'How-to'	20
Hobbies, 'How-to'	14	Reference, study	20
Reference, study	14	Literature	10
Literature	11	Children's	9
Religion	5	Socio-political	4
Socio-political	1	Travel	3
Others	2	Others	5
TOTAL	100		100

Source: New Zealand Book Trade Organisation

198

Chapter Eight

THE PRICE OF BOOKS

Books are extremely difficult to price. No two books are identical, and determining expected sales volume is very hazardous for a significant proportion of the product range. Does one opt for a low price in the hope of attracting a more than compensatory increase in volume, or a high price to maximise profit per unit at the risk of selling very few copies? Should guaranteed best sellers be over-priced because losses are certain on other parts of the product range? Should stock items be sold forever at the original published price, or repriced in line with current prices for similar titles?

The questions can only be answered by the individual publisher. The only question which one can attempt to answer is the aggregate one concerning whether book prices have any tendency to rise faster than prices in general, since a publisher has to consider the question of potential resistance by the consumer should he have reason to believe, rightly or wrongly, that books are poor value for money. In order to shed some light on the value for money issue, we must examine the question of converting the money price of a book into a real price.

Adjusting for Inflation

Throughout this text we have been adjusting for inflation, primarily by recourse to the consumer price indices set out in table 8.1. This procedure is, however, open to objection. At a fundamental level it can be argued that the construction of a conventional price index for books is impossible. For such an index the same 'basket of goods' must be priced over a period of at least two years. However, no two books are exactly alike, so one year's publications cannot truly be compared with another's. Nor is the price of a particular type of book necessarily likely to move in price at the same rate as any other type of book. Just occasionally one comes across a book which is reprinted every year, but not enough to be statistically significant.

TABLE 8.1 CONSUMER PRICE INDICES 1975 = 100

Unit: Annual averages

	Australia	Canada	France	Italy	Japan	Nether-lands	United Kingdom	United States	West Germany
1970	61.4	70.2	65.5	58.5	58.0	66.1	54.2	72.2	74.2
1971	65.2	72.2	69.0	61.3	61.5	71.1	59.3	75.3	78.2
1972	68.9	75.7	73.3	64.8	64.3	76.6	63.6	77.7	82.5
1973	75.5	81.4	78.7	71.8	71.9	82.7	69.4	82.5	88.2
1974	86.9	90.3	89.5	85.5	89.4	90.7	80.5	91.6	94.4
1975	100.0	100.0	100.0	100.0	100.0	100.0	100.0	100.0	100.0
1976	113.5	107.5	109.6	116.8	109.3	108.8	116.5	105.8	104.5
1977	127.5	116.1	119.9	138.3	118.1	115.8	135.0	112.6	108.4
1978	137.6	126.5	130.8	155.1	122.6	120.5	146.2	121.2	111.3
1979	150.1	138.1	144.8	178.0	127.0	125.6	165.8	134.9	115.9
1980	165.2	152.2	164.5	215.5	137.2	133.9	195.7	153.1	122.2
1981	181.3	171.0	186.5	257.5	143.9	142.8	219.0	169.1	129.5
1982	201.5	189.6	208.5	295.9	147.7	151.4	237.8	179.3	136.3
1983	221.8	200.8	228.5	339.0	150.5	155.6	248.7	185.1	140.5

The only way in which to overcome this difficulty is to use a technique which, instead of pricing a constant basket of goods, prices a constant set of price-relevant characteristics of the goods. In this case, although the books themselves change from year to year, one holds constant such characteristics as the number of pages, the type of binding, or the subject matter class, in order to construct the index. An attempt has been made to apply this technique to data for Canada, the USA and the UK[1], but the model probably needs refinement before it can be said to be worthy of more serious consideration.

United Kingdom

In the absence of more sophisticated methods, one is obliged to resort to the generally available arithmetic means of prices. The UK has possibly the most interesting set of indices available, and these are set out in table 8.2. The RPI and BPI are produced by the government statistics services. The *Bookseller* index is based upon the prices of books listed at the end of each weekly edition of the journal, but excluding government publications. It is, therefore, based upon a very comprehensive sample. The library series are constructed in order to shed light upon the prices of books bought by libraries, so the base sample is less comprehensive but still statistically significant. The LMRU series is concerned only with the prices of academic books.

[1] G.Rosenbluth, *An Index of Book Prices 1967-1979*, Discussion Paper 83-18, Department of Economics, University of British Columbia (July 1983)

TABLE 8.2   UK: ANNUAL PRICE INDICES

	Retail price Index (RPI)	Retail prices Books (BPI)	The Bookseller			Library Association			LMRU[1]		
			Money	Real (RPI)	Real (RPB)	Money	Real (RPI)	Real (RPB)	Money	Real (RPI)	Real (RPB)
1975	100	100	100	100	100	100	100	100	100	100	100
1976	117	117	126	108	108	128	109	109	135	115	115
1977	135	141	141	104	100	156	116	111	166	123	118
1978	146	163	157	108	96	161	110	99	179	123	110
1979	166	180	169	102	94	189	114	105	195	118	108
1980	196	212	195	100	92	218	111	103	206	105	97
1981	219	249	215	98	86	231	105	93	218	100	88
1982	237	280	245	103	88	257	108	92	257	108	92
1983	249	334	288	116	86	234	94	70	244[2]	98	73
									(331[2]	133	99)

[1] Library Management Research Unit;

[2] an increasing number of academic items in the *British National Bibliography*, from which this series is derived, have been appearing without prices. In 1981 this was considered to account for only a 1% underestimation, but in 1983 a large sample of unpriced items were eventually priced, and this suggested an under-estimation of 35.5%.

Quite a number of reservations can be expressed about basing indices upon simple arithmetic means of price. They are calculated on the basis of titles published rather than taking account of the number of copies sold; there is an enormous price range between cheapest and dearest; between paperback and hardback; and the mix of low-priced to high-priced tends to fluctuate over time; the indices apply only to new titles and reprints and shed no light upon variations in the prices of backlist titles; the average length of books varies from year to year, and there are changes in production processes.

These objections tend to render any individual index invalid as an accurate estimate of the average prices ruling in any individual year. Nevertheless they may well prove useful as a means of evaluating changes over time since if an index is consistently defined from year to year it would take fairly profound changes in the product mix, which one has no reason to believe actually occur, to invalidate such comparisons.

What then do the series show? The first and obvious point is that the two official series do not tell the same story, which is not altogether surprising since the BPI is but a small sub-set of the RPI. In every year from 1976 onwards the BPI has stayed ahead of the RPI, the difference remaining fairly static between 1978 and 1981, but shooting ahead subsequently. Since these series are to be used for adjusting for inflation the size of the current gap between them presents difficulties in interpreting real price trends. Until 1980 the LMRU series stayed ahead of the other two, but subsequently the relationship became more erratic. It now appears, as the footnote explains, that the present position is deceptive, and that the index should reach a figure far greater than originally estimated. Of the other two series the LA had its nose in front of the *Bookseller* until 1982, but the latter index leapt ahead in 1983, whereas the former actually declined (technically possible, given the difference in samples, but a little difficult to accept).

Both the RPI and BPI have been used to deflate the money prices in the three indices. Where the RPI is used virtually every entry shows real prices running ahead of their level in 1975, but the picture is erratic over time and the present position arguably not too bad, with one series actually showing a reduction. Clearly there is no tendency for the real price of books to accelerate. Using the BPI presents a very rosy picture indeed in recent years.

One reason why real prices tended to rise during the mid-1970s, subsequently to fall, is that the price of paper rose by 82% between 1973 and 1975, and stocks bought at this time would have been turned into books in the following period. The real price of paper subsequently fell during the period 1975-1981, thereby easing pressures on prices. Other influences on book prices, such as price trends for competitive products, have counteracted one another somewhat, so the net effect was to help keep book prices fairly well in line with prices in the general economy. In conclusion, it may be argued that, taken as a whole, books are not becoming unreasonably expensive in the UK. Because many people purchase only occasionally they may get the opposite impression, but the fact that money prices do indeed rise inexorably can easily produce that illusion. Furthermore, quite a lot does depend upon the particular books which are purchased, as the table below illustrates.

TABLE 8.3   UK: ANNUAL PRICE INDICES, SUB-CATEGORIES 1975-1983

	1975	1976	1977	1978	1979	1980	1981	1982	1983
The Bookseller									
New books	100	121	138	153	167	189	209	240	276
New editions	100	143	150	171	174	214	238	262	333
Cloth fiction	100	117	130	151	169	196	214	236	260
Library Association									
Adult fiction	100	121	135	146	169	194	218	227	237
Adult non fiction	100	128	160	163	192	220	238	259	239
Reference	100	138	195	203	245	308	396	476	339
Children's fiction	100	124	131	140	169	181	221	210	246
Children's non-fiction	100	118	106	107	122	161	200	208	238
LMRU									
Hardback	100	141	169	181	—	—	—	—	212[1]
Paperback	100	138	159	169	—	—	—	—	314[1]
Hardback/paperback	100	132	148	170	—	—	—	—	151[1]
RPI	100	117	135	146	166	196	219	237	249
BPI	100	117	141	163	180	212	249	280	334

[1] undervalued by 35% according to recent CLAIM report

The *Bookseller* data suggest, for example, that new books represent better value than new editions. The LA data indicate that children's books have remained remarkably cheap in real terms although many parents would doubtless argue the opposite view on the basis of selective buying. Herein, of course, lies the difficulty for the book industry, namely how to project to the general public the basic proposition that books are not priced in an unreasonable manner, but generally reflect the same forces which account for why the prices of virtually everything are rising. In this respect the industry could, perhaps, do better.

United States

A great deal of information about prices is published by the R. Bowker Co for the USA, but the same issues arise as have been discussed in the above section, so we will simply examine below the general issue of whether book prices are rising in real terms, and which books are a good or bad buy in general.

Table 8.4 examines price trends over the past six years. The general picture is clouded somewhat by the absence of data on mass-market paperbacks prior to 1981.

TABLE 8.4   US: AVERAGE PER-VOLUME PRICES

Unit: $		1977	1980	1981	1982	1983
Hardcover books	Money	19.22	24.64	26.63	30.34	30.84[1]
	1977 prices	19.22	18.12	17.73	21.36	18.76
Hardcover books	Money	17.32	22.48	24.33[1]	23.26	23.38[1]
$80 or less	1977 prices	17.32	16.53	16.20	14.61	14.22
Mass market	Money	n.a.	n.a.	2.65	2.93	3.13[1]
paperbacks	1977 prices	n.a.	n.a.	1.76	1.84	1.90
Trade	Money	5.93	8.60	9.76	12.32	11.64[1]
paperbacks	1977 prices	5.93	6.32	6.50	7.74	7.08

Note: [1] provisional
Source: R. Bowker Co

The different categories of books analysed show rather differing pictures. Hardcover prices, adjusted for inflation, fell appreciably from 1977 to 1981, rose sharply in 1982 and settled back in 1983 to a figure not greatly above that of 1980, and below that of 1977. Only philosophy/psychology and science books showed increases in money terms considerably higher than the average, whereas general works and travel rose by much less than the average. Eliminating high priced titles results in inflation-adjusted prices falling continuously throughout the period, with all categories broadly following this experience. Mass-market paperback prices, on the other hand, rose in real value between 1981 and 1983. Many categories moved erratically, but 75% of these paperbacks are fiction titles so their price changes in effect determine the average change as well. Trade paperbacks rose steadily in real terms from 1977 to 1981, rose sharply in 1982, then settled back in 1983.

Only the prices of agricultural titles rose by appreciably more than the average, whereas languages, law, poetry and drama and fiction rose by significantly less than the average. The sharp change in 1982 was caused by the behaviour of biography and sociology/economics titles, the latter being much the biggest individual category. Both declined to normality in 1983. The reasons for these changes are unknown.

Overall the picture is not easy to interpret, primarily because we must wait for the 1984 data before we can put the erratic movements in 1982 into their proper perspective. However, it would appear that the bulk of the books being bought in the USA are more expensive in real terms than they were at the turn of the decade.

West Germany

As indicated in the following tables, the West German experience with respect to book prices has not differed greatly from that in the UK. Taking books as a whole the indices moved as follows:

TABLE 8.5   WEST GERMANY: BOOK PRICE AND CONSUMER PRICE TRENDS

	1977	1978	1979	1980	1982
Total book prices	100	106.4	108.0	115.4	121.1
Consumer prices index	100	102.7	106.9	112.7	125.7

Source: Consumer Price Index

Hence, despite running ahead of inflation during the late 1970s, the position has now reversed itself with general prices currently running ahead of book prices. The differences are not, however, significant, so the same conclusion can be reached as in the case of the UK, namely that book prices generally move in line with other prices in the economy. A more detailed picture is presented in the two tables below, but the same conclusion applies even though there are significant fluctuations in the prices of books in individual subject categories, partly because the sample size is often quite small.

TABLE 8.6   WEST GERMAN HARDCOVER AND SCHOLARLY PAPERBACK
BOOKS: AVERAGE PRICES 1980-1982[1]

Unit: DMark

	1977 Average price	1980 Average price	1981 Average price	1982 Average price
General, library science, college level textbooks	82.28	86.93	73.66	87.18
Religion, theology	27.67	28.63	26.24	25.47
Philosophy, psychology	40.38	38.14	44.68	42.13
Law, administration	37.50	50.79	70.32	55.88
Social sciences, economics, statistics	32.20	39.71	39.90	45.81
Political and military science	27.85	32.52	33.07	33.95
Literature and linguistics	40.90	36.06	42.57	31.18
Belles lettres	7.48	8.20	9.82	11.05
Juvenile	12.86	12.69	11.54	9.54
Education	18.19	19.40	23.07	20.66
School textbooks	10.98	11.79	13.80	13.64

Continued...

Table 8.6 continued...

	1977 Average price	1980 Average price	1981 Average price	1982 Averge price
Fine arts	58.51	63.70	65.08	56.45
Music, dance, theatre, film, radio	37.89	38.73	46.13	41.26
History, folklore	49.82	53.43	54.73	44.62
Geography, anthropology, travel	34.76	34.05	35.19	32.59
Medicine	61.55	68.47	76.41	75.31
Natural sciences	131.28	118.89	143.29	149.80
Mathematics	32.83	41.55	46.60	44.69
Technology	45.39	67.79	60.87	68.00
Touring guides and directories	22.94	34.08	33.80	30.26
Home economics and agriculture	31.49	31.38	33.90	35.21
Sports and recreation	24.55	28.51	29.97	27.70
Miscellaneous	11.71	14.32	12.63	19.08
TOTAL	27.68	32.18	35.39	33.74

[1] Indexes are tentative and based on average prices unadjusted for title production for numbered paperback books (Taschenbucher). Figures for 1981-1982 were compiled by Peter Graham and Paul Peters from *Buch und Buchhandel in Zahlen* (Frankfurt, 1982 and 1983). The index year 1977 has been adopted to conform to the year used in the US government's Consumer Price Index

TABLE 8.7   WEST GERMAN PAPERBACK BOOKS: AVERAGE PRICES 1980-1982[1]

Unit: DMark

	1977 Average price	1980 Average price	1981 Average price	1982 Average price
General, library science, college level textbooks	6.47	8.71	13.04	10.73
Religion, theology	7.03	7.29	8.92	8.79
Philosophy, psychology	8.06	9.44	9.18	9.75
Law, administration	8.95	13.41	10.42	12.04
Social sciences, economics, statistics	10.02	10.75	11.06	12.14

Continued...

Table 8.7 continued...

	1977 Average price	1980 Average price	1981 Average price	1982 Average price
Political and military science	8.24	9.34	10.08	9.88
Literature and linguistics	8.36	10.21	10.02	10.59
Belles lettres	4.89	5.70	6.21	6.85
Juvenile	4.77	5.51	5.59	6.17
Education	10.88	11.63	10.70	11.86
School textbooks	2.52	3.12	3.05	3.85
Fine arts	10.28	11.77	11.11	11.45
Music, dance, theatre, film, radio	8.11	8.60	9.64	10.78
History, folklore	8.35	9.22	10.75	11.57
Geography, anthropology, travel	6.82	9.09	9.90	10.29
Medicine	10.42	12.15	10.58	11.97
Natural sciences	10.85	12.31	12.86	12.92
Mathematics	15.00	16.21	17.53	16.74
Technology	20.63	28.22	36.72	33.17
Touring guides and directories	7.11	10.46	9.93	10.00
Home economics and agriculture	6.77	7.38	8.25	8.53
Sports and recreation	6.81	7.69	8.24	9.28
Miscellaneous	5.00	8.87	8.73	8.51
TOTAL	6.69	7.76	8.13	8.57

[1] indexes are tentative and based on average prices unadjusted for title production for numbered paperback books (Taschenbucher). Figures for 1981-1982 were compiled by Peter Graham and Paul Peters from *Buch und Buchhandel in Zahlen* (Frankfurt, 1982 and 1983). The index year 1977 has been adopted to conform to the year used in the US government's Consumer Price Index.

France

The position in France is apparently extremely satisfactory, as shown in the table below. Prices generally are running well below the rate of inflation, although the information is not very detailed. Given the large numbers of titles produced, it is difficult to understand why prices have been so much lower in real terms compared to the UK and West Germany.

209

TABLE 8.8   FRANCE: BOOK PRICE TRENDS

	Average price (francs)		Price index (1979 = 100)	Consumer price index (1979 = 100)
	1979	1982	1982	
School textbooks	14.03	19.68	140.3	
Scientific and technical	49.93	72.98	146.2	
Human sciences	27.98	28.46	101.7	
General literature	11.04	13.82	125.2	
Encyclopaedias and dictionaries	55.95	84.54	151.1	
Fine arts	55.18	90.97	164.9	
Children's books	7.66	12.25	159.9	
Practical books[1]	24.21	21.45	88.6	
TOTAL	17.22	21.22	123.2	144.0

Note: [1] excludes atlases etc
Source: SNE/Euromonitor

Retail Price Maintenance

Retail price maintenance (rpm) is probably the issue which has raised most hackles around the world since the Second World War. Trade association officials invariably support it without much qualification, and shower abuse upon those who don't, and especially upon economists even though the latters' preference for abolishing rpm is generally ringed with qualifications. Economists are accused of failing to understand what the public interest means, although there is clearly no universally agreeable definition. Furthermore, it is essential to appreciate from the outset that in many countries only a limited number of products are currently subject to rpm, and since in the case of books it is by no means intuitively obvious that books are indeed different from other consumer products such as records and tapes, the special status of books is bound to be periodically called in question.

   The arguments concerning rpm on books are presented below in the context of the UK, since the issues have been thoroughly aired in that country. They should, however, be regarded as equally applicable to the great majority of other countries.

United Kingdom

The Net Book Agreement[1] currently in use came into being in 1957. It contains a number of conditions of sale of which the most important is that a net book may be sold or offered for sale to the public at less than the net published price only if

a) it has been held in stock by the bookseller for a period of more than twelve months from the date of the latest purchase by him of any copy thereof and
b) it has been offered to the publisher at cost price or at the proposed reduced price whichever shall be the lower and such offer has been refused by the publisher.

The Agreement covers the vast majority of new books other than school books, and is binding upon members of the Publishers' Association who publish net books.

Prior to 1956 a list of Recognised Booksellers, known as the Register, was used by publishers to determine the terms they would offer to individual booksellers. The 1956 Restrictive Practices Act prohibited collective enforcement of restrictive practices, and as an example of such enforcement the NBA was investigated by the Restrictive Practices Court, the Judgement being delivered in October 1962. This allowed the NBA to continue to force. Where a publisher discovers that his books are being sold at less than their net prices he may now obtain a legal injunction to restrain the bookseller, and the Publishers' Association may require him to take such action. In practice, no injunction has ever been taken out, mainly because entry into the Register, now called the Directory of Booksellers, which in effect guarantees preferential treatment to those listed, requires acceptance of the NBA, and it is not in the interests of the listed booksellers to infringe its Conditions of Sale.

The NBA is not a typical form of restrictive practice. In the first place it specifies a minimum price but not a maximum, although repricing is rare, partly because of fears about loss of sales at higher prices, and partly because prices are often stamped on books by publishers. Secondly a publisher is free to designate a book as either net or non-net, to

[1] for a full analysis of the Net Book Agreement see P.J.Curwen, *The UK Publishing Industry,* (Pergamon Press, 1981) chapter 3.

211

transfer it between categories, to fix the price at any level, and to supply anyone he so chooses. In addition, books may be sold at less than net prices during the two week National Book Sale.

The Restrictive Practices Court in 1962 accepted that the termination of the NBA would lead to (1) fewer and less well-equipped stockholding bookshops (2) more expensive books (3) fewer published titles. Higher prices would result because, in the absence of stockholding bookshops, publishers would have to be more cautious about their publishing strategies, reducing print runs and hence forcing up prices. Price cutting was expected to be selective rather than widespread, perhaps in the form of loss-leadership whereby a non-bookstore would attract customers by offering cheap books. The Court considered that such tactics would merely transfer demand from one outlet to another and deter bookshops from ordering stocks of books likely to be used as loss-leaders. Their profits would be damaged, and they would demand higher discounts by way of compensation, which would force up prices across the board.

An interesting argument took place before the Court about the relationship between risk and discount. The highest discounts are offered on fast moving stock which, with a sale or return facility, constitute low risk stock to the bookshop. One would expect a high discount to constitute a reward either for a high level of risk or for an exceptional level of service, yet neither of these apply in the case of books which attract high discounts in practice. One consequence is obviously that large and efficient bookshops have the leeway to meet price competition head-on should it be necessary, although smaller ones do not.

But would abolition of the NBA result in fewer and less-well equipped stockholding bookshops? The absence of price competition clearly holds back any restructuring of the industry, and open price competition would undoubtedly send some bookshops into liquidation. It is interesting to note that many bookshops are very unprofitable despite the apparent protection of the NBA, yet there is no shortage of newcomers to the trade, so the NBA may be fairly immaterial in this respect. It may be that some towns would lose bookshops whilst others gained them, but the existing distribution is essentially random and it is not, therefore, particularly beneficial for the existing distribution to be supported by the existence of the NBA.

What is rather clearer is the effect of abolition upon the quality of services provided by stockholding bookshops. Most would obviously

212

have to rationalise their stock and eliminate those titles with an unaccept-ably slow stockturn. Given that few bookshops stock even as much as 10% of titles in print, this would be unlikely to have much effect upon the relationship between stocked and ordered items, but would affect books in certain categories much more than those in others. The main problem would arise were it to become necessary, as many argue it would, to charge for the obtaining of titles not held in stock, since this would undoubtedly discourage purchases. It may be argued that poorer people who buy mass-market paperbacks are currently subsidising free services which are used only by richer, educated people who want books not held in stock. The only effective reply to this line of argument is that it would be disadvantageous culturally to remove the subsidy. If books with limited appeal could be obtained only by payments for special orders, or at generally higher prices, library provision would suffer, and anyone seeking to improve their knowledge, whether rich or poor, would be discouraged.

We must also ask whether books would in general be more expensive. There is no clear cut answer to this question, only a balancing of proba-bilities. Since mass-market paperbacks would undoubtedly come down in price this would benefit consumers on a simple head count basis. But it may be argued that this principle should be adjusted to give more weight to regular book buyers as compared to those who only make the occa-sional purchase. Furthermore, if one accepts that anyone should be entitled to expect a wide range of books at reasonable prices, however narrow or esoteric his interests, then abolition of the NBA would prove detrimental because the prices of slow turnover books would typically rise. In all probability more books would go up in price than would go down, but the average price level would probably go down. Insofar as the number of titles published would be affected, it would almost certainly go down as duplication of titles was eliminated and lists were pruned to remove uneconomic short-run titles. The latter would in many cases be concerned with the higher reaches of literature with cultural overtones.

Overall, therefore, the predictions of the Court in 1962 still probably hold good. What is far less clear is the effect upon the public interest. From an economic viewpoint abolition is undoubtedly called for. The NBA serves to rigidify the existing structure of the book trade, yet neither its distribution, nor its profitability, nor the relationship of prices to supply costs, nor the number of titles, nor the cross-subsidisation of some customers by others, is remotely optimal. Therefore, the justifica-tion for the continuance of the NBA must rest upon non-economic

213

grounds. In the course of his 1962 Judgement, Mr Justice Buckley uttered the now famous words, 'Books are different'. Books unquestionably have a special cultural, social and educational role to play. It may therefore be argued that this role both is, and always has been, the only justification needed for the continuance of price maintenance on books both in the UK and throughout the world. This does not, however, imply that economic factors should be disregarded, since there are many respects in which trade practices could be improved without bringing the continuance of price maintenance into question.

France

The position of France is especially interesting because price controls on books there have been both abolished and restored within recent years. It was decreed on January 1st 1979 that the prix conseillé would be abolished on July 1st. Prices would, as from that date, no longer appear on book covers, nor in catalogues and advertising matter. Prior to 1979 it was not illegal as such to sell below the recommended price, and discounting inevitably crept in, particularly in the case of FNAC, a discount house which offered a 20% reduction across the board. The Monory decree was intended to restrict the activities of discounters, and achieve lower prices through competition.

By early 1981 it was clear that the response among the French book trade was one of virtually unanimous disapproval. It was felt, in particular, that there had been a substantial shift away from traditional bookshops in the purchasing of their profitable quick-selling titles, and that discounters didn't need to spend money on advertising because customers assumed, not always correctly, that they were going to get a big discount.

Traditional bookshops sometimes raised the prices of slow-selling stock by way of compensation, but allegedly with little success, and publishers reduced the number of such titles since fewer bookshops wanted them in stock. As a consequence the division between success and failure with respect to both firms and titles became more marked. The larger bookshops profited because they had more control over their marketing strategies than before, but smaller ones found pricing a time-consuming and costly exercise. Technically they could be compensated by quality of service discounts from publishers, but earning enough, and getting them paid, proved difficult.

214

In February 1980 price differences of 100% were noted among different forms of sales outlet, and prices rose outside the main urban centres. Prices of books rose faster than prices generally as printers and publishers took their opportunity to pass the buck to booksellers, but the latters' price raising on specialist books also disinclined their publishers to keep trade prices down. Overall, therefore, the forces of competition appeared to be working rather perversely, and the new Socialist Government, elected in mid-1981, introduced a law enforcing rpm on books as from 1st January 1982. The Lang Act required that the publisher's fixed price be printed on all titles, and that booksellers sell at not less than 95% of the published price for the first two years after publication. Subsequently they could lower the price only if they had had the title in stock for at least six months, and they could refer to this reduced price only on point-of-sale labelling, not in other forms of advertising. Books sold by mail order could not be offered at reduced rates within nine months of publication. The Publishers Association guaranteed that its members would keep prices down and would discontinue the practice of giving massive trade discounts based solely on quantity rather than on the quality of the service offered to the public.

The required review, eighteen months later, came out unequivocally in favour of the new system, claiming that it had clearly benefited the trade. The booksellers' associations, which had initially favoured freedom to fix prices, were no longer of that mind, but voiced a major grievance over the awarding of quality discounts. They claimed that publishers were reluctant to pay up, and rewarded services which benefited themselves rather than services to the customer. A further bone of contention, this time with the authorities, concerned the continuation of discount selling. Lower courts ruled against such discounters when they were taken to court by local booksellers' associations, but the appeal courts found in favour of the discounters, a result which encouraged further discounting to take place. Subsequently writs and injunctions flew freely, to the joy of the legal profession, and the current position is indeterminate. Hostilities will resume in October, by which time the European Court in Luxembourg will have ruled on the validity or otherwise of the Lang Act in relation to the Treaty of Rome.

Rpm in Europe

In addition to the UK, rpm is the general rule in West Germany, the Netherlands, Austria, German-speaking Switzerland, Denmark and Norway. Evidence concerning trade practices, either in countries with rpm or without it, remains largely anecdotal. Ironically, one of the criticisms levelled after the collapse of rpm in Italy was that this compelled booksellers to work on inadequate margins.

In terms of trade between fellow European states, mention should be made of recent European Commission rulings. In November 1981, the European Commission ruled that an rpm agreement between the book trade associations of Flanders and the Netherlands was contrary to EEC competition rules. An appeal was lodged, but was eventually rejected in January 1984.

The rpm systems in Flanders and the Netherlands require publishers to fix book prices both at home and for books shipped across the Dutch-Flemish border. The EEC Commission ruling stated that while it recognised the benefits of rpm in general, 'it should be possible to achieve those aims without collective resale price maintenance crossing the member states and being imposed by member associations'.

In its Judgement the European Court rejected the argument that inability to impose prices within the single language area could itself lead to unfair competition, or that this was sufficient reason to exempt an entire sector from EEC competition rules.

The Court held that legal practices or legislation in one country cannot be imposed in another to restrict competition. Arrangements within the UK or Germany where borders are not national means that the judgement may not apply in any other case in practice.

Rpm outside Europe

United States: The size of the country deterred agreements among trade members, and widely dispersed bookshops would anyway be extremely difficult to monitor. As a consequence rpm never got to first base, nor is there any reason to expect that it ever will. The trade argues that consumers are therefore suffering a loss of service. Evidence is lacking.

216

Canada: Price maintenance has been illegal for decades. Evidence of detriment caused thereby was considered significant in the UK case in 1962, but subsequent commentaries cast doubt on the evidence, and the Canadian authorities remain unmoved.

New Zealand: Rpm has no legal backing, but recommended prices are supported by traditional bookshops. Widespread discounting elsewhere is currently putting their loyalty to the test.

Australia: Rpm was abolished in 1972 as a result of the Tribunal placing more confidence in the assertions of economists than in the dire predictions of members of the book trade. The Tribunal concluded that prices would fall; that there would be no reduction in the range of titles on offer; that booksellers' services would be maintained; and that booksellers would continue to stock up on titles which were likely to be the subject of price competition. A survey in 1975 supported the Tribunal's findings for the most part. Subsequently Zifcak has many times asserted that prices have tended to rise; services to be cut; stocks to be reduced; special orders to be charged for; and more remainders to be sold. As a consequence bookselling has remained economically viable through the sacrifice of cultural responsibility. The reading public are, therefore, the prime sufferers. This is necessarily rather difficult to establish. The fact that discounters have not taken over the market is rather more concrete in the evidence stakes.

Chapter Nine

COPYRIGHT

Issues relating to copyright have increasingly come to the fore around the world in recent years. One aspect is piracy, discussed later in this chapter. Piracy does not, however, affect the home markets of the publishers concerned, and is therefore more of a nuisance than a life or death issue. The latter is commonly perceived as being rooted in the increasingly widespread use of photocopying facilities, and it is this issue which we will explore below.

It is not altogether easy to address the issue of copyright in the abstract because, over time and in different countries, the established justification for copyright protection has varied considerably. Copyright involves philosophical as well as economic issues, but whereas the latter are in principle verifiable, virtually no evidence of any kind exists of the link between the copying of copyright material and the economics of publishing books and articles. This means, ultimately, that the issues involved in copyright may well only be resolved by recourse to legalistic interpretation of copyright statutes in individual countries. It may be observed that in a good many countries this will first of all require such statutes to be introduced! The most obvious justification for copyright protection is that a writer is entitled to a property right in his creation. To allow such a right does not deny any rights to anyone else. Hence the writer should be rewarded for allowing others to share in his creation. A second argument relates to the fact that any publication increases the welfare of society. It is therefore undesirable to allow barriers to publication to arise unnecessarily. The expectation that potential infringement of copyright will destroy the economic viability of a publication obviously constitutes such a barrier. The solution is to guarantee a recompense to both publisher and author for such infringements, thereby maintaining the viability of books which need to be printed in smaller editions.

It is possible to photocopy entire books for less than their purchase price. The end result is not, however, anything like as satisfactory as the original, so the real problem typically arises either in the form of copying chapters or sections of books, or of copying the whole or greater part of articles in journals. In the great majority of cases the problem arises in the context of information provision as part of the educational system.

On the one side are lined up academics and librarians. The former argue that knowledge is a right, rather than a marketable commodity, and should not have to be bought when the scholar is not using it to earn money himself. The latter are concerned to provide a library service as cheaply as possible, and consider that inter-library loans and multiple photocopies held on a restricted loan basis are cheaper than a substantial enlargement of the book stock or additional subscriptions to journals. The opposing view taken by publishers is essentially that for a photocopy to be taken an original must already exist. This sets up a vicious circle because photocopying erodes potential sales; therefore fewer copies are printed at a higher price; therefore fewer libraries can afford to buy; therefore more copying occurs. In many cases, publication of certain types of books ceases to be viable and the academic community ultimately suffers. Everyone agrees this may happen, but whereas publishers say it is widespread, their opponents claim the effects are very limited. Since no one can quantify the effect with any precision, it ultimately depends upon whether governments can be persuaded by either side to intervene in the dispute.

In order to get some idea of how the authorities tend to react, we can examine certain aspects of the international situation.

There are two worldwide conventions relating to copyright proper, namely the Berne convention of 1886, last revised in Paris in 1971, and the Universal Copyright Convention (UCC) of 1952, also revised in Paris in 1971.

The Universal Copyright Convention 1952

This provides a minimum term of protection, both for a country's own citizens and for those of other countries who are published in that country, of life of the author plus 25 years, or, where the term of protection dates from publication, 25 years from that date. The revision in 1971 was mainly concerned with provisions allowing developing countries which were members of UCC wider rights in the compulsory licensing field.

The UCC arose because the United States were unwilling to join the Berne Convention. It provided a relatively low standard of protection, and this was of concern to existing Berne Convention Members who were afraid that countries would leave the Convention and opt for lower protection. A safeguard clause was therefore inserted to prevent a country which left the Berne Convention from being able to claim protection on the basis of UCC from other Berne Convention Members. This provision was waived in 1971 in the case of developing countries.

The Berne Convention 1886

The original text has been extensively revised. In the course of the 1967 Stockholm revision specific reference was made for the first time to the issue of making copies of a copyright work. At the time, all Convention members had individual approaches to the issue, which, whilst all accepting the need to provide protection, differed in the exceptions to be allowed. The over-riding need, therefore, at the 1971 Paris revision was to find a compromise formula to which all members would agree.

Article 9(1) of the Paris text of the Berne Convention provided that authors should have the exclusive right of authorising the reproduction of their protected works in any manner or form. Article 9(2), however, allowed countries to permit the reproduction of works in certain special cases, provided that the reproduction does not conflict with normal exploitation of the work, and does not unreasonably prejudice the legitimate interests of the author.

The official explanation of this provision is as follows:

'If it is considered that reproduction conflicts with the normal exploitation of a work, reproduction is not permitted at all. If it is considered that reproduction does not conflict with the normal exploitation of work, the next step would be to consider whether it does not unreasonably prejudice the legitimate interests of the author. Only if such is not the case would it be possible, in certain special cases, to introduce a compulsory licence, or to provide for use without payment. A practical example might be photocopying for various purposes.

'If it consists of producing a very large number of copies it may not be permitted, as it conflicts with the normal exploitation of the work. If it implies a rather large number of copies for use in industrial undertakings, it may not unreasonably prejudice the legitimate interest of the author provided that, according to national legislation, an equitable remuneration is paid. If a small number of copies is made photocopying may be permitted without payment particularly for individual or scientific use.'

221

It is clear that the regulation of reprography in detail is essentially a matter for national laws. Thus each country would be free to adopt any appropriate measures which, while respecting the provisions of the conventions, establish whatever system is best adapted to meet its own educational, cultural, social and economic requirements. The position in a number of countries is set out below for illustrative purposes.

The United States

Revisions to US copyright law came into force in January 1978. The new law prohibited copying beyond the limits of fair use, and also systematic library copying of copyright material. Inter-library lending was permitted provided a library did not receive copies in such aggregate quantities (a maximum of five) as to substitute for a subscription to, or purchase of, such work. The first quinquennial report of the Register of Copyrights on library photocopying, issued in January 1983, was critical of the lack of balance between library photocopying practices and publishers' rights as defined in the law. The report indicated that libraries misinterpreted Section 108 of the Copyright Act to authorise copying in excess of fair use, and that the relationship between Sections 107 (on Fair Use) and 108 (on Photocopying) should be reconsidered. The report considered that far too much photocopying was job related and that libraries were virtually setting themselves up as republishers of copyright works. The solutions recommended were either to surcharge library photocopying equipment or collective licensing agreements through a licensing agency.

The library community responded that prior reports indicated they were acting within the legislative guidelines with respect to inter-library loans, and that library copying in excess of fair use was not considered unlawful. The solutions offered were therefore rejected outright. A number of ways of revising the Copyright Act have been proposed by the two sides but little progress has been made.

The fair use section of the Copyright Act guaranteed the right of teachers to duplicate published material for classroom distribution. The congressional reports accompanying the Act included an 'Agreement on Guidelines for Classroom Copying in Not-for-profit Educational Institutions'. The amount of fair use copying indicated in the Guidelines was not, however, considered sufficient for college teaching practices, and this led to a case whereby it was charged that New York University professors collaborated with a commercial copying shop to reproduce copyrighted books of assigned readings. The case was settled out of court with New York University agreeing to restrict copying in line with the Guideline provisions. Other institutions have subsequently also fallen into line.

The United Kingdom

The position in the UK developed along similar lines. The Whitford Committee was set up in 1964 to consider the need to revise the law on copyright and designs. It published its Report in 1977. Its starting point was a joint statement on fair use copying issued in 1965 by the Publishers' Association and the Society of Authors entitled 'Photocopying and the Law'. In this they agreed that where, for the purposes of research or private study, a single copy is made from a copyright work of a single extract not exceeding 4,000 words or a series of extracts (none exceeding 3,000 words) to a total of 8,000 words, provided that in no case the total amount copied exceeds 10 per cent of the whole work, then that copy would be regarded as fair dealing. In essence this did not mean that these limits had any backing in law, but rather that publishers did not want to be bothered with requests to copy unless the limits were exceeded.

Under Section 7 of the 1956 Copyright Act anyone wanting to make a copy from library material has to sign a declaration that the copy is for research or private study. But these terms are ambiguous and were interpreted as allowing every student in a large class to make a personal copy from the same material. In addition most libraries happily allowed the setting up of limited access sections containing multiple copies of copyrighted material. The Whitford solution was to propose a system of blanket licensing whereby individual publishers and authors would not be responsible for collecting their own royalties. Indeed, payment at a standard rate would be collected by a central collecting agency which would then distribute the proceeds to the copyright owners.

The blanket licence would reduce the need for making large numbers of individual requests to copy, but would require a royalty to be paid for single copies which were previously supplied free. Not surprisingly this went down like a lead weight with the academic community, and there were those who argued fiercely that the Copyright Act did not lend support to the Whitford position.

223

However, publishers, sensing their advantage, pressed ahead with the setting up of a Copyright Licensing Agency to enable institutions to photocopy within an agreed system, and subsequently made it clear that the codes of practice favoured by libraries would no longer be accepted as an alternative to licensing. The CLA proposed the introduction of an audited scheme, similar to the US Copyright Collecting Centre's licence, whereby records need to be kept of copying for a 90 day period only, the figures gathered then being used as a base for extrapolation to an annual sum. Just recently the associations of local authorities for England, Scotland and Wales have agreed an experimental scheme to licence photocopying in schools, to start in November 1984. The scheme will allow copying well beyond the provisions of the Copyright Act in return for payment of a lump sum. It will run for one year, and the records kept will provide the basis for subsequent negotiations over the fee to be paid for a permanent licence.

Whether higher educational institutions will join in is as yet unclear, but the recent case in which certain institutions in Manchester were forced to pay damages for abuse of copyright has sent waves throughout the UK, and resulted in massive shedding of material from libraries. For this material to be reintroduced copyright permission will have to be sought and a fee paid.

West Germany

Under Article 54(2) of the German Copyright Act 1965 authors have the right to remuneration in respect of reproduction for commercial purposes. Single copies may be made without charge only for strictly personal use. As a result of a decision by the Federal Court of Justice in a case involving photocopying from scientific journals by an industrial firm, an agreement resembling a blanket licence was concluded between the Federation of German Industry and the Exchange Association of the German Book Trade. This covered photographic reproduction from scientific and technical periodicals of domestic origin carried out for the internal use of firms. Licence fees are paid in a variety of methods to a collecting agency which then redistributes the income, less expenses, to authors and publishers.

Sweden

Sweden often takes a more progressive stance than most countries in social and educational problems. In this case, under the Swedish Copyright Law of 1960, archives or libraries can copy literary works 'for the purpose of their activities', and 'for personal use'. Libraries do not pay royalties in respect of photocopying, but must inform the Swedish Fund for Authors of copies made, subsequent to which the State pays recompense through the fund to authors.

Photocopying of copyright works in schools was the subject of a 1973 agreement between the Government of Sweden and a group of organisations representing authors and publishers. These organisations agreed to give general permission to school teachers to make photocopies within certain limits, eliminating the need to ask for specific permission each time, and the Government undertook to pay fees for this permission based upon actual copies made.

Conclusion

The two general conclusions to be drawn from the above discussion and examples are firstly, that copyright law can provide endless problems of interpretation. Very few countries have an up to date Copyright Act, and in many cases the Acts were legislated prior to the widespread introduction of photocopying, so their lack of precision in this respect is hardly surprising. Secondly, insofar as publishers around the world are clearly becoming increasingly impatient with the abuse of copyright, their attempts to restrict such abuse are beginning to bear fruit. Just where the line is to be drawn in fair dealing is inevitably going to vary from country to country, but the evidence from the USA and the UK clearly indicates that where publishers stand prepared to defend their interests, if necessary by recourse to law, they are likely to force the educational communities to make significant concessions.

Piracy

Where the developed and less developed publishing nations come most obviously into conflict is over the issue of piracy. Book piracy was worth perhaps $500 million in 1981 (not as bad as for records and cassettes, but hardly a sum to brush aside), and the ultimate key to its continuing success is that it results in price reductions in countries where money to spend on books is not plentiful. Under such circumstances not all governments are madly keen to take action on the matter.

Not that low prices mean low profits for pirate publishers. The UK Book Development Council has produced some sample costings to illustrate this point.

TABLE 9.1   UK: COMPARISON OF COSTS — LEGITIMATE AND PIRATE PUBLISHERS

	Legitimate publisher	Pirate 1	Pirate 2
Retail price	100	50	80
less			
Discount	20	10	30
Royalty	8	—	—
First costs	8	½	½
Production	8	5	5
Stocking/distribution	15	3	3
Marketing	11	—	—
Overheads	15	2	2
= profit	15	29½	39½

Source: UK Book Development Council

The most obvious conclusion to draw is that the legitimate publisher has no room to manoeuvre on price, because even if he did cut his price the pirate could easily match any reduction.

The UK Publishers' Association proposes a number of reasons for controlling book piracy, namely (1) stealing copyright is no easier to justify than stealing anything else. Countries may try to avoid this implication by failing to sign international agreements on copyright, but inexcusable as this is it is far worse when, as in Singapore, they fail to enforce their own internal law on copyright. (2) competition among pirate editions of popular titles may make them uneconomic even for pirate publishers and deter bookshops from stocking any which they think may be sold in other pirated editions elsewhere. (3) royalties required for an authorised reprint or translation are quite small, and their payment would not cause prices to rise by as much as is often claimed.

The main offenders are currently Korea, Taiwan and Singapore, although piracy is common throughout the Middle East and South East Asia. The only lasting solution must be in persuading the governments of countries concerned either to introduce copyright laws or to enforce those that already exist, but it would certainly help if in the first instance publishers in the countries concerned took action to protect their own interests.

Copyright and Piracy: A Case Study

During the late 1970s and early 1980s a number of factors combined to enhance opportunities for piracy and copyright infringement in India. In the first place, because of the dominance of institutional buying mentioned elsewhere, reductions in institutional budgets such as occurred in India in the late 1970s drastically reduced the market for legitimate publishers, who understandably responded by pruning their publishing operations, especially with respect to books for higher education. In the second place, the literate population, loosely defined, rose by getting on for 100 million during the 1970s, and per capita incomes also rose, albeit slowly. The personal market therefore offered opportunities which the major publishers, locked into institutional sales, were in a poor position to meet.

As a result private editions began to proliferate, and American editions of popular titles were increasingly imported. These practices were defended as providing more books more cheaply, but the Government accepted the need to stamp out these practices, and in August 1984 the Indian Parliament passed the Copyright (Amendment) Bill which sought to introduce 'stringent legislative and enforcement measures' against piracy. The main provisions of the Bill were:

1. to increase penalties for piracy

2. to empower the police to seize pirate copies without requiring a warrant

227

3. to remove any time limitation upon taking proceedings against private publishers.

In addition, Penguin has recently obtained a favourable judgement against one of the biggest importers of books which infringed Penguin's market agreements, and although the matter is not fully resolved other publishers are now likely to follow suit. Finally, the Indian Government has curtailed book imports along the lines of the Paris Copyright convention, thereby offering additional protection to indigeneous publishers.

Chapter Ten

BOOK PRINTING

The main purpose of this section is to review some of the major issues relating to book printing which are currently of concern around the world. Printing is increasingly an international activity, and we will also examine some of the considerations which determine where publishers choose to buy printing capacity.

Europe vs America

The differing treatment by America of printers in Europe and the USA has long been a cause of discontent in Europe. In essence this is because the European market is open to all whereas US printers are protected from competition in their home market. Historically, US copyright law specified that all work containing 'non-dramatic literary material that is in the English language' which was first printed in the USA, or whose authors were citizens or residents of the USA, had to be manufactured in the USA in order to obtain copyright protection in, and be imported into, the USA. This meant that the text of all copies, excepting only up to 1500 copies of any book or periodical first published outside the USA and imported within five years of first publication, had to be printed and bound in the USA, and that the printing had to be done from type set in the USA or from plates made in the USA from type set there. Where text was produced by lithographic process or photoengraving process, this had to be performed wholly within the USA.

In 1976, America was persuaded to amend the Act, commencing on January 1st 1978, in order to:

a)   exempt Canada;

b)   exempt up to 2000 copies of a title;

c)   exempt works by American authors domiciled outside the USA for at least one year before the date of importation;

d)   exempt works to which foreign authors have contributed a substantial part even if an American author is also a contributor;

e)   define in a more clear-cut manner the processes that constitute manufacture.

None of these amendments were of particular significance in practice. The key issue was a commitment to repeal the clause protecting the US market as from 1st July 1982. But Congress passed a Bill on 15th June 1982 setting back the date of repeal to 1st July 1986. This was vetoed by President Reagan but promptly restored by Congress. De facto, therefore, the clause remains in operation. Furthermore, due to definitional difficulties, it is unclear whether certain illustrated texts are exempt or not, and publishers are bound to err on the side of caution in directing such work to US printers.

The nub of the problem is, therefore, that whereas US printers have a stranglehold on the US market, literary work manufactured in the USA can, and does, enter the EEC free of all non-tariff and virtually all tariff barriers. Given the widespread use of English within the EEC, and not merely in the UK, and given the facilities which printers have throughout Europe to print in English, these non-reciprocal arrangements are most unfavourable to EEC printers.

All EEC member states are signatories to the Florence Agreement which, in the cause of the free exchange of ideas, extends duty-free treatment to works printed overseas on behalf of EEC publishers in addition to works published overseas. America profits from the Agreement but refuses to reciprocate. This results primarily from a report presented to Congress by the US Copyright Office in June 1981 which concluded that between 10% and 19% of book printing protected by the Act might end up overseas. In addition, the US Department of Labor estimated that repeal of the Act would cost between 170,300 and 366,500 job losses overall, of which between 9,000 and 13,000 would occur in book printing.

In response to these claims, EUROGRAF submitted counter-arguments to the US International Trade Commission in March 1983. They pointed out firstly that publishing, as distinct from printing, activities were not protected and would be unaffected by repeal. Secondly, that printing overseas for ease of distribution to export markets would be unlikely to rise significantly because US publishers were not in any event great exporters. Thirdly, that if overseas printing resulted in reduced costs then more books ought to be sold in aggregate in the USA, thereby creating more jobs. Overall, therefore, job losses in the USA would be very small.

With respect to import penetration, this would not be affected greatly by repeal. The great bulk of American books are destined for the home market, so they would have to be transported back to the USA at a cost which would offset a good part of the potential savings in production costs. If the UK publishing industry does not find it economic to buy extensively outside Europe, presumably US publishers would not find it economic to buy extensively outside North America. Although this might seem to suggest that the argument isn't worth pursuing, it must be remembered that the US market is very large, and for European printers to obtain, say, one half of American imports of printing would constitute a significant improvement in their turnover.

United Kingdom

The country most obviously affected by the above is the UK, because of the linguistic connection. Unfortunately, this is by no means the only difficulty which affects the UK printing industry, although some of these difficulties also affect its main competitors.

This has not always been so. Historically, all was well with UK printing until well into the 1960s. The market for books both at home and, especially, abroad was buoyant, and it was the custom for the main UK printers to get together annually to thrash out a pay award with the unions which was then promptly passed on to publishers. The increases were generally modest, providing little incentive to look elsewhere even if they had known where to look. Even when printers began to negotiate wages individually, they found it in their mutual best interests to compete on service rather than price. In response, some of the major publishing houses such as Longmans began to look to the Far East for printing capacity, especially for books destined predominantly for export markets. By 1974, UK publishers were alleging that they would be unable to survive in the face of rising domestic printing prices. Material costs rose by 29.7% that year, but subsequently fell back to 0% in 1977. Printers' non-material costs, chiefly wages, did rise sharply in money terms during the mid-1970s, but not by much after adjusting for

231

inflation, and there is evidence that printers were unable to pass on all of the increases in their costs despite the consequent deterioration in profitability. In essence, therefore, there was still no enormous incentive for UK publishers to go abroad unless it was, for example, to obtain high quality reproduction in colour.

However, the situation changed quite significantly in the late 1970s. Not merely was UK inflation high by international standards, with printing wage increases in 1979 of 15% on average, and in 1980 of 20% on average, but the exchange rate rose sharply with an equivalent effect upon UK printers' prices converted to foreign currencies. Given that UK wages were low by comparison with our main European competitors, UK printers would still have managed adequately were productivity not so poor that it completely offset the wage cost advantage even after a decade of substantial investment in new equipment. As a consequence, an increasing number of UK publishers began to look abroad for printing capacity, and in Hong Kong they found, for example, both lower wages and high productivity.

To some extent, the UK printing industry was cushioned by the inevitable loss of control which publishers faced when printing at a great distance, and by the heavy shipment costs of bringing the product home, provided the final market was not primarily Asia or Australasia. Most UK printers had little choice, however, but to raise productivity, reduce manning levels, and hold down prices and profits. Some succeeded and some did not. It is estimated that as many as 30% of jobs in book printing have disappeared since 1980 in the UK. Several well known companies such as the Fakenham Press and Oxley Printing have either disappeared or cut back hugely. The low exchange rate will now help stem the outflow of work, but there can be no doubt that UK publishers are now much more sophisticated in seeking out the optimum combination of price, quality and delivery. An illustration of what they might find was provided in the March 1981 Production Supplement of *Printing World*. This contained quotations for the printing and binding of 50,000 copies of a 496 page colour encyclopaedia containing 500 illustrations, half in colour, as follows:

TABLE 10.1 COMPARISON OF INTERNATIONAL PRINTING AND BINDING
COSTS

Unit: £ per copy	Different quotations given			
Hong Kong	1.89	1.98	2.23	
Singapore	1.93	2.03	2.04	
UK	2.40	2.43	2.66	2.78
USA	2.19	2.30		
Spain	1.83	1.86	1.95	
Italy	2.14	2.14	2.37	
Belgium	2.08			
Holland	2.18			

Note: see previous text for specifications
Source: *Printing World,* March 1981

On this occasion, Spain won the day, though currency fluctuations
could wipe out the price advantage for a particular country. What is most
obvious is that such fluctuations would not help the UK printers making
quotations given the scale of their competitive disadvantage. At the end
of the day, there can be no doubt that UK printers are currently in an
invidious position, for not merely are they largely excluded from the
USA, but many Far Eastern markets are heavily protected by tariffs,
which means that printers in Hong Kong and Singapore need to compete
most effectively in the UK's traditional English-speaking markets.

Elsewhere in Europe

The main difference between the UK and other European countries
relates to the scale on which book publishing takes place. In most other
respects, the problems and the opportunities are the same, for example,
with respect to the USA. Variations in the rate of inflation and in
exchange rates favour first one country then another. In 1982, for
example, the Belgian printing industry enjoyed an upturn after years of
stagnation, but it still represented a further minor setback in real terms.
Investment was heavy in order to improve the industry's competitive
position. In West Germany things were no better. Production activity
declined sharply with capacity utilization falling below 80% for the first
time since 1975. Real turnover just held its own, and a large number of

233

printing bankruptcies were recorded. White and blue collar redundancies were necessary. As in the UK, small offset printing was increasingly marked by the exigencies of short deadlines, rapid order completion and smaller and fast changing printings.

In France, on the other hand, printed tonnage of books rose by 17% between 1979 and 1980, and held its own the following year, the best performance of all printing categories. However, although turnover rose by 20% in money terms over the two year period, this failed to keep up with inflation. In Italy, the inflationary situation was much worse, with labour costs rising by 20% in 1982 following on a mere 15% in 1981. Unsurprisingly, remaining competitive against countries such as Spain is a serious problem.

Finally, the Netherlands also had a bad year. Bookprinting volume fell slightly and real turnover fell by several per cent, causing redundancies to take place. Overall, therefore, it may reasonably be concluded that printing throughout the EEC is going through a bad patch which all must confront in much the same way in the face of growing external competition.

The Developing Countries

Like his counterpart in the developed countries, a publisher in a developing country may choose where to obtain his printing capacity. However, his requirements may well differ from those of his European counterparts, and there will inevitably be difficulties arising from the use of uncommon languages, climatic conditions and lack of contacts. He therefore needs a viable local printing industry.

Information about printing is difficult to obtain for developing countries, but the results of a major survey were published some years ago by UNESCO[1]. Smith compiled a table showing variations in manufacturing cost elements in relation to a list price chosen by the publisher.

[1] Datus C. Smith, 'The Economics of Book Publishing in Developing Countries', Series: *Reports and Papers on Mass Communication, No.79* (UNESCO, Paris, 1977)

TABLE 10.2   MANUFACTURING COST ELEMENTS AS % OF LIST PRICE IN DEVELOPING COUNTRIES

	In edition of 1,000 copies	In edition of 5,000 copies	In edition of 10,000 copies
Composition			
Asia	12.9	4.9	2.8
Latin America	15.1	9.5	7.1
Middle East	17.4	5.2	3.7
Arica	21.8	9.5	6.3
ALL AREAS	15.1	6.9	4.6
Presswork			
Asia	4.7	4.2	3.8
Latin America	5.7	5.2	5.1
Middle East	7.0	3.9	3.6
Africa	8.1	7.7	8.2
ALL AREAS	5.7	5.0	4.5
Binding			
Asia	2.7	3.8	4.2
Latin America	2.0	3.2	3.5
Middle East	3.1	5.0	5.6
Africa	8.0	4.4	4.6
ALL AREAS	2.6	4.1	4.3
Paper			
Asia	10.3	15.5	17.0
Latin America	5.6	9.0	10.2
Middle East	11.5	15.6	17.2
Africa	8.0	11.6	15.2
ALL AREAS	8.9	14.0	14.9
Total manufacturing cost			
Asia	30.6	28.4	27.8
Latin America	28.4	26.9	27.8
Middle East	39.0	29.7	30.1
Africa	40.8	33.2	34.3
ALL AREAS	32.3	30.0	29.3

Source: D.C.Smith, op.cit., p.15

As can be seen, there are significant variations in the proportions in different regions, with paper relatively expensive in Asia and the Middle East, and composition, presswork and binding in Africa. In aggregate, Africa comes out very badly compared to Latin America, although curious things appear to happen as editions get bigger with, for example, the proportion rising as editions grow from 5,000 to 10,000 copies in many regions. Differences between regions are far less significant for large editions, but the fact is that editions rarely exceed 5,000 copies in Africa.

Obviously the cost/price relationship involves decisions by publishers about the appropriate retail price for editions of different sizes. This factor can be removed by examining manufacturing cost per copy in units of local currency, which appears as table 10.3 below.

TABLE 10.3   MANUFACTURING COST PER COPY

Unit: local currency	In edition of 1,000 copies	In edition of 5,000 copies	In edition of 10,000 copies
Asia	100	54	47
Latin America	100	45	38
Middle East	100	55	45
Africa	100	49	41
ALL AREAS	100	51	44
A highly developed country	100	29	21

Source: D.C.Smith, op.cit., p.17

The table shows that there are very big savings to be made as editions rise from 1,000 to 5,000 in size, and some additional, but limited, savings arise if the edition increases to 10,000. This pattern is similar to that found in a typical developed country, but as the table shows, costs in the latter decline much faster for editions above 1,000 copies, leaving developing countries at a significant competitive disadvantage.

This factor is by no means unrelated to the technological issue.

Table 10.4, below, shows the comparative costs of different methods of composition.

TABLE 10.4   COMPOSITION: COMPARATIVE COST BY DIFFERENT METHODS

Unit: %

	Linotype or monotype	Typewriter	Hand composition	Photo composition
Asia	100	74	103	209
Latin America	100	57	175	172
Middle East	100	68	141	374
Africa	100	69	107	206
ALL AREAS	100	69	119	231

Source: D.C.Smith, op.cit., p.17

For all editions up to 10,000 copies, letterpress is cheaper than offset, significantly so in Asia and Africa. Typewriter composition can only be used with offset printing and is therefore generally not the answer, though it is cheap. Hand composition, even in regions of plentiful labour, is surprisingly expensive. A final conclusion is that advanced technology will generally not provide the answer to cost reduction. Operating skills are in short supply in developing countries, the equipment difficult and costly to repair, and climatic conditions unconducive to its use. The traditional hot metal processes must, therefore, remain the bastion of the printing industries in developing countries except where the vagaries of individual languages allow little latitude for anything other than hand composition.

With respect to binding, table 10.5 shows clearly that stapling is by far the most economical solution.

Perfect binding is in any event susceptible to climatic conditions because it involves adhesion. Here again, the solution differs from that typically found in developed countries.

TABLE 10.5   BINDING: COMPARATIVE COST BY DIFFERENT METHODS

Unit: %

Copies per edition	Asia	Latin America	Middle East	Africa	All areas
1,000					
Staple	100	100	100	100	100
Sew	164	156	120	344	166
'Perfect'	147	204	76	127	140
5,000					
Staple	100	100	100	100	100
Sew	167	161	114	341	170
'Perfect'	150	215	77	122	158
10,000					
Staple	100	100	100	100	100
Sew	165	161	117	340	166
'Perfect'	148	222	79	122	144

Source: D.C.Smith, op.cit., p.18

An inhibitory factor in developing countries is undoubtedly the price of paper, and local production does not necessarily resolve the problem. The rate of decline as edition size grows in the table below is unexpectedly slow and cannot therefore be relied on.

TABLE 10.6   PAPER COSTS IN DIFFERENT AREAS

Unit: $US per copy

	In edition of 1,000 copies	In edition of 5,000 copies	In edition of 10,000 copies
Asia	0.18	0.16	0.16
Latin America	.19	.19	.19
Middle East	.31	.29	.28
Africa	.50	.43	.43
ALL AREAS	.24	.23	.23

Source: D.C.Smith, op.cit., p.18

Between 1970 and 1978, the number of countries producing more than 80% of their paper consumption rose from 5 to 8 in Latin America, from 7 to 11 in Asia and from 4 to 7 in Africa. Its cost nevertheless remains a major factor affecting the profitability or otherwise of printing and publishing in developing countries.

Technological Change

It is beyond the scope of this text to enter into a lengthy exposition of what the future holds with respect to printing techniques[1]. It is clear, however, that significant changes are taking place which will offer both much greater flexibility to publishers and opportunities for those printers who invest wisely to meet changing demands. Letterpress is practically obsolete in developed countries, although it can still be used economically where low quality paperbacks are required. It has been replaced primarily by offset lithography, and to a lesser extent by gravure, which is held back by the high cost of preparing the cylinders.

The key to the future lies in automation, with the widespread introduction of mini-computers and microprocessors in order to raise productivity and improve consistency. Electronic composition and the automatic setting up and running of the printing press and bindery operations are already with us. The critical issue from a printer's viewpoint is to utilise the technology to produce what the publisher wants, and one obvious example of this, which results from the previously mentioned relationship between title output and turnover, is the need to produce print runs which are short, and on a time-scale which is short, by historical standards. Computerized Web offset presses are currently the answer here, and printers who hope to survive will have to invest in these or alternative machines. Another challenge, especially for UK printers, is the economic production of high quality colour work for small editions.

The relationship between publishers and printers is obviously important. Printer/publishers have always been the exception rather than the rule, especially for paperback publishing. No publisher likes to be so committed to a single printer that something like a strike could disrupt

---

[1] for a detailed discussion see, for example, P.Hills (ed), *The Future of the Printed Word*, (Frances Pinter Ltd, 1980)

239

his publishing programme. On the other hand, switching continuously from printer to printer causes enormous problems of control, especially where quality and house style are important. Printers' machinery necessarily becomes obsolescent, and no publisher wants to be tied too closely to a printer who is unwilling or unable to remain at the forefront of technology. On the other hand, a printer will normally offer better terms for a larger volume of work. At the end of the day, it is the printer's task to provide an economic service, and the publisher's task to obtain the best deal available. So long as printers and publishers are largely independent this will result in UK publishers testing the water overseas even if they ultimately decide to stay at home. The smarter UK printers now know this only too well, but it is conceivable that changes in the exchange rate, or a shortage of capacity resulting from the closure of inefficient firms, will swing the pendulum more in favour of the printers who remain, although the balmy days of the 1960s will never return.

Training

There are two facets to the training issue. In the first place, as already indicated, the lack of suitably trained personnel can be a major inhibiting factor in the development of a printing industry in a developing country. However, the increasing sophistication of production techniques, and the widespread introduction of computerisation, also represent a challenge in developed countries. Typically, training takes place in colleges which have a modest range of traditional equipment, and in many cases this remains adequate even today, simply because an awful lot of printing is still being done by small companies using small-scale unsophisticated equipment. But book printing for major publishing houses is an increasingly capital intensive high technology business, and no individual college, or indeed individual printer, can reasonably expect to be able to offer a training in the full range of techniques available. Furthermore, rather fewer operatives are going to be needed because computers increasingly do the work, and therefore both these pressures lead inexorably to the conclusion that a relatively small number of centralized facilities will be needed in each country to satisfy its training needs. With so many vested interests, this process is inevitably slow, but the pressures of international competition may eventually force the issue to a head.

A related issue concerns the preparation of the original manuscript. Here again the traditional methods of transferring the author's typed copy into a second format ready to be printed is time consuming and expensive. Computers now make it possible to produce the text on a screen for easy editing, and the edited version can then either drive a type-setter or create a master copy for the printer. The word-processing function is well within the grasp of the original author or his secretary, so it is increasingly going to be a case of training the originator rather than the printer's employee. The computer can, of course, perform more sophisticated tasks, such as moving blocks of text and graphics around, although the cost of equipment and software is likely to remain beyond the scope of individual authors for some time to come.

Chapter Eleven

ELECTRONIC PUBLISHING

The aim of this chapter is to describe the extent to which electronic publishing has affected the book market and describe developments taking place that might have an impact in the future. Wherever possible, examples of current commercial ventures will be used to illustrate conclusions. That electronic publishing will replace the book in all its aspects is not in question. The threats posed by electronic publishing are more diverse and less dramatic than that: but there nonetheless.

The traditional print publishing market is segmented into many specialised markets. This is even more true of electronic publishing. The range of electronic publishing ventures discussed in this chapter should illustrate this.

Users of electronic publishing services, on the whole, pay only for the information that they use, so the publisher gains a very accurate idea of how much of the information is used. This gives publishers a much clearer view of who their audience is and where its special interests lie.

In some cases however, especially information of a very specialist nature, a subscription charge is paid in advance and subscribers can use the service as many times as they wish. This has advantages for both parties involved, in that the database providers know how much money they are getting in advance while the user also knows in advance the financial commitment involved, which can be very useful for budgetary purposes.

US Domination in Electronic Publishing

We discuss here many projects that have been developed in the United States and have not been introduced to the British market. The reason is that many innovations in electronic publishing come from the United States. It is there that the financial and intellectual resources exist to get electronic publishing projects underway. There are several competing data networks in the United States, which has helped development to progress while in the UK this has been hampered by the restrictions of first the Post Office monopoly and now British Telecom and its inherited out-of-date equipment.

As electronic publishing relies on the existence of high-quality telecommunications rather than physical communication, the Atlantic Ocean does not pose a problem or barrier. Where a computer file is located does not matter so long as the dialup connection is good. Many of the projects begun on the other side of the Atlantic have found their way here and have displaced attempts to provide a British alternative. The British market is especially susceptible to US-originated products as much scientific and business communication is now carried out in Amerenglish. The national markets in European countries have developed more independently because they do not have a common language.

It is noteworthy that almost all of the European electronic publishing ventures are either government-inspired or government subsidised. The small size of the European markets makes commercial ventures virtually impossible on a national basis. There are commercial European publishers, but they offer products that are of interest to an international market: Reuter's financial information services, for example. US electronic publishing has a much stronger commercial foundation, and therefore tends to look to expanding its market as the next target after satisfying its domestic audience.

What is Electronic Publishing?

The different types of electronic publishing are teletext, videotex, online databases, cable, videodisc and CD-ROM.

There are a number of ways of looking at electronic publishing. It can be considered in the light of what is published electronically and who uses electronic publications. We will discuss both these in separate sections later.

Both these divisions apply just as much to conventional as electronic publishing. Many discussions of electronic publishing focus on something that is not normally considered important in conventional publishing: the technology used in the different systems. Indeed, the existence of such 'systems' is strange in itself when compared with conventional publishing and its reliance on one basic system.

Why should technology be so important? There are two reasons: first, the industry is partly 'technology-driven' (that is, the market is forced by new technical possibilities as well as commercial requirements); secondly, technological divisions also mark out divisions in the market and applications of the different types of electronic publication.

Rather than describe each different electronic publishing technology in abstract. Selected examples from each field are used.

i   Ceefax

Ceefax is an example of *teletext*. It offers users over 200 'pages' (screensful) of information on their television sets. The information available includes news summaries, weather forecasts, travel information and television programme information. The user selects the item he wants by keying-in the number of the appropriate page on a numeric keypad. After a few moments' delay the page appears on the television screen.

The user requires a television set that is fitted with a special adaptor to receive teletext information. This includes the keypad used to select the pages required. The pages are broadcast continuously in an unused part of a conventional television picture. Each page is cycled through the transmitter, and pages specified by the user are caught by the adaptor as they go past. This is why there is some delay between specifying the page required and seeing it.

Teletext is a broadcast technology. In Britain there are three services: Ceefax is run by the BBC, Oracle by the IBA and 4 Tel by Channel 4.

ii   Prestel

Prestel is an example of *videotex* (formerly called 'viewdata'). Users connect an adapted television set to their telephone, and then select the information needed from a series of multiple-choice menus that lead eventually to a page containing the relevant information. They make their choice of pages using a keypad similar to that used by Ceefax. There are many files of information (databases) available through Prestel, including information from travel organisations, newspapers, stock-market information services and many businesses. Users can also send information back to Prestel, and this facility can be used to order products sold through the system.

245

Prestel requires users to make a telephone connection to the computer that holds the information. They also need a television set or special terminal to use the service. The service needs no training and is aimed at users who are not familiar with computers.

Prestel is operated by British Telecom, but all the information is provided by outside publishers who charge a rate for each page displayed on the user's screen.

iii Compendex

Compendex is an example of an *online database*. Users will be using the system to identify relevant journal articles on engineering subjects. They need a computer terminal which is connected to a telephone line. The words that will identify the item of interest are typed into the terminal together with some special command words that will instruct the computer that holds the information. If the search is successful users will see abstracts of the articles displayed at their terminal, together with references to the original material.

The information is stored on a computer in the form of a database of many thousand items. The computer is programmed to respond to the commands issued by users at their terminals. The user has to learn these commands before using the system.

Compendex is published by Engineering Information Inc. It duplicates a printed abstracting service, Engineering Index. The computer on which the database is held is not run by EI, but by a specialist bureau, Lockheed Information Services. The user is charged by Lockheed for the time spent using the system and the amount of information retrieved from the database.

iv Qube

Qube is an example of a *cable* service. Users have a conventional television set, connected to a cable network instead of an aerial; they can select from among thirty television channels, including specialist channels for news, sport and current feature films. Qube is unusual as it is interactive: it allows the user to send a signal back to the cable centre. It can therefore be used to supply videotex services as well as television

246

programmes. The user also has access to shopping and banking services through the system.

Information supplied over cable systems resembles videotex information and uses very similar technology. The television component of the service is exactly the same as conventional broadcast television.

v   Academic American Encyclopedia

This is an example of *videodisc* electronic publishing. A videodisc is similar in size to an LP, but carries colour television pictures and sound. It is played on a special player that reads the disc using a small laser instead of a stylus. Users can select exactly which position on the disc they wish to see, and this has opened up the possibility of setting up an encyclopedia with text accompanied by pictures and sound. It is also being used in a CAL (Computer Aided Learning) role especially for staff training by various companies.

A new development which has emerged recently is CD-ROM (Compact Disc Read Only Memory) whereby, instead of a videodisc, a much smaller compact disc, capable of storing large quantities of information, is used and utilizes a microcomputer and specially adapted peripherals. These compact discs have a memory of 520 megabytes and are able to store around 300,000 A4 pages of text, which makes them especially suitable for use as encyclopedias and other reference books.

What is Published Electronically?

In this section many of the underlying trends of electronic publishing will become apparent, as will the threats and opportunities for the book industry. Most electronically published information is based on journals and periodicals (journal-related) rather than books. This is because electronic publishing originated in scientific and technical information publishing. Information that parallels that which is generally found in books has been much slower to find its way out through electronic publishing. There are signs that this is now beginning: some of the most important recent projects have overlapped with books, either by publishing book materials directly (as in the Academic American Encyclopedia) or by offering new indexing tools (Super-index).

247

There is also a growing field of information that is published *only* electronically. This is usually where the information is not suited to print in the first place since it may be of a form which needs to be constantly updated on a large scale.

i Journal-related electronic publishing

Most journal-related electronic publishing is through online databases. Two types account for most of the market: *source* databases and *reference* databases. Source databases offer online access to the full text of the original material. Reference databases offer access to abstracts and indexes that will guide the user to the original print publication. Reference databases are the more common.

There are at least 400 databases of scientific abstract information, available through twenty-five different computer services ('hosts'). Examples are Chemical Abstracts, Biological Science Information Service, Geoarchive (geology information) and Inspec (electronics and physics information). One of the most successful publications of this kind has been Medline, an online version of Index Medicus, which gives index information for virtually every medical journal published. Almost all scientific fields are covered and there is a tendency for services to become more and more specialised. There are also reference database services for business and economic information. ABI/Inform indexes management literature and Predicasts offer international coverage of trade publications and business newspapers as well as the general press. Business services are growing in importance.

The main advantages for users of these services are that searching for information is far quicker electronically, and they are being offered the chance to pay for just what they use. Large advance subscriptions are no longer necessary. This has made these services available to much smaller organisations. At the same time it has affected the financial position of the publisher, who is now much less certain about his revenue.

Full-text or source services offer users information that is much more detailed than that offered in reference databases but are usually more expensive to use and require considerable investment in software and hardware on the part of the publisher. For that reason they are much rarer. They are also less wide-ranging in their coverage. The source database market is newer than reference databases, and the pattern it will

248

take has not yet become clear. It does seem to have a professional/business bias rather than a scientific one at present, though. Significant publications are the Harvard Business Review, which is now simultaneously published online and in print, and Lexis, a service that offers lawyers the full text of many law report series usually published in sections throughout the year.

There is one special case of journal-related publishing: patent abstracting and indexing. This has been one of the most successful electronic publishing fields. Derwent Publications, a British company now part of the Thomson Organisation, has made a very successful business out of turning its patent abstracting (reference) service into a computer database. Patents are notoriously difficult to locate manually, and the Derwent service (though expensive) offers many advantages to its users.

Videotex has not made much of information derived from journals. Some journal publishers have set up videotex databases, but general problems with the small videotex market in Britain have affected these too and many have now ceased their videotex activities. The Institute for Scientific Information (publishers of Science Citation Index) has been one such. Newspaper publishers have also set up videotex services, and this development is becoming popular in the United States, where newspaper publishers often have a wider range of information-and-communication activities (including, for example, owning television and cable stations) than their British counterparts.

ii   Book-related electronic publishing

Electronic publishing has not affected book publishing to the extent that it has journal publishing. The reasons are that computer storage costs (although now falling) have limited the willingness of publishers to store large quantities of text; the existing electronic publishing market is journal-oriented in its interests; and thirdly, no-one had really seen a clear application for an online book that offers enough advantages to get people to pay for it. Most books, such as novels, biographies and poetry, are better presented in book form and are also cheaper for the purchaser to buy. With journal-related databases it was often possible for a library or information unit to replace the printed publication with access to an electronic version. This is less likely to be the case with book-related electronic publishing as, unless the full text is published, a printed copy will be necessary for reference.

Recently there have been some interesting projects that do use book material or aim at a book-using market. Three of these, the Academic American Encyclopedia, Superindex and BRS/Colleague, are discussed in more detail later. None covers the general book field, although the encyclopedia does appeal to a general audience. The important class of books being affected by electronic publishing at the moment is scientific and technical reference books. These are used by the same kind of readers who use reference databases and therefore are used to the idea of online retrieval. The advantages they are being offered are fast access to the right material, which may not be located in the reference book they would usually turn to; and the ability to search for items of interest in more than one book simultaneously. They are not being offered a cheaper alternative to printed books, as users of journal-related electronic publications are.

Among the longest-established book-related electronic publications are the online version of the British National Bibliography and the catalogue of the US Library of Congress. Both these aim to record the book-publishing output of their countries and make the results available to libraries. Full bibliographic details are given for each book, together with recommended classmarks. Both files offer access to a retrospective database going back some years, and are a valuable tool for librarians who need to locate and classify books in all subjects.

All three examples are available through online services. Only the encyclopedia is available on a videotex service. The technical limitations of early Prestel-type videotex services made full-text a difficult proposition, but some of the newer ones that resemble online services much more closely can handle it.

iii   Directory-related electronic publishing

Directory publishing is a special class of book publishing and needs to be considered separately. Directory information is much more suited to electronic publishing: it changes each year and it is used mostly by businesses. Many directories are already produced with the assistance of computers, only the changed information being rekeyed each issue. Publishing directories electronically also means that the data can be

250

changed as soon as the publisher becomes aware of new information. Users no longer have to wait months or even years for new editions.

Directory information is available on online database services and on videotex services. The most extensive project at the moment is French: the French telecommunications authority aims to give every household access to an electronic telephone directory using videotex terminals. This will open the way for other videotex services and is a pump-priming operation. Videotex is suitable for simpler directories, but with large databases it can take a long time to reach the information needed. Some directory publishers have consequently adopted online database technology.

The largest such service is probably the electronic version of the US Yellow Pages. This contains the ten million entries from all 4,800 printed directories, and can be searched by town, industry and company name. In France, the French edition of Kompass is available online. In Britain, companies such as Dun and Bradstreet have databases in-house, and have made them available to the public through Pergamon InfoLine.

Other online directories include a directory of published market research (Harfax) and the International Directory of Microcomputer Software. Gale Research, a large US directory publisher, has mounted its Encyclopedia of Associations online: this is perhaps the most significant standard reference book so far published electronically.

Directory publishers have the same difficulties as journal datbase publishers: they have to face the problems of converting their income from advance payments to payment for information as it is used. The smaller directory publisher must therefore approach the field with caution. The main threat to such publishers is that the sophistication of computer retrieval will allow users to get much of the information they are presently getting from specialist directories from much larger, comprehensive databases. It is thought by some that the CD-ROM will be the most favoured medium for directories which can not show a cost-benefit to online users. The advantage of CD-ROMs is that they can carry a mass of data, they are cheaper to produce than books containing a similar amount of data, they can be updated as frequently as demand requires, are cheap to distribute and can be searched by traditional online techniques.

251

iv Material only published electronically

There is much information that has no print equivalent. There are a number of computer bureaux who have compiled large files of statistics on trade or economics, and they make these available to users. They have complex associated software that allows the user to manipulate the data and make calculations and projections. Such information can only be made available by computer, and is generally considered to be a special branch of electronic publishing.

Parallel to these statistical services are rapid business information services like Datastream, which provides information on share prices as they change on stock markets, and Reuter's foreign exchange system, which offers users up-to-the-second information on foreign exchange prices and also a communications network for dealers to carry out transactions with one another. A current affairs and news information service called World Reporter is offered by Datasolve, which is updated on a daily basis and is supplied with information by the BBC, the Economist and the Associated Press general news wire for Europe.

Another service available is Pergamon InfoLine, which carries over 30 different data bases some of which overlap with directory-related electronic publishing. For example Key British Enterprises and Who Owns Whom, published by Dunn and Bradstreet, are available on InfoLine together with data from a number of trade and research organisations and journals.

There have also been some ventures into publishing abstracting services as computer-readable databases only: Inspec's Electronic Materials Information Service is an example. This field will probably expand, but few publishers are willing to venture into a field whose economics are so little understood.

Electronic Publishers

The largest electronic publishers are American; inevitably, in view of the size of the American market. Most publishers have come into electronic publishing from print publishing: Chemical Abstracts, Engineering Information (publishers of Engineering Index) and the Institute for Scientific Information were among the major publishers of scientific abstracting services who migrated to electronic from conventional publishing. One reason for this was that these publishers were already using computer typesetting for their printed publications, and the source tapes for the typesetting operation could be processed to make up online databases.

The most important British publishers who have a place in the international market are: Derwent Publications (patent information); Institute of Electrical Engineers (the Inspec series of databases on physics, electronics and computers) and Reuter's (international money-market services).

There are a number of British publishers who have specialised databases, important in their own fields and with international appeal, who do not fall into the 'major publisher' category. These include: Commonwealth Agricultural Bureau, British Hydromechanics Research Association, Rubber and Plastics Research Association and the Library Association.

This picture of subject-specialist publishers is beginning to change as the industry diversifies. Large general publishers are moving to electronic publishing commercially rather than experimentally, although many publishers have become cautious of electronic publishing after seeing the losses made by some companies who provided information for Prestel in its early days. It will take some time to get over these suspicions.

The Users of Electronic Publications

The market for electronic publications is still a segmented and specialised one. There are two types of users: end-users, who search for their own information, and intermediaries, who search for information on behalf of someone else. Librarians and information managers make up the intermediary market; the end-user market includes both business users and the small number of home users.

i Librarians

This is probably the largest field numerically. Librarians use online databases almost exclusively. They use them to answer requests for relevant literature put by researchers. Because of the command languages needed to search these databases specialists do most of the work: the individual

253

researcher cannot usually practise often enough to become a skilled searcher.

The most popular databases are limited in number. Out of the total of over 400 available, only a handful are widely-used. The most popular are Chemical Abstracts, Medline and Derwent (patent information). Many of the smaller databases in less popular subjects can only continue with support from governments and public institutions.

ii Professional users

There are some specialised systems that are based on a professional market. The largest such group is lawyers, who have very clear information needs. In Britain they are served by Lexis and in the United States by Lexis and Westlaw. Another group recently identified is the medical market. In the United States, with its heavy emphasis on private medicine, publishers such as BRS have set up special systems to provide textbook information to doctors. Drug information is also popular in the medical market. The next development in this field will probably be on-line 'diagnostic aids' that will offer a doctor advice on how to treat a particular case.

iii Business users

Business users are the largest group of Prestel users (around 55% of the total). These are almost all used by end-users, not librarians or information specialists. Business users are now starting to use the more sophisticated online database services, though the difficulties in learning the command languages needed is still inhibiting this from developing rapidly. Business videotex users are interested in travel information, financial information such as Datastream's stock-market prices and news services.

The statistical timesharing services and the financial information services have always been the province of the end-user rather than the intermediary, though in this case the end-user is more likely to be a statistician than a manager. This is because the provision of information is only half of the service: the other half is the computer software used in modelling projections based on the data retrieved.

254

iv Domestic users

The mass-market has remained untapped by electronic publishers. Prestel intended to appeal to this market, but has not progressed as well as expected.

Videotex services have attempted to reach the home audience. They have been more successful in the United States, where it has been established in trials that what makes users subscribe is the availability of interactive services (such as banking and shopping using videotex links) as well as information services.

Videotex encyclopedias have been well-received in the United States tests which have been carried out. They need a more sophisticated system than the rigid 'tree' structure that characterised early systems. The newer videotex services offer this. The publisher of the Academic American Encyclopedia is now planning a videodisc encyclopedia to accompany the videotex one.

The long-term future of videotex in the United States is probably assured. This is not so in Britain. The Prestel scheme has created much scepticism as to whether videotex can ever make money for anyone. At the moment, Prestel is trapped in a cycle: few terminals sold mean that it is not worth setting up a database; the lack of databases means that no-one wants to buy Prestel terminals.

There is a way out of this cycle, and it has been taken up already in the US, and more recently in the UK. Two US services, The Source and CompuServe, have been marketing videotex services to personal computer owners. The personal computer, even the simplest type, can be programmed to act as a videotex terminal. All that is needed is a suitable set of programs and a modem to connect the computer to the telephone line. By definition, computer users have some form of screen attached to their computers (often a conventional colour television used for computer purposes and normal television viewing). These computer users are hobbyists rather than people using their computers in business, and are very interested in computer-related information. They are also interested in communicating with other computer users. CompuServe and The Source (marketing slogan, inevitably, "may The Source be with you") offer a variety of such services: electronic mail, databases of computer software that users can load into their own computers and retain, and electronic publishing services. Grolier offer the Academic American encyclopedia through CompuServe, for example. Stock market prices, financial news and other current information is also offered, just as it is on conventional videotex services.

In the sophistication of some of their facilities, these services are approaching the online databases. However, their market is the domestic one, typically videotex. A new service on Prestel, Micronet 800, has looked at these lessons and acted accordingly. The Micronet service for home computer users is described in more detail later. For the time being, it is worth noting that there are nearly two million microcomputers in British homes, and that anyone who has bought a computer has demonstrated an interest in information technology which means that half the selling job has already been done.

The only form of electronic publishing that has yet made any impact on the domestic market is teletext. In a quiet way, teletext has succeeded where Prestel has not. Nearly one million sets equipped with teletext decoders have been sold through conventional television retailers and rental companies in Britain. The extra cost of a teletext set is not great, and once it has been bought there are no further charges to pay for information used. The very modesty of the service has probably ensured its success.

The next product to be sold to the domestic market will be the videodisc and also CD-ROM. If a market base is established among users who buy videodisc players to view feature films, the way will be open for encyclopedias and manual publishing using the new medium. This market may take some time to develop, though, as few videodisc players have been sold in Europe yet, unlike the United States.

CD-ROM is still very much in the early stages and, unlike videodisc, requires the possession of a microcomputer and a specially designed peripheral, although it is able to store much more information. The technology for 'read-back' facilities is also being developed, but it will be some time before this is available for general use.

Some Key Projects

Here five projects are examined, as an indication of the possible impact of EP on the book market. They are multi-media publishing ventures, an online encyclopedia, a medical 'quick reference system' and a computerised back-of-book index for collection of textbooks. Three out of the five

256

come from the United States but, as pointed out earlier, it is there that the developments are happening that will eventually affect Europe.

i *Academic American Encyclopedia*

The new Academic American Encyclopedia is available as an electronic as well as a print product. The full text of the encyclopedia, 28,500 articles, was keyed into the computer. This was used to create the type-setting tapes for the conventional, printed version of the twenty-one volumes, and to set up a database. One of the most interesting points about the scheme is that the publisher, Arete, began creating the encyclopedia in 1977 with both traditional and electronic publishing in mind from the outset.

The electronic version of the encyclopedia was tested in an experiment carried out in Ohio. The text was made available to 200 homes taking part in a videotex trial installation, and the results were monitored. Although users were provided with the service without charge, most said that they would be prepared to spend up to $15.00 per month to have access to it. Many users browsed in the system, looking through the classified lists of articles as well as reading specific items. As the computer-system used was a videotex-based one, users had to get at particular articles through the usual series of videotex menus, and those who used the system with any frequency soon found this to be too slow, suggesting that there was need for a more sophisticated way of accessing the database, perhaps using an alphanumeric keyboard to search for particular words. The encyclopedia has been mounted by one online service, the New York Times Information Service. Online access allows much more sophisticated searches to be made.

Grolier Publishing, the company who have taken over the project, have also been experimenting with a videodisc encyclopedia. This would allow all forms of communication: still and moving pictures, sound and text. A complete encyclopedia will probably take up three or four discs, but will still be able to sell at around half the price of a printed version. It is possible to go to one place on a videodisc very fast, and as videodisc players can be linked to microcomputers the two together can be used as a powerful home information system. Both are becoming commonplace technologies, and may be expected to sell widely over the next few years, so a user base will exist by the time publishing projects are coming to fruition. The development of CD-ROM, as mentioned earlier, which is ideally suited to this type of publishing, opens up still further opportunities in this field.

ii   BRS/Colleague

BRS (Bibliographic Retrieval Services) is a New York-based company that has been running online database services for some years. They have now launched a reference system that uses microcomputer and videodisc technology. BRS/Colleague is a medical service, aimed at busy hospitals which need to offer emergency critical care. Its main components are the full texts of medical reference works and videodisc recordings of the accompanying illustrations.

The text part is held on BRS's computer near New York. Users have a terminal that can be used to locate relevant passages to the cases they are dealing with. Connected to the terminal is a videodisc player which will then display the illustrations that accompany that text. Users can magnify parts of the illustration they are interested in, or pull back for an overview. The advantage for the user is that instead of having to check the text of up to twenty-three textbooks he can search the indexes of all the books simultaneously and accurately, and come up with directly relevant material and an illustration within seconds. The texts stored on the system include *Gray's Anatomy* and *Schwartz's Principles and Practice of Emergency Medicine*.

BRS see the system as being most useful in busy hospitals at times when more experienced staff are not available (evenings and weekends, for example) but when patients may well enter the hospital requiring emergency treatment. The system will be able to offer very rapid support to a junior doctor presented with an unfamiliar illness or injury.

iii   Superindex

Superindex was set up as a joint experiment between several European and American academic publishers, including Elsevier, McGraw-Hill and Springer-Verlag. It consists of a combination of the traditional indexes to over 644 scientific and technical textbooks and handbooks. These were mounted as a computer file, and librarians and researchers could search the file through the Dialog computer in California. The total size of the index was 651,000 items. No text from any of the books was put into the file, and the purpose of Superindex was to cut down time spent looking through the indexes of several texts to find relevant information, and to be able to use the indexes of texts not held in the user's own library. A large number of users also said that using the service had led them to relevant information in textbooks that they would not previously have considered relevant, and therefore would not have bothered to look at.

The ten most cited books in the test were handbooks of hard data and reference information. Users expressed a desire to have this information instantly available, and an expansion to the system to allow it to display tables and other structured information is being planned. This takes it into the field of content as well as indexing, and will no doubt result in some falling-off of enthusiasm among some of the participants.

Superindex is going ahead on a commercial basis now the test has demonstrated that it will be well-used. Its publishers hope that they will eventually be able to include all relevant titles from 'quality' publishers.

iv   Mitchell-Beazley/Thorn-EMI joint venture

Mitchell-Beazley have set up a special video publishing unit, and part of their work will be carried out as a joint venture with Thorn-EMI. The significance of this is that, unlike the traditional printing process, the company who will *manufacture* the finished product is to be involved in the publishing process from the outset.

Mitchell-Beazley's first project has been a multi-media photography training package. A series of programmes was broadcast on Channel 4 television, accompanied by a complementary book. The television programmes have now been released on videotape. The book and the videotapes are designed to provide different materials for the user, and to be used together.

v   Micronet 800

Micronet 800 is the first British venture trying to tap the large base of home computers. Micronet offers subscribers two things: access to all public Prestel databases and access to its own Prestel database of computer software, news and information.

Micronet is run by Telemap which is a partnership run by EMAP (East Midlands Allied Press), with the majority holding, British Telecom and Tele Direct, the publishing arm of Bell Canada. Its availability on Prestel would qualify it to be considered as electronic publishing, but its real claim to electronic publishing status is that one of the services available to users is the purchase of computer software direct from the Micronet database. A user can see a demonstration of the program he is interested in, check the price, and order it. The software is not packaged and sent to him through the post, it is 'downloaded' direct over the telephone line into his computer, where it can be stored for later use on tape or disk. The user is charged on his Micronet quarterly bill.

Software publishing has not been very different from conventional publishing. Even booksellers have been offering program tapes as a sideline to their computer books, with prices usually between £5 and £10. Is the user likely to want also to order manuals and books on computing through Micronet? Very likely, and at the moment these would have to be sent through the post in traditional printed form: the memory and storage capacity of most microcomputers would not allow the downloading possible with software.

Implications of these Projects

All of these projects intrude into the book market in some way. They are all to some extent dealing with specialist publications, even those which approach a mass audience. The most important point to note about them is that none of the projects is a simple conversion from traditional to electronic publishing: they all offer some *enhancement*. In the case of the videotex version of the Academic American Encyclopedia this is a chance to 'pay-as-you-use' rather than putting up a lump sum for a multi-volume work. For the online and videodisc versions of the encyclopedia, though, there are more significant benefits: online permits very sophisticated searches and videodisc a completely new approach to publishing. Arete also began their programme with electronic publishing in mind from the outset, using one computer-generated tape for both conventional and electronic applications.

BRS/Colleague makes a very interesting use of new technology in a specialist environment. The use of videodisc players linked to microcomputers or videotex terminals is perhaps the most important electronic

260

publishing technique in use at the moment. It offers true multi-media facilities at comparatively low cost. A number of companies are developing training courses based on this technology. Its interactive facilities outstrip videotape and it has none of the limitations associated with computer graphics and sound. For these reasons it will almost certainly achieve a prominent place in many forms of education.

Note that it has taken much of its basic material from conventional sources not created with any form of electronic publishing in mind. This is also true of Superindex. Both offer particular advantages of speed of access rather than anything new in the way of communications.

Mitchell-Beazley's and Pergamon's involvement shows that book publishers are considering the market, and in involving an electronics company from the start consider that electronic publishing is not the same type of process as print publishing. Their choice of material indicates again that it is reference books and manuals that are likely to be published electronically for a popular audience.

Micronet is the first serious attempt to broaden the British user-base for electronic publishing. The main point a publisher should take note of is that it will encourage an activity that may replace reading for many people. Some studies have shown that computer enthusiasm is growing rapidly because it is *active:* the computer user is learning a skill and solving problems, not passively absorbing information and entertainment. It may therefore come to be seen as a much more productive way of passing time, particularly in a 'leisure society'.

However, it must always be remembered that for some types of information, such as fictional works, there is little advantage offered by electronic publishing — books still have the edge. In contrast, for information of a fast-moving nature or which is part of a large mass of data, electronic publishing offers advantages which can not be matched by traditional book publishing.

On Demand Publishing

There is one field that has not yet been considered which might have a considerable impact on the book market. This is the field of on-demand publishing using new printing technology. On-demand publishing happens when a book or journal paper is printed only when it is requested by a specific user. It has always been possible to print direct from a computer text-file using conventional computer printers. However, these are slow and would not have produced an acceptable finished result. The method has been used largely to produce copies of computer-software manuals as they are needed. For a high-quality print result it has been necessary to link the computer to a phototypesetting machine to produce a plate, and then use conventional lithography to do the printing. The advantages of the computer are largely lost under this system.

Two new types of printer, laser printers and ink-jet printers, can produce high-quality printed material direct from a computer file without the need for an intervening phototypesetting and plate-make stage. They function much like a computer printer, but offer much higher quality print, choice of fonts and point-sizes. Both types are instantly reconfigurable: that is, to set up a different page takes only a moment as the computer controls the whole process. As the configuration is instantaneous and requires no physical change to the printer, one copy of a book can be printed in sequence at a unit cost not far different from that of a run of 10,000.

Storing the text itself as a computer file is not expensive, and it is cheaper to prepare a text in the first place using an integrated computer system than it is using conventional methods. This opens up the possibility of printing a book when the reader asks for it, not printing a run to be stocked in a warehouse. The first such on-demand printing system (now collapsed) was Adonis, a consortium of academic publishers who intended to use it to print journal articles rather than books. It is still likely that this will be the first application to see light of day and commercial use. In the longer-term it may be more economical to offer on-demand printing of specialist works rather than extensive print runs.

As the whole process is computerised, this offers the possibility for a reader to order a copy of a required book direct from a computer or videotex terminal, and have it delivered by post within a few days. This is not much slower (and could be much faster) than ordering a non-stock item from a bookseller or library. For an organisation with the financial resources it could be possible to maintain a laser printer in-house to print the material straight away, the delivery being over the telephone in this case.

The advantage of on-demand printing to the user is that it results in a finished product that is acceptable, being book-like and usable as a book. The advantage to the publisher is that it eliminates one area of financial risk in book-publishing: the print run. It has the effect of shifting the economic emphasis on to the cost of creating the original document rather than printing and selling it. This shift is true in general with electronic publishing systems and has been one of the major impacts of the new technology.

Electronic Publishing and the Book Market

In the early days of electronic publication there were many claims and counter-claims about the imminent demise of print publishing and its assured and prosperous future. As readers will have gathered by now, electronic publishing is not going to replace the book.

i Electronic publishing as an alternative publishing system

There are very few books available in full-text through electronic publishing systems. The Academic American Encyclopedia and Colleague are the most important at the moment, but neither has affected the British market. Both fill very specialist niches in their own fields, and while have significance they do not presage a full-scale move to new media in encyclopedia or medical publishing. The point they make is that careful selection of market and service can result in a successful venture. Anyone who tried to mount a whole library online would probably end up with losses that exceeded even those of Prestel information providers.

The major limitation to the acceptance of electronic publishing is that present systems demand that the user has a terminal, and that this terminal has to be connected by telecommunications to a remote computer. Even for videodisc a player is still needed. Both terminals and videodisc players are not common in households, so the general reader will have no access to any electronic publishing service, so the days of the electronic book are still some way off.

The second reason is that, in itself, the conventional book is accepted and popular to an extent that even a user-friendly, portable, free-roaming terminal might not be. It is free from constraints about power, and it offers far more immediate choice of reading material and environment than electronic systems will be able to offer for many years. Publishers, readers and commentators on the industry seem to agree about this.

263

It is clear that the most successful electronic publishing ventures are the ones which identify a market with distinct special needs, and devise a service that will offer enough advantages to be worth paying for. Companies such as Lexis, Derwent and Datastream have realised this. These companies should be the model for any company that wants to begin electronic publishing, whether of books or journals.

ii   The threat from alternative activities

Electronic publishing does not, in itself, threaten the book market seriously. However, many developments in electronic publishing are related to new technologies that may lead people to diversify the ways in which they spend their time. The two most likely to affect the use of time are cable television and the growth of home computing.

The threat presented by cable is that it increases the choice of conventional television programmes that are available. This might well erode one of the main advantages of the book— readers have always had much more control over what to read when. Television has never managed to cater satisfactorily for special-interest groups as there has not been the broadcast time available. The introduction of cable (particularly if it is to be pay-per-view cable) will make users check more carefully on how they are to use both their financial and their time resources, and more attractive television appealing to their own particular interests may detract from time spent reading. It is too early to say for certain whether this will happen, but US experience suggests that it does.

The increasing interest in home computers will also divert resources away from reading. Its active rather than passive nature has already been mentioned and interest has been fuelled by much media attention recently. The indications are that microcomputer users are now moving out towards communicating with other users and with database services as they discover the limits of what they can achieve with just their own resources. The low cost of microcomputers and associated software will lead users to make comparisons between, say, purchasing a program and purchasing a book.

STATISTICAL APPENDIX

APPENDIX TABLE 1 MAJOR INTERNATIONAL TRADE FLOWS IN BOOKS

£ m¹ 1982

Exporters \ Importers	Australia	Austria	Belgium	Canada	France	Hong Kong	India	Ireland	Italy	Japan	Mexico	Netherlands	New Zealand	South Africa	Spain	Sweden	Switzerland	UK	USA	West Germany
Australia													11.1 / 11.7					0.9	0.7 / 1.0	
Austria									0.4			0.2			0.1		1.6 / 1.8	0.1	0.3 / 0.6	24.4 / 22.4
Belgium				2.1 / 1.8	24.9 / 26.9							23.6 / 17.3				2.8 / 2.0	2.1 / 2.0	3.5 / 3.9	3.5 / 3.4	2.1 / 2.9
Canada	0.6		1.1		5.3 / 1.4													2.1	43.9 / 27.1	
Denmark					2.5 / 2.0							0.9 / 1.3				4.5 / 4.9		2.5 / 3.0	1.3	2.8 / 2.9
Finland																2.7 / 2.4		0.7		0.4
France			30.2 / 20.5	13.7 / 12.8					3.5 / 2.6	1.3		2.1 / 2.1			2.5 / 1.3	0.3	21.2 / 18.4	2.2 / 3.0	4.1 / 3.7	5.9 / 5.4
Hong Kong	11.0 / 10.0			1.1	3.1		0.3			1.0		0.6	1.7		2.0	0.4		14.6 / 21.5	8.1 / 11.0	
Italy		0.7	1.6	0.9	14.7 / 32.4	0.8						3.0			0.1	4.1	7.5	9.7 / 13.6	4.6 / 8.9	5.4 / 7.2
Japan	1.8 / 3.4			0.6	0.8	0.8	0.5 / 0.7					1.0 / 1.3	0.7					2.6 / 4.2	16.7 / 26.8	2.0
Mexico																1.9			1.3 / 4.0	
Netherlands		1.9 / 2.4	24.4 / 33.7	0.9 / 1.1	6.2 / 6.2					2.2					0.2	2.4 / 2.0	2.0	8.5 / 10.5	6.9 / 5.4	10.9 / 7.2

Continued....

Appendix Table 1 continued . . .

Importers

£ m[1] 1982

Exporters

Exporters ↓ / Importers →	Australia	Austria	Belgium	Canada	France	Hong Kong	India	Ireland	Italy	Japan	Mexico	Netherlands	New Zealand	South Africa	Spain	Sweden	Switzerland	UK	USA	West Germany
Norway																			0.1	0.6 / 0.8
Singapore	6.3 / 5.6					1.0	1.0 / 0.5			0.4			0.7 / 0.7					2.6 / 3.1	1.0 / 3.0	
Spain			0.4	1.8 / 1.6	14.9 / 13.0				1.6		25.7 / 24.5	3.7 / 5.2				0.5		6.8 / 6.1	8.9 / 9.5	1.7 / 1.2
Sweden					0.2							0.2						0.4	0.3 / 0.6	0.5
Switzerland			2.3 / 1.6	0.6 / 0.9	20.6 / 15.8				1.4 / 1.1	1.3		0.9 / 0.8	0.6		0.5	0.9		2.6 / 3.2	3.8 / 4.0	
UK	37.6 / 45.2	0.8	2.5	10.8 / 10.6	7.8 / 6.2	7.6	6.8 / 5.4	13.9 / 13.0	3.9 / 3.5	5.4 / 9.3		13.9 / 12.6	8.2 / 11.7	20.6 / 19.5	3.4 / 2.1	6.2 / 5.9	3.0 / 2.2		50.4 / 48.6	8.3 / 8.4
USA	32.6 / 41.0		1.1 / 1.6	135.8 / 188.8	2.9 / 4.9	3.2 / 5.7	3.5 / 3.6	5.7 / 2.6	3.1 / 2.0	14.2 / 21.8	8.9 / 6.4	9.9 / 10.9	4.7 / 9.1	7.0 / 8.5	1.3 / 1.6	1.6 / 2.2	3.8 / 3.5	47.2 / 68.5		6.8 / 12.6
West Germany	49.5 / 47.8	1.0	1.0	6.2 / 4.9	11.1 / 10.4				6.9 / 2.8	5.5 / 6.9		14.8 / 11.6			2.6 / 0.9	2.4 / 2.5	47.1 / 45.3	4.0 / 4.1	14.4 / 9.4	

Notes: [1] Top figure represents amount of exports by column country to row country. Bottom figures represent amount of imports by row country from column country.

APPENDIX TABLE 2   TRANSLATION OF TITLES BY ORIGINAL LANGUAGE AND BY SELECTED LANGUAGES INTO WHICH TRANSLATED IN 1978

Translated from	English	French	Spanish	Russian	Arabic	German	Italian	Japanese	Dutch	Danish	Norwegian	Swedish	Polish	Turkish
Albanian	18	28	14	9	1	10	1	0	1	3	0	1	7	11
Arabic	34	58	57	11	—	21	0	4	9	8	1	3	0	44
Armenian	3	8	0	36	0	2	0	0	0	0	0	0	0	0
Bulgarian	19	16	7	84	3	31	1	1	0	0	0	2	9	18
Chinese	42	191	9	7	0	24	3	22	10	3	0	4	0	14
Czech	67	56	15	51	0	165	9	7	20	8	4	6	37	0
Danish	50	77	92	13	1	103	8	2	45	—	66	102	6	0
Dutch	100	79	33	0	0	158	13	7	—	21	4	11	4	3
English	—	4,922	2,760	453	59	4,878	808	1,568	2,129	1,022	619	759	199	299
Finnish	3	7	0	15	0	12	1	0	2	2	2	21	4	0
French	886	—	1,467	125	15	1,231	476	280	434	177	32	83	94	95
German	810	999	854	154	9	—	250	236	751	227	53	103	105	56
Greek (classical)	39	78	57	3	3	52	20	4	28	12	2	4	9	5
Greek (modern)	7	31	2	3	0	8	1	0	0	0	0	0	3	0
Hebrew	95	50	10	6	7	29	10	1	12	3	1	0	0	2
Hungarian	95	45	13	79	1	127	7	1	7	2	2	5	19	10
Italian	178	534	435	13	0	275	—	22	33	25	5	10	17	9
Japanese	97	44	1	10	2	27	4	—	9	2	1	1	2	1

Continued....

Appendix Table 2 continued...

Translated into

Translated from	English	French	Spanish	Russian	Arabic	German	Italian	Japanese	Dutch	Danish	Norwegian	Swedish	Polish	Turkish
Latin	82	112	51	3	0	69	37	5	15	5	2	21	4	0
Norwegian	30	19	6	3	0	29	1	1	6	76	—	50	4	1
Polish	108	69	11	83	0	124	5	9	3	3	1	6	—	3
Portuguese	25	39	75	5	0	23	8	5	3	2	0	1	6	2
Romanian	111	73	19	43	0	71	1	1	1	0	0	4	5	0
Russian	668	552	361	—	110	680	71	108	71	34	20	52	191	79
Sanskrit	47	18	9	2	0	10	2	1	1	2	0	0	0	0
Serbo-Croatian	43	31	18	27	6	45	19	1	0	0	1	1	13	8
Slovak	1	1	0	6	0	18	1	1	1	0	0	0	11	0
Spanish	111	237	—	28	3	129	60	18	38	16	10	15	26	10
Swedish	102	81	21	5	0	181	5	8	54	349	184	—	9	7
Turkish	6	5	0	15	3	8	0	0	2	1	1	3	0	—
Ukranian	15	8	2	58	0	9	0	0	0	0	0	0	10	1
Urdu	7	2	0	0	1	1	0	0	0	0	0	0	0	0
Yiddish	9	10	0	6	0	13	0	0	1	0	0	5	1	0

Source: UNESCO Statistical Yearbook

APPENDIX TABLE 3   BOOK PRODUCTION : NUMBER OF TITLES BY UDC CLASSES

Country	Year	Total	Gener-alities	Philos-ophy	Religion	Social sciences	Pure sciences	Applied sciences	Arts	Litera-ture	Geog/history
Africa											
Nigeria	1980	2,316	130	42	52	856	104	470	104	328	230
Tanzania	1980	512	31	4	94	151	50	66	57	39	0
All other	1980	2,529	110	23	360	727	296	274	50	517	172
North America											
Canada	1980	19,063	577	762	454	3,853	1,805	2,641	1,111	2,248	932
Cuba	1981	1,438	150	2	0	770	24	180	31	263	18
Dominican Republic	1980	2,219	46	82	70	1,360	98	227	250	23	63
Guatemala	1981	574	55	0	1	203	11	38	155	41	70
Mexico	1981	2,954	112	194	53	857	136	414	133	852	203
USA	1981	76,976	1,448	1,193	2,086	8,760	2,850	7,638	2,793	3,044	2,673
All other	1981	310	34	4	4	136	19	41	13	34	25
South America											
Argentina	1981	4,251	247		542	944	313	606	616	914	69
Bolivia	1979	596	36	8	17	222	14	74	23	129	73
Chile	1981	918	24	26	69	416	29	114	62	84	94
Colombia	1980	5,492	700	70	151	1,408	430	671	441	1,277	340

continued....

Appendix Table 3 continued...

Country	Year	Total	Gener-alities	Philos-ophy	Religion	Social sciences	Pure sciences	Applied sciences	Arts	Litera-ture	Geog/history
South America cont...											
Peru	1981	767	12	17	16	344	40	109	12	144	73
Uruguay	1981	837	0	34	35	238	80	189	32	163	66
Venezuela	1981	4,200	151	90	92	1,241	233	636	307	807	643
All other	1981	81	6	0	2	51	3	7	2	9	1
Asia											
Bangladesh	1980	542	11	12	104	97	29	53	21	115	100
China	1981	22,920	0	2,559	0	3,901	5,862	0	0	3,934	0
Cyprus	1980	1,137	12	4	70	529	52	208	68	143	51
Hong Kong	1980	4,851	100	47	137	704	519	563	428	1,874	479
India	1981	11,562	243	371	929	3,956	813	803	214	3,368	865
Indonesia	1981	1,836	253	33	87	646	73	361	82	106	195
Iraq	1979	1,204	114	22	102	373	31	127	58	258	119
Israel	1979	2,397	46	57	264	319	179	136	51	980	325
Japan	1981	42,217	1,340	1,416	611	7,512	2,735	6,134	6,195	13,355	2,919
Korean Republic	1981	25,747	375	1,056	1,988	5,606	1,054	2,309	1,552	10,943	864
Malaysia	1981	2,356	43	6	155	425	428	375	35	743	146
Pakistan	1980	1,279	31	15	406	239	29	58	10	413	78
Singapore	1981	1,783	28	10	174	612	95	121	118	545	80
Sri Lanka	1981	2,352	29	48	314	1,287	72	154	29	357	62

continued....

Appendix Table 3 continued...

Country	Year	Total	Gener-alities	Philos-ophy	Religion	Social sciences	Pure sciences	Applied sciences	Arts	Litera-ture	Geog/history
Asia cont...											
Thailand	1981	4,498	380	104	264	1,838	304	894	193	328	193
Turkey	1981	4,793	813	82	329	1,093	131	707	192	961	485
Vietnam	1981	1,495	143	14	12	638	70	156	72	341	49
All other	1981	1,358	111	17	256	237	215	155	23	270	74
Europe											
Albania	1981	1,043	7	3	0	252	178	236	57	271	39
Austria	1981	6,214	116	281	208	1,367	771	1,258	479	1,144	590
Belgium	1981	9,736	111	224	365	1,580	673	1,220	916	3,584	1,063
Bulgaria	1981	5,036	221	56	10	1,426	289	1,246	268	1,180	340
Czechoslovakia	1981	10,493	807	140	56	1,963	1,080	3,153	722	2,215	357
Denmark	1981	8,563	228	234	220	1,628	638	2,042	562	2,211	800
Finland	1981	8,227	347	217	366	2,273	743	2,001	410	1,500	370
France	1981	37,308	1,007	718	1,338	12,435	1,027	5,530	2,948	9,723	2,582
East Germany	1981	5,979	79	116	245	774	437	929	437	1,616	305
West Germany	1981	56,568	3,681	1,838	3,082	14,896	2,626	6,974	5,052	14,087	4,332
Greece	1980	4,048	60	124	455	943	89	450	192	1,317	418
Hungary	1981	8,810	350	123	85	1,941	784	2,495	794	1,756	482
Ireland	1981	715	22	3	56	228	29	58	53	172	94
Italy	1981	13,457	334	660	1,075	2,820	701	2,026	1,329	1,320	1,192

continued...

273

Appendix Table 3 continued . . .

Country	Year	Total	Gener-alities	Philos-ophy	Religion	Social sciences	Pure sciences	Applied sciences	Arts	Litera-ture	Geog/history
Europe cont...											
Netherlands	1981	13,939	159	520	635	2,313	968	1,668	894	5,739	1,043
Norway	1980	5,578	170	94	274	1,144	541	1,122	263	1,567	403
Poland	1981	10,435	434	154	252	2,125	877	3,266	754	1,835	738
Portugal	1981	6,714	406	133	239	1,252	559	1,140	924	1,596	465
Romania	1981	7,242	126	141	78	1,231	1,010	2,174	425	1,720	337
Spain	1979	24,569	3,915	1,180	1,497	3,692	1,626	2,257	1,870	6,852	1,680
Sweden	1981	8,582	243	150	277	1,837	422	1,582	305	2,360	587
Switzerland	1981	10,544	126	422	662	2,084	820	2,300	991	1,822	794
United Kingdom	1981	42,972	1,491	1,455	1,530	8,286	3,884	8,079	3,989	10,234	4,024
Yugoslavia	1981	11,088	125	141	294	4,003	384	1,530	1,466	2,700	445
All other	1981	738	79	13	125	197	11	43	74	111	85
Oceania											
Australia	1980	7,856	288	91	166	2,548	553	1,448	699	1,319	744
New Zealand	1981	2,499	100	23	69	816	260	478	324	239	190
All other	1980	447	8	'10	0	157	38	47	20	45	42
USSR											
USSR	1981	83,007	2,471	1,453	227	21,128	8,174	32,870	2,559	12,271	1,854
Byelorussia	1981	3,189	127	45	12	931	207	1,293	100	425	49
Ukraine	1981	8,450	301	204	39	2,295	1,055	2,926	177	1,311	142

Source: UNESCO Statistical Yearbook

APPENDIX TABLE 4   UK: PA STATISTICS COLLECTION SCHEME — EXPORTS

Unit: £ million

	Mass-market paperback		School		University		Specialised		General		Total	
	1982	1983	1982	1983	1982	1983	1982	1983	1982	1983	1982	1983
Western Europe	6.6	8.4	9.4	11.4	13.1	15.2	1.8	1.8	7.4	7.9	38.3	44.7
EEC	4.7	6.5	6.9	8.3	9.9	11.5	1.3	1.4	6.1	6.4	28.9	34.1
Non-EEC	1.9	1.9	2.5	3.1	3.2	3.7	0.5	0.4	1.3	1.5	9.4	10.6
Eastern Europe	0.1	0.1	0.1	0.1	0.7	1.0	0.1	0.1	—	0.1	1.0	1.4
Indian sub-continent	1.2	1.4	0.1	0.1	2.5	2.1	0.2	0.2	0.5	0.8	4.6	4.7
Middle East/N.Africa	0.9	1.2	5.7	7.6	6.5	2.6	0.5	0.5	0.9	1.3	14.5	13.2
Africa	5.8	6.3	12.4	6.7	5.7	5.3	1.6	1.6	4.3	4.3	29.9	24.1
Southern	4.9	5.3	2.5	2.5	2.1	2.2	0.9	1.2	3.4	3.7	13.8	14.8
East/Central	0.3	0.4	1.2	1.3	0.6	0.8	0.1	0.1	0.4	0.4	2.6	3.0
Nigeria	0.6	0.5	8.1	2.5	2.8	2.2	0.5	0.2	0.4	0.2	12.5	5.7
Other West	—	0.1	0.6	0.4	0.2	0.1	0.1	0.1	0.1	—	1.0	0.6
Australia	10.9	15.0	1.6	1.7	2.8	2.8	1.3	1.6	6.7	9.3	23.3	30.3
New Zealand/Oceania	2.7	2.5	0.4	0.4	0.6	0.6	0.3	0.4	1.6	2.2	5.6	6.1
Far East/S.E.Asia	2.3	2.9	2.8	3.3	5.9	6.7	1.0	1.2	1.8	2.2	13.8	16.3
America/Caribbean	5.5	6.2	5.5	5.2	12.0	16.5	2.8	3.8	9.2	12.9	35.0	44.8
USA	1.9	2.1	0.6	1.4	9.5	13.8	2.0	2.7	6.6	9.2	20.7	29.2
Canada	2.1	2.5	0.3	0.3	1.3	1.6	0.4	0.8	1.6	2.6	5.6	7.8
Central/South	0.9	0.8	2.0	0.8	0.4	0.2	0.2	0.1	0.3	0.4	3.8	2.4
W.Indies	0.6	0.8	2.6	2.7	0.8	0.9	0.2	0.2	0.7	0.7	4.9	5.4
Other	0.3	1.0	0.5	0.6	1.9	2.9	0.4	0.6	1.0	0.9	4.0	6.0
TOTAL	36.3	44.8	38.6	37.2	51.6	55.7	10.0	11.8	33.4	41.9	170.0	191.6

APPENDIX TABLE 5 LIBRARIES AND THEIR HOLDINGS[1] BY CATEGORY OF LIBRARY, WORLDWIDE SURVEY

Country	Year	Category of library	Number of libraries	Number of volumes (million)	Additions per year (000 vols)	Registered borrowers (000s)
Africa						
All countries[3]	1979	National	17	3.8	99.7	41.8
	1979	Public	378	4.8	344.0	563.6
	1979	Higher				
		education	6	0.3	10.0	5.2
	1979	School	231	0.7	28.8	60.1
North America						
Canada	1950	Public	791	45.6	3,875.2	n.a.
	1977	Higher				
		education	255	43.6	2,661.4	n.a.
	1977	School	8,692	49.4	n.a.	n.a.
USA	1978	National	3	20.8	359.7	n.a.
	1978	Public	8,456	439.5	26,007.3	n.a.
	1979	Higher				
		education	3,122	519.9	21,608.0	n.a.
	1978	School	70,854	531.5	28,599.0	n.a.
	1977	Special	1,143	19.8	877.7	n.a.
All other[2]	1979	National	8	5.9	103.5	339.7
	1979	Public	795	6.5	126.3	4,818.7
	1979	Higher				
		education	291	5.0	195.3	8,196.4
	1979	School	2,110	4.2	57.9	11,085.4
	1979	Special	116	2.1	n.a.	5,993.8
South America						
Argentina	1977	Public	1,528	9.5	n.a.	4,201.2
French Guiana	1980	Public	1	18.7	1.6	0.7

Continued...

Appendix Table 5 continued...

Country	Year	Category of library	Number of libraries	Number of volumes (million)	Additions per year (000 vols)	Registered borrowers (000s)
South America continued...						
All other	1979	National	7	6.8	128.1	n.a.
	1979	Public	706	5.9	151.8	119.9
	1979	Higher education	193	4.1	n.a.	n.a.
	1979	School	426	0.6	15.9	n.a.
	1979	Special	761	0.2	n.a.	n.a.
Asia						
India	1977	Higher education	93	12.5	540.1	n.a.
Japan	1980	Public	891	58.8	5,338.0	6,521.0
	1977	Higher education	1,112	106.4	6,353.9	n.a.
	1977	School	41,163	200.8	11,661.5	n.a.
	1978	Special	2,019	31.2	n.a.	n.a.
	1980	Non-spec.	928	80.2	9,104.0	8,621.0
Korean Republic	1977	Higher education	159	7.6	311.6	4,357.3
	1977	School	3,954	11.3	1,046.3	n.a.
All other	1979	National	17	11.0	335.1	n.a.
	1979	Public	1,216	9.4	1,230.2	4,335.7
	1979	Higher education	105	1.8	399.7	n.a.
	1979	School	2,790	2.5	91.9	n.a.
	1979	Special	567	5.3	n.a.	n.a.
Europe						
Albania	1980	Public	3,631	5.7	740.4	n.a.

Continued...

Appendix Table 5 continued...

Country	Year	Category of library	Number of libraries	Number of volumes (million)	Additions per year (000 vols)	Registered borrowers (000s)
Europe continued...						
Austria	1977	Public	n.a.	5.5	n.a.	718.5
	1977	Higher education	742	10.8	n.a.	n.a.
	1977	School	5,600	9.5	n.a.	n.a.
	1977	Special	212	7.7	n.a.	n.a.
	1980	Non-spec.	66	17.4	466.9	n.a.
Belgium	1979	Public	2,372	23.9	n.a.	1,590.7
Bulgaria	1980	Public	5,808	48.9	2,908.2	2,282.0
	1977	School	3,700	13.2	938.2	836.1
	1977	Special	10,290	59.5	4,184.4	3,110.2
	1980	Non-spec.	27	8.1	420.6	314.5
Czechoslovakia	1980	National	15	17.2	467.6	292.8
	1980	Public	10,157	50.5	3,047.2	2,625.8
	1977	Higher education	1,701	11.9	434.5	242.8
	1977	Special	14	15.0	421.0	208.2
Denmark	1981	Public	247	30.7	n.a.	n.a.
	1977	Higher education	17	6.1	254.0	n.a.
Finland	1980	Public	464	23.3	1,344.3	1,841.6
	1981	Higher education	26	6.8	n.a.	n.a.
France	1981	National	1	10.0	60.0	n.a.
	1980	Public	1,028	50.5	2,938.7	4,917.0
	1976	Higher education	47	14.4	437.5	440.0

Continued...

Appendix Table 5 continued...

Country	Year	Category of library	Number of libraries	Number of volumes (million)	Additions per year (000 vols)	Registered borrowers (000s)
Europe continued...						
German Demo-	1980	National	2	9.8	179.1	54.9
cratic Republic	1980	Public	7,271	45.8	4,094.4	4,816.8
	1977	Higher education	532	20.6	478.5	212.9
West Germany	1980	National	3	10.0	391.9	n.a.
	1980	Public	n.a.	62.2	n.a.	n.a.
	1980	Non-spec.	76	65.1	2,360.0	n.a.
Hungary	1980	Public	2,241	40.8	2,028.3	2,242.5
	1977	School	4,680	14.9	1,245.1	848.0
Ireland	1980	Public	31	7.4	688.7	719.0
Italy	1980	National	9	11.7	206.1	32.7
Netherlands	1980	Public	475	30.7	4,517.4	4,008.4
	1976	Higher education	346	10.0	455.7	n.a.
	1976	Special	466	9.7	276.9	n.a.
Norway	1980	Public	454	14.0	644.0	1,059.0
	1981	Higher education	206	5.9	n.a.	n.a.
	1978	School	3,720	5.4	n.a.	n.a.
Poland	1980	Public	9,315	94.5	6,928.0	7,388.0
	1977	Higher education	89	30.5	1.7	785.0
	1977	Special	5,462	19.1	n.a.	1.1
	1980	Non-spec.	126	11.9	363.5	172.3
Portugal		Public	118	6.3	272.2	2,303.9

Continued...

Appendix Table 5 continued...

Country	Year	Category of library	Number of libraries	Number of volumes (million)	Additions per year (000 vols)	Registered borrowers (000s)
Europe continued...						
Romania	1980	National	2	13.4	n.a.	29.0
	1981	Public	6,303	61.1	2,732.9	3,841.3
	1980	Higher education	43	19.3	n.a.	252.0
	1980	School	10,850	47.1	n.a.	2,930.0
	1980	Special	3,948	19.3	n.a.	843.0
Spain	1980	Public	1,396	11.7	601.7	1,308.0
	1977	Higher education	323	6.7	314.9	229.6
	1977	Special	452	8.1	256.3	144.2
Sweden	1980	Public	408	39.0	2,330.0	n.a.
	1977	School	413	27.9	n.a.	n.a.
Switzerland	1980	Non-spec.	33	12.3	269.3	149.6
United Kingdom	1980	National	1	14.6	n.a.	n.a.
	1980	Public	160	131.3	12,667.0	n.a.
Yugoslavia	1980	National	8	8.1	208.8	103.8
	1980	Public	2,101	24.1	1,417.9	4,367.7
	1978	Higher education	425	9.6	285.8	498.6
	1977	School	8,411	27.4	1,536.9	n.a.
	1977	Special	1,072	10.9	n.a.	313.8
All other	1980	National	28	35.1	862.0	n.a.
	1980	Public	4	0.2	1.1	n.a.
	1980	Higher education	231	9.4	276.7	n.a.
	1980	School	6,996	n.a.	n.a.	n.a.
	1980	Special	458	10.2	198.3	n.a.

Continued...

Appendix Table 5 continued...

Country	Year	Category of library	Number of libraries	Number of volumes (million)	Additions per year (000 vols)	Registered borrowers (000s)
Oceania						
Australia	1977	Higher education	92	16.3	1,232.0	354.0
New Zealand	1979	Public	209	6.1	529.7	1,150.8
USSR						
USSR	1980	Public	132,000	1,824.0	n.a.	143,700.0
	1976	School	154,000	602.0	n.a.	n.a.
Byelorussia	1980	Public	6,957	87.1	n.a.	5,416.0
Ukraine	1980	Public	26,233	370.7	n.a.	31,386.0
	1976	School	25,700	125.3	n.a.	n.a.

[1] countries listed by separate category where over 5 million volumes held. Data not necessarily available for categories not listed

[2] mainly Mexico

[3] definitions of data for separate countries available in source document

Source: UNESCO Statistical Yearbook

APPENDIX TABLE 6   FOREIGN EXCHANGE RATES — ANNUAL AVERAGES

	US dollars	Belgian francs		Swiss francs		French francs		Italian lire		Netherlands guilders		German deutschmark		Japanese yen	
	£	£	$	£	$	£	$	£	$	£	$	£	$	£	$
1976	1.81	69.74	38.58	4.52	2.50	8.61	4.78	1,497	832	4.78	2.63	4.55	2.52	535	296
1977	1.75	62.51	35.83	4.19	2.40	8.57	4.91	1,540	882	4.28	2.45	4.05	2.32	468	268
1978	1.92	60.34	31.45	3.42	1.79	8.64	4.51	1,627	848	4.15	2.16	3.85	2.01	403	210
1979	2.12	62.20	29.32	3.53	1.66	9.02	4.25	1,762	831	4.26	2.01	3.88	1.83	466	219
1980	2.33	67.97	29.20	3.89	1.67	9.82	4.22	1,992	856	4.62	1.99	4.23	1.82	526	226
1981	2.03	74.81	37.15	3.97	1.96	10.94	5.44	2,287	1,138	5.03	2.50	4.56	2.26	445	220
1982	1.75	79.84	45.78	3.55	2.03	11.48	6.59	2,364	1,355	4.67	2.67	4.24	2.43	435	249
1983	1.52	77.47	51.16	3.18	2.10	11.55	7.63	2,301	1,520	4.33	2.86	3.87	2.56	360	237

Source: Bank of England Quarterly Bulletin

APPENDIX TABLE 7   EFFECTIVE EXCHANGE RATES — ANNUAL AVERAGES

	£	US dollars	Belgian francs	Swiss francs	French francs	Italian lire	Netherlands guilders	German deutschmark	Japanese yen
1975	100.0	100.0	100.0	100.0	100.0	100.0	100.0	100.0	100.0
1976	85.7	105.9	101.8	108.8	95.8	82.8	102.9	105.3	104.5
1977	81.2	105.4	107.8	111.7	91.3	76.0	110.0	113.7	115.4
1978	81.5	96.4	111.9	138.8	91.5	71.6	115.3	120.9	141.3
1979	87.3	93.7	114.3	144.7	93.0	69.6	118.6	127.8	131.0
1980	96.1	93.8	114.5	114.3	93.9	67.2	119.8	129.0	126.2
1981	95.3	105.6	106.6	139.2	83.8	58.1	111.4	119.5	142.8
1982	90.7	118.1	96.0	147.9	76.0	53.9	116.2	124.6	134.5
1983	83.3	124.9	92.3	151.2	69.5	51.1	117.1	127.4	148.5

Source: Bank of England Quarterly Bulletin

LIST OF TABLES

Continued...

Continued...

Continued...

Continued...

Continued...